Reawakening the Soul

Patty,

Enjoy the journey!

Happy Birthday

Carrie

Once upon a time, I tapped my heels three times saying out loud,"There's no place like Om" . . . to my surprise, I was activated by the Rainbow of Eternal Light—which contained the pot of gold!

Reawakening the Soul

A Journey to Discover & Express Your True Nature

Sundara Fawn
सुनदअरअ उअडन

Reawakening
Publications

To my beloved Gurudeva
Paramahansa Yogananda ~
whom God has sent to me through my
yearning for truth and whose voice gently
whispers behind my words, art and actions.

CONTENTS

Acknowledgments

This book would not be in existence if it were not for the teachings and guidance I receive from my beloved Guru, Paramahansa Yogananda, founder of Self-Realization Fellowship.

Over 25 years ago, I had a profound and lucid dream that I documented in my journal. This memory is as vivid to me today as it was the morning that I awoke from it. I was on an airplane with my identical twin sister and I was trying to convince her to jump out of the plane with me. I kept pleading with her, telling her that we were dreaming and to trust me. After no avail, I decided to jump alone. There was absolutely no fear or doubt in my mind—I was jumping no matter what! So, I anxiously leaped out of the plane. I'll never forget the exhilarating feeling, as I swept through the clouds plunging down to earth. While gliding through the air, I was waiting to "wake up"—but I didn't. A slight panic filled my mind as I raced through the air, "Oh, no . . . what did I just do?! Maybe I'm not dreaming after all!" Then I noticed the vast ocean below me and I found myself landing into the water. When I looked up, there came a man with long black hair, wearing all orange falling through the air coming to save me. I wrote, "but I didn't want to be saved . . . or did I?"

Approximately ten years after this dream, I had an experience that would forever change my life. There was a pivotal moment for me where my confusion about the concept of God came to a peak. Growing up Catholic left me with many bewildering questions and uncertainty. My inner conflict entailed the fear of what I was taught about God and my soul's longing to know and to love God. I was sobbing out loud from the deepest depths of my heart with complete reverence in my desire to know God. I sunk to the floor, pressing my hands to my heart to ease the gripping pain of tireless longing. I remember being coiled up in the fetal position as I cried out, "God, I just want to know you!" I repeated it over and over again until I collapsed from exhaustion.

The very next day, a friend of mine handed me a large photo of Yogananda and said, "I thought that you may want this." As I took the picture in my hand to look at it, my entire body began to vibrate. Yes, his beauty was captivating, but there was something much deeper, way beyond words. Although I had no awareness of gurus, I placed the picture on my wall next to my bed and my heart smiled each time I glanced at it. Within days after receiving the photo, another piece of literature happened to come my way. I loved the inspiration I read and then I noticed the author's name appeared on the back of the booklet along with contact information. I remember feeling such excitement when I noticed it was the same name, which during that time seemed completely baffling to me. I read that there were Self-Realization Fellowship Lessons offering spiritual and scientific techniques of meditation—a way-of-life series. I instantly mailed a request to receive the lessons and eagerly awaited their arrival. I remember going out to the mailbox day after day in anticipation of my lessons and when they arrived my life forever changed. It was my Guru who came to save me in my nightly dream and in this earthly dream!

My blessed Master is with me for eternity, guiding me to the awakening of my soul. His wisdom encourages me to reclaim my divine nature and to awaken the love of God in all hearts. This project is a result of his everlasting, unconditional love for me. Through the grace of God and Guru, I was sent angels—my confidants that believe in my work and me, and who lovingly continue to support me.

I wish to thank Syvanah Bennet, my beautiful talented daughter for allowing me to receive such intimate gifts of motherhood, compassion and unconditional love. Your freedom of artistic expression has opened my eyes and heart into the depths of my own creativity.

I offer special gratitude to one of my dearest friends and editor, Angela Wilson. You have been by my side for 15 years pouring your heart into this project and offering your incredible gifts. Your editing has truly been a magical blessing to me, as your pure desire is beautifully aligned with the same love of truth. I treasure our friendship and love you beyond measure. I am speechless when it comes to conveying what my heart feels for all the gifts you have given to me. Your countless years of patience, dedication and honorable service to this Divine work makes my heart smile with joy. Our baby is finally being born!

I cherish Dr. Shannon South for being my number one angelic cheerleader, spiritual reflector and best friend! Your wisdom, laughter and joy light up my world. You are an inspiration to me and I value all your encouragement and support.

I am deeply grateful to another sacred angel and dearest friend, Ellen LaPenna. Your sincere love for God is heart warming and uplifting. Your additional support with final editing throughout the years means so much to me. Your wondrous gifts, prayers, love and grounded divine presence is deeply appreciated.

Altar Raye, my beautiful karmic partner—thank you for believing in me! You have brought fresh air into my art, giving it new life through your passion in video art. I admire your patience and growth during the creative process of making the video journeys for each one of my wisdom cards. You allowed them to come alive, to sing their unique soul songs. Thanks for riding on this beautiful magic carpet with me in this dream called life!

My heart is filled with gratitude for my twin sister, Jeri Antonette (Moondara), who is forever inspiring me to keep moving forward. Your enthusiasm and reinforcement to complete this project has driven me to stay focused.

A special tribute to all you incredible angels (you know who you are) whose light has shined into my heart, encouraging me to "be all that I can be" in the army of love, authenticity, integrity and power.

Introduction

After countless years of perseverance, dedication and continually moving through limiting beliefs and self-doubts, I am humbly honored to share this precious and intimate part of my life's work. This project has been a labor of love; it is a creation much like my own baby. I never imagined that this moment of completion would be so emotional for me. As tears of wonderment flow down my cheeks, I am fully aware that this project has been birthed through the pure grace of God. As I reminisce and glimpse a taste of this holiness, I view how my life has been orchestrated with such absolute perfection. It is now crystal clear to me how I was destined to use my artistic gifts, desire for truth and creative imagination as a catalyst to ignite the Supreme love latent within my soul. Such delicate rewards flow to me as I share this enchanting treasure of joy!

Reawakening the Soul Exploration Guidebook was birthed from the passion of my two greatest loves—my love for God, and my love for creating art that expresses Divine beauty. This book contains the ingredients from my own intimate self-discovery journey back to my soul. My pilgrimage brought me to yoga—the scientific union of bringing my soul back to Spirit, using the science of meditation for God realization through the teachings of my guru, Paramahansa Yogananda. (See Acknowledgments.) The gifts of creativity so graciously bestowed upon me through Spirit have allowed a natural way for me to share Divinity in material form. My wish for you is that you feel this heavenly love pulsating from the depths of this book, flowing into your heart, allowing this sacred transmission to awaken your transcendental immortal Self!

My heart softly smiles as images float through my mind . . . visions such as the thought of this book now being nestled in the hands of a special angel, the individual who is ready to spread his or her wings and fly back home into the wisdom of their own soul. This book was created for the one who truly appreciates the beautiful mystery of life and searches for understanding that leads to self-mastery. It is intended for one who desires to earnestly awaken in this cosmic dance of creation with a burning desire to feel the absolute truth of their existence, and wishing to experience, express and live this truth. I have written this especially for the one who feels the longing for a deeper, more meaningful and purposeful relationship with themselves and their Almighty Creator. To the gentle soul whose pure heart knows that they came into this world to make a difference and who strives with a determined attitude to put forth the effort to attain their highest aspirations . . . here you are, beautiful angel!

With a creative childlike imagination, art allows me to explore and experience truth for myself. With unflinching determination, my vision is to free my soul from the delusive bondage of physical matter in order to unite with God. For me, creativity is the highest expression of God. With excitement, I envision the very first sublime spark of Creation and realize that everything in the universe, including us, comes from this same Infinite Source. The more I feel the presence of Oneness and allow myself to create from this space, the more I feel my consciousness expand. Creativity feeds my soul and burns passionately throughout my consciousness, seeking expression. When I engage in art, I become one with creation and my Creator. The awareness of this sacred spirit flowing through me during the creative process brings ecstatic joy and soul fulfillment. We are all innovative light beings, creating how we choose to experience the world around us, so let's have fun! Let's all become special and unique emissaries of love and share the precious gifts bestowed upon us from our omniscient Creator. I am honored to meet you here in the magical realm of Spirit. Close your eyes, take a deep breath and feel my heart connect to yours, as we take this sacred journey together towards reawakening our souls.

Every page of this book encompasses the awareness of my participation in this worldly dance of duality. Throughout this journey, I'm dancing . . . learning how to balance the polarities of light and dark, good and evil, happy and sad, personality and soul, Spirit and nature—all along trying to replace ignorance with wisdom. I'm excited to dance with you! Since duality is interpreted by perception, my concept is to change the way in which I view the world. I wear rose-colored glasses to bring out the best in all circumstances and to utilize all of life's experiences, as they are the guides that help me navigate my way back home. The Universal law of cause and effect, which governs everything, is constantly in motion with the desire for expansion. We are all a part of this perfect divine order and we are here to expand! Everything in this material world is Spirit—and this Spirit makes up all of creation. I behold the waves of Spirit's intelligent consciousness as orbs of light, which you will see floating throughout my paintings within the pages of this book.

During the design and layout of this book, I felt like a little girl creating my own unique scrapbook, which contains the contents from the longing of my soul to know God and expressing this love. All the while I was inwardly feeling as though I were on a vision quest, chasing after the rainbow in search of that pot of gold—everlasting truth! I was endowed with unflinching faith and trust that I would find the gold . . . and I did! I discovered that the treasure is found in the realization of the Infinite life force flowing through me during each eternal present moment while creating here on earth. Accepting, allowing, loving and embracing every precious second as an unfolding blessed gift, along with experiencing the Supreme presence of everlasting joy brings forth the absolute wealth of true abundance. Now, I settle into peace and relaxation as I experience deep, profound fulfillment during every process of this creation—having no need to chase anything anymore.

Paramahansa Yogananda said: "The sun shines equally on a piece of charcoal and a diamond placed side by side in the sunlight, but the diamond reflects the light while the charcoal does not. Those who have become spiritual diamonds reflect the sunlight of God's consciousness, they become sons of God." So, how many lifetimes will it take for this spiritual warrior to become the spiritual diamond? How many battles will I have to face? How much pain and suffering must I endure in order to feel the truth of my existence? I guess it's all up to me how much spiritual effort I apply in order to accomplish my Supreme goal. And thus far on this journey, I've come to fully recognize that the joy obtained from my dedicated spiritual practice far outweighs the old feeling of my soul being paralyzed and suffocated by the illusion of fear.

There was a time when it was unimaginable for me to even think that I would be doing this work. There is a deep side of me that craves silence and solitude, and the forests could easily capture me forever as I roam quietly amongst their whispering wisdom. My outlook changed when I read this quote by my guru.

"To seek one's own salvation and then not use it to benefit others is extreme selfishness. But to seek salvation for oneself so that ultimate freedom may be shared with others is divine."

I instantly knew that it was time for me to share the sweet nectar that I have gathered from my secret creative love affair. I feel absolutely no need to hide any longer. I live every day as if it were a dream; I am the dreamer and God is dreaming through me. With this conception, I am learning how to transform earthly nightmares into peaceful dreams.

My intention is to use every one of my God-given gifts in a positive way to bring the Supreme spark of truth back into the awareness of humanity and to share the awareness that God is approachable and His Eternal bliss can be experienced. By developing a loving relationship with our Creator and ourselves, we begin to feel the truth of our existence. We begin to live this truth and create our lives accordingly. Meditation is the way in which we come into contact with our soul's intuition and experience ourselves as Spirit. We have been dreaming that we are mortal, here on earth struggling and suffering. Well now it's time to reawaken our souls and arouse our knowing that we are immortal beings here on earth to express the Infinite consciously and to serve.

In this guidebook, I share my favorite spiritual tools that have proved successful and effective during my life and trials. These tools are a blessing to help you shift your consciousness and regulate your emotions, therefore, creating a brighter future. By regular use of the information and tools provided, you'll soon discover the duration of your suffering becomes shorter and shorter, until it has no need to exist and naturally fades away. Through application and practice, you come to understand that everything in life is a choice and you learn to make wise decisions because you know truth as an actual intuitive experience in your body, mind and soul. You will experience life through the wisdom of your soul, as you spend your time creating in the present moment rather than clinging to past stories. You'll see every opportunity the Universe provides for you and learn from its blessed lessons, knowing that each one is a part of your spiritual evolution. You will utilize the full capacity of your free will to make conscious decisions, choosing happiness over suffering. You become conscious of your thoughts, as you understand that each one acts according to its nature and is divinely orchestrated as a part of Spirit's perfect plan. In this space of awareness and vulnerability, with fear dissolved, you see faith, love and courage take their place. You will realize that the greatest accomplishment is to know your Creator! With practical application, you re-wire old thought patterns and you notice the world around you reflecting this change as your soul reawakens gradually to receive the blessings of the Lord's peace, love, joy, power and wisdom!

Welcome to discovering what you are, why you are here and becoming the very best of that. Congratulations on your journey towards victory over your mind and Mastery of your Self!

Editors Note

I am so grateful for the honor and privilege to be a small part of the creation and birth of *Reawakening the Soul Exploration Guidebook for Self-Discovery*. The card deck is a treasure chest of wisdom, beauty and exploration. Every word in this guidebook is infused with so much love and intention. In the process of editing each card message, every journey was a co-creative adventure where Sundara took my hand and led me to new insights, growing me with every heartfelt word. I created my own sacred ritual for each card as I edited, which brought so much joy to the process. May each reader create their own sacred way to enjoy these magical cards and may each person benefit from Sundara's positive messages as much as I have.

~ Angela Wilson

Using Reawakening The Soul

The artwork in *Reawakening the Soul Exploration Guidebook* is derived from my original paintings carefully chosen over the past 30 years, along with the direct personal message that was received from each one. After listening to the guidance of Spirit, I transformed my paintings into a 38 Wisdom Card Deck. There are 33 cards representing a particular aspect or energy reflecting your soul's wisdom along with 5 Elemental cards (Earth, Water, Fire, Air and Ether) offering guidance for supportive energy. This guidebook shares the wisdom of each painting through: Inspirational Quote, Affirmation, Card Message, Card Symbology, Meditation Journey, Introspection, and an EFT/Tapping exercise. This book can be used alone or as a companion to the Wisdom Card deck and Vision Quest Workbook.

Inspirational Quote: An inspiring quote pertaining to the energy contained in the painting to stimulate the hope latent within your soul.

Affirmation: When saying an affirmation, relax, still your mind and close your eyes. Begin to verbally state the affirmation out loud a few times, and then gradually repeat it, each time lowering your voice until you are mentally chanting it in your mind. Become absorbed in the vibration of the truth that you are stating. The repetition of a positive and powerful concentrated thought with intensity, sincerity, conviction and faith will naturally create the change desired. The power of strong determination and devotion will strengthen the attitude of your mind. By using affirmation, you begin to reprogram your subconscious mind with wisdom, which in time influences your superconscious mind, bringing forth the desired outcome at will.

Card Message: Delivers the universal divine message and meaning of the subject found on each wisdom card, along with spiritual insights that offer profound understanding and wisdom. Each message offers you a fresh new insight into the energies swirling around and within you in this physical plane of existence.

Card Symbology: An intuitive spiritual message with descriptive spiritual meanings of the symbols, colors and images contained in the painting. The mystical artwork shares a personal secret message, in which your soul comprehends the direct meaning. The text is uniquely written according to Spirit's dictation in various tenses in order to best articulate the personal direct message given during that specific time. Understanding the hidden language behind each brush stroke reveals deeper and profound insights. Relax and take a deep look into the painting to receive the activating intelligent consciousness that resides within it. Allow this energy to infuse you with Cosmic Consciousness and baptize you with the Holy Spirit, the identical Spirit in which exists in you, as you.

Journey: Offers a guided meditation and journey to reawaken your soul. In this space, you are encouraged to leave your old story behind in order to create a new one—one that is aligned to your higher Self. As you journey into your soul, you begin to behold your eternal true nature as Spirit. The more energy and time you devote in realizing your divine essence, the less time you will spend identifying with the limited senses, which are influenced by the subconscious mind. The subconscious energy contains beliefs, patterns and habits derived from programming and conditioning. The soul contains the nectar of superconscious energy offering divine intuition, inner-joy and happiness. These journeys are designed to bring your soul out from identification with the ego/physical world and into the depths of your intuitive soul to unite with your Creator.

I invite you to explore another dimension of consciousness by journeying through video and audio. A transcendental video and guided meditation audio journey is created specifically for each card and is available on my website at: www.SundaraFawn.com.

Introspection: Self-inquiry through introspection can lead you to an increased understanding of your spiritual values, the meaning of life and your true purpose, along with increased clarity about who you are. These questions stimulate and enhance your inquisitive mind allowing you to dive deeper into truth through knowledge. The kind of questions you ask determine the kind of life you lead. Questions trigger their own set of answers, which lead to certain emotions, actions or inactions and insights followed by results.

EFT/Tapping: Emotional Freedom Technique or Tapping exercises allow you to release past emotional blocks, which are buried in the physical body. Founded by Gary Craig, this fundamental principle is the basis of meridian tapping. EFT is similar to acupuncture as it achieves healing through stimulating the body's meridians and energy flow. Negative emotions are felt through a disruption of the body's energy and physical pain and disease are intricately connected to negative emotions. Tapping on these meridian points, while concentrating on accepting and resolving the negative emotion(s) will release blocks, restoring your body and mind. This highly effective exercise is simple to use and offers instant results. You can apply it to yourself, whenever you want, wherever you are. It gives you the power to heal yourself. Refer to the diagram, which shows the points along with the abbreviations that are used under the specific EFT exercise in the book. For a video demonstration of the tapping points and how to tap, visit: www.SundaraFawn.com. Also available are downloadable audios and CD's for each individual EFT/Tapping exercise.

EFT Sequence:

1. Identify the energy that arises for you from the card message before you begin and breathe into it. It may be a general anxiety, or it can be a specific situation or issue that causes you to feel anxious.

2. Consider the problem or situation. How do you feel about it right now? Rate the intensity level of your anxiety, with zero being the lowest level of anxiety and ten being the highest.

3. Begin with the set up statement labeled KC (karate chop) acknowledging the energy pertaining to the wisdom card. The setup statement is repeated three times. Proceed forward by tapping on the remaining points while reading the exercise.

4. When complete, tap your inside wrists stating the affirmation three times. Take a deep breathe in, relax and rate the intensity level of your anxiety as you did in step 2. Notice how your body feels. Notice how your mind feels. Pay attention to any body shifts and let only the negative go.

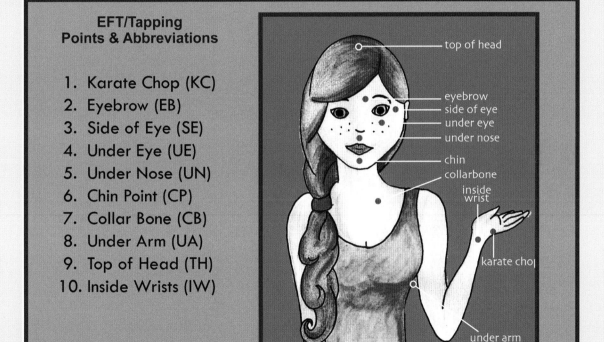

EFT/Tapping Points & Abbreviations

1. Karate Chop (KC)
2. Eyebrow (EB)
3. Side of Eye (SE)
4. Under Eye (UE)
5. Under Nose (UN)
6. Chin Point (CP)
7. Collar Bone (CB)
8. Under Arm (UA)
9. Top of Head (TH)
10. Inside Wrists (IW)

Drawing by Syvanah Bennett

"Everything in the future will improve if you are making a spiritual effort now."

~ Swami Sri Yukteswar

Another highly beneficial tool I use regularly is Ho'oponopono, which is an ancient Hawaiian practice of reconciliation and forgiveness created by Dr. Ihaleakala Hew Len. This Hawaiian healing practice is personal and universal and means "to make things right." There are four simple steps to this method: repentance, forgiveness, gratitude and love— by saying and feeling the words: *I'm Sorry, Please Forgive Me, Thank You, I love you.* Repeat these phrases as many times as needed in order to feel the truth within them around the energy you wish to transmute. Since you are responsible for everything you think, you can purify your mind and energetic field. The words used with intention are vibrations that break up old patterns of fear, negativity and victim mentality. Use this exercise on yourself along with others with whom you wish to clear any emotional blocks stopping you from truth.

Throughout this guidebook you will find many names for God: Cosmic Consciousness, Infinite, Divine, Absolute, Creator, etc. The word and meaning of God conveys something different for each individual and deserves respect. The way in which God is referred to in this guidebook is universal, omnipresent, omnipotent, and omniscient.

Understanding the Five Elements

The Cosmic Vibration, or Aum, structures all physical creation, including your physical body, through the manifestation of five elements: earth, water, fire, air, and ether. Matter appears in five varieties; solid, liquid, gaseous, fiery, and ethereal—from the action of the five elemental vibrations. These elements are structural forces, intelligent and vibratory in nature. God in matter is vibrating intelligent energy and acting in your mind as the vibration of intelligence. Your consciousness consists of various rates of intelligent vibration, and matter consists of various vibrating electrons.

By deepening your understanding of the elements and the energetic roles they play in your existence, you will be able to draw in their healing properties to balance your body, mind and soul. Through this awareness, you begin to feel yourself as Spirit manifested in the physical world and you naturally relax and flow within the currents of life.

Earth represents the solid state of matter and is considered a stable substance. The earth vibration current flows into the coccygeal plexus (the small bone at the base of your spine.) In your body, the parts such as bones, teeth, cells, and tissues are manifestations of the earth.

Water represents the liquid state and is a substance without stability. The water vibration current flows into the sacral plexus. A large part of your body is made up of water. Your blood, lymph, and other fluids move between your cells and through your vessels, bringing energy and carrying away wastes along with performing many other active duties.

Fire is the power to transform solids into liquids, to gas, and back again. Without the fire element, there would be no heat. It is considered a form without substance, as it possesses the power to transform the state of any substance. The fire vibration current flows into the lumbar plexus. The fire energy in your body binds the atoms together, converts food to fat, energy, and muscle. It creates the impulses of nervous reactions, your thought processes and also your feelings.

Air is the gaseous form of matter and is existence without form. The air vibration current flows into the dorsal plexus. Your body uses air (oxygen) as the basis for all energy transfer reactions. It is a key element needed for fire to burn.

Ether is the background space upon which all the other combined elements are displayed. The ether vibration current flows into the cervical plexus (neck.) Paramahansa Yogananda spoke of ether as the background on which God projects the cosmic motion picture of creation. Space gives dimension to objects; ether separates the images. This "background," a creative force that coordinates all spatial vibrations, is a necessary factor when considering the subtler forces—thought and life energy, the nature of space and the origin of material forces and matter. It is the field that is simultaneously the source of all matter and the space in which it exists.

Let the Magic Begin . . .

Earth

Earth is the element on which we are born and sustained.

*"And forget not that the earth delights to feel your
bare feet and the winds long
to play with your hair."*

~ Kahlil Gibran

Affirmation

I receive support and connection
from the element of Earth.

Card Message

Call upon the earth's precious resources and anchor yourself with grounding energy. The feminine energies of Mother Earth are adaptable and flexible and can be called on for inspiration and creativity. Earth Element is the great balancer of your mental, emotional and physical energies, which is why there is so much green on our planet. Your body consists of approximately 12% of the Earth Element. Breathe in the sweetness from your blessed Mother Earth, for you are her child. Remembering your Mother's caress keeps you feeling nurtured, supported and safe. Call upon her energy and remember to feel her presence. Let her revitalize your physical, mental and emotional state. Every day, take off your shoes and ground with her energy for Earth is your source of stability. The Earth pulls your negative energy out and radiates positive light back to you. Recharge your soul with nature's spirit; walk in a forest or in luscious garden to connect. Her magnetic life force is necessary for your spiritual nourishment.

Elemental Earth is ruled by the direction of the North, the ending of life, and winter. North is a place to go deep within yourself, to hibernate, meditate and feel your connection in unity with your Earth Mother. For it is in this place where you draw upon your intuition by silencing your mind. North is the place to obtain wisdom and knowledge. Elemental Earth of the North is the place of sleeping and dreaming, solitude and spiritual introspection. Connect with Spirit and commune with the unseen worlds. It is the place of the night, winter and where you go to receive guidance. Earth nurtures and sustains you, providing you with living food. A place where you quiet your actions, activity and mind and draw upon the wisdom of your blessed soul. Give thanks to the bounty of nourishment from Elemental Earth.

Card Symbology

The figure sits upon the lotus flower of wisdom in deep introspection with the root chakra harmoniously connected to the Earth's vibration. Surrounded by nature and rooted like the large tree beside her, she draws upon the guidance and wisdom of Earth. Spirit Below, Mother Earth, beautiful and spontaneous, ever-changing. She is always in motion, never the same from one moment to the next. Surrounded by the color green, which symbolizes growth and hope with the anticipation of things to come. Green is also rejuvenating and nurturing as it revitalizes us when we are physically, mentally or emotionally exhausted.

Journey

Find a quiet place where you can relax undisturbed. Sit comfortably with your spine straight. Take a deep breath in, tensing your body from your feet to your head. Bring awareness to each body part, as you tense each muscle one by one, within the same inhale. As your entire body is tensed with energy, hold your breath until you are ready to exhale and release. As you exhale, make any audible sounds to expel all tension from your body. Repeat this exercise three times or until you feel relaxed. Gently begin allowing your natural breath to move in and out. With each inhale, silently chant: "I am grounded." With each exhale, chant: "And supported by Earth." Repeat this chant several times as you naturally breathe in and out. Remain in this state for as long as needed, feeling all distracting thoughts subside.

Experience the Transcendental Video & Audio Journey on my Website to Feel more Connected!

You are now entering into the dark silence beneath the earth. It is quiet, still, and safe like a cave of peace. You are in a deep connection with the Spirit that moves through all things. As unconditional love pours into your being, you feel your heart supported by the Spirit of Mother Earth. You feel your own imaginary roots, going down from your body and plunging into the depths of the earth and spreading out, just like the roots of the tree. Your roots extend downwards below the surface, expanding from your root chakra at the base of your spine. You allow all the negative energy to be released out from your body, and into Mother Earth. Feel all this conflicting energy leave your entire physical body. It is now completely gone, and you feel clear, open and purified. You are now ready to draw the essence of Spirit into your field. This force is infused with the positive frequency of Mother Earth. Fill yourself with this highly charged life force, for you are beautiful, spontaneous and ever-changing, just as Mother Earth. Your soul is now recharged with pure nature energy from the light of Spirit. You now feel the awareness of your Godly nature. You sense a great sustenance and support guiding your inner self, leading you to truth.

You are in the magnetic North where you have time to be introspective, imagine, and dream in solitude. Feel your connection with Spirit and commune with unseen worlds. There is no rush, nowhere to go, you have time to contemplate. As you stop and pause, scan your past life here on earth. Review your journey thus far and give deep thanks to where it has led you. Be grateful for all the joy and wisdom that you have been blessed with along your journey. Be grateful for all the hardships you endured because each of them strengthened you and made you exactly who you are this very moment. Remain in this sacred space of stillness, reflecting with sincere appreciation for being here on earth.

Return back to the present moment and receive the activation of wisdom from the energies of Earth, direction of North and Spirit Below. Allow this penetrating vibrant green energy to fill your entire being. This deep inner reflection brings forth insights, guidance and direction to your future path. Remain in this space and receive the wisdom. Give thanks to the blessings you received from the sacred transmission from Elemental Earth. You are now grounded in strength, wisdom and the truth of your connectedness with all that exists. You feel rejuvenated, nurtured and harmoniously balanced, mentally, emotionally and physically. Anchor and draw upon Mother Earth's energy every day, for she is always willing and ready to give.

When you return from your journey, take a deep breath and reflect on the insights you received. Smile inwardly into your heart and thank your Godly self for the work you have done to accept life, yourself and others. Record any insights or awakenings in your copy of the *Reawakening the Soul Vision Quest Workbook*.

Introspection

Do I spend enough time in solitude to receive guidance and wisdom?

How can I spend more time connecting to Earth energy to feel more grounded and centered?

Am I willing to learn how to completely stop my mind and connect more deeply with Spirit?

EFT/Tapping

KC: Even though I don't feel grounded or connected, I completely accept the way I feel.

KC: Even though I don't feel supported, I deeply and completely love myself.

KC: Even though I feel scattered, I accept the way I feel.

EB: I don't feel grounded.
SE: I don't feel very clear.
UE: And I don't feel supported.
UN: I feel a bit scattered.
CP: My mind is always racing with thoughts.
CB: How would I feel differently if I were grounded?
UA: I would be more present.
TH: I would be able to think more clearly.

EB: I would feel supported and safe.
SE: All of this feels really good to me.
UE: I'm willing to explore how to be more grounded.
UN: I want to feel connected.
CP: I want to feel peace.
CB: I am now choosing to take action.
UA: Because these things feel aligned to me.
TH: I am willing to meditate every day.

EB: And spend some time alone in nature.
SE: I will do whatever it takes to receive Earth's energy.
UE: I will make an effort to ground myself barefoot outside.
UN: And lay upon Mother Earth's bed.
CP: And connect with her healing energy.
CB: I am beginning to feel excited.
UA: I feel rejuvenated just thinking about it.
TH: I am connected to earth.

EB: I am connected to all that is.
SE: I am Spirit.
UE: I am grounded in truth.
UN: I am love.
CP: I am supported.
CB: I love my earth.
UA: And I love my Mother.
TH: Thank you Mother Earth.

EFT
Audio Available
For Deeper
Grounding &
Support!

EB: I honor and respect your wisdom.
SE: I will do my best to take care of you.
UE: I feel so nurtured.
UN: And safe.
CP: And loved by you.
CB: Thank you.
UA: For sustaining me.
TH: I love you.

Water

Water opens your energy channels and allows mystery to flow into your life.

"You can't cross the sea merely by standing and staring at the water."

~ Rabindranath Tagore

Affirmation

I flow effortlessly and harmoniously like water.

Card Message

Your body is made of approximately 72% water, which is almost the exact percentage of the earth's water. You are universally connected to the earth's flowing water. Water is the element associated with purification, healing, depth, mystery and the unconscious dimension of your psyche. Pay attention to how life appears to be flowing for you. Is it calm and peaceful or like wild crashing waves? Your emotions may be heightened right now, so be sure to keep everything in proper perspective. On the path through water, you begin to open, empty, cleanse and flow.

Elemental Water is ruled by the direction of the West. It signifies ending or completion as it reflects the setting sun at the end of the day and the fall of the year. At the end of each day, take time to be introspective to see how you have behaved. Take note and make any necessary changes. Water Element governs the past, so if you have any negative emotions lingering from the past, revisit them and allow them to float away. In the West is where you face your emotional pain, losses, and any grief you have accumulated throughout life. Get in touch with any part of your self that is dying, worn out or no longer serving you.

Always remember that you are flowing in the rhythm of Spirit in this cosmic world. You are like the little wave within the vast ocean of Spirit. You are never separate from the infinite ocean of oneness and your natural rhythm is to flow in unison with ease and grace. It is when you forget who you are; a divine being of love and light, that you experience the changing tides of life as crashing waves, which keep you in the illusion of separation. Learn to accept and embrace each current of life, because it is an important aspect of your eternal soul's development. Realize that every circumstance is playing its role as a part of your spiritual evolution, always changing with constant motion trying to bring you back to your true nature.

Card Symbology

The central figure is filled with the movement and natural flow of water, sometimes gentle, and other times rough and wild. The image floats with the setting sun and symbolizes the cycle of endings and the past. Water encourages the release of the old and is the place to honor any emotions that need to be released into the water.

The sacral chakra spins within the moving waters stimulating passion, creativity, spontaneity, and movement. Use this energy to put into motion any creative ideas you are passionate about. Now is a great time to flow within the present moment and allow the healing waters to carry you forward on your dreams and visions.

The lotus flower, which represents purity and beauty, grows out of the murky darkness of the water. The flower is a reflection of our own purity and wisdom that progresses from the lowest to highest states of consciousness. The lotus flower inspires us to continue to grow through the trials of our life so we can bloom and reach our highest potential. It reminds us that there is beauty in every aspect of life. Thus spiritual unfolding can be achieved by fully surrendering to our Creator. The sacral chakra spins within the figure stimulating passion, creativity, spontaneity and movement.

Journey

Find a quiet place where you can relax undisturbed. Sit comfortably with your spine straight. Take a deep breath in, tensing your body from your feet to your head. Bring awareness to each body part, as you tense each muscle one by one, within the same inhale. As your entire body is tensed with energy, hold your breath until you are ready to exhale and release. As you exhale, make any audible sounds to expel all tension from your body. Repeat this exercise three times or until you feel relaxed. Gently begin allowing your natural breath to move in and out. With each inhale, silently chant: "I flow like water." With each exhale, chant: "gracefully and naturally." Repeat this chant several times as you naturally breathe in and out. Remain in this state for as long as needed, feeling all distracting thoughts subside.

Your body is made up of mostly water. You can feel the multitude of water droplets forming your physical body. You understand that water evaporates and changes form and you know yourself as ever-changing, ever-existing consciousness, which is constantly transforming. You realize your body is not as dense as it appears to be. It is rippling with life force. You feel a deep sense of truth that you are vibrating spirit, dancing upon the waves of creation.

You feel yourself flowing within the rhythmically moving cosmic waters. You have nothing to resist. You just float and trust the tides of Spirit to move you in the right direction. If there are areas in your life appearing motionless and not flowing as you wish, release your expectations into

Experience the Transcendental Video & Audio Journey on my Website to Flow Gracefully with the Tides of Life!

the magic waters. The water wishes to take all of them, so keep letting them go until you dance in harmony with the movement of the waters. Now that you have given your expectations away, you have freed yourself from forcing things to happen. As you release these energies into the sacred waters, you notice how calm and expanded your body feels. Your whole being expands as it fills itself with glorious healing light. You trust the perfection of life and flow naturally with the tides.

West is the direction of the dying of old patterns that make way for new life. Now look into the past for reference to heal affliction, misery and resentment. Scan your past and let go of any pain, suffering or resentment. Gently embrace each emotion that presents itself into your being. Intentionally allow them to transform by flushing them from your field. You are aware that these situations are the gateway to reawakening your soul, for each one has made you the special you that you are. Now that you have courageously completed your work, you experience your heart filled with stillness and deep peace.

You are a mature light being, and choose to die to your childish ways, and to realize who you are. You are ready to embrace your wholeness in order to discover a larger dimension of your essential self and your place in this great mystery. You understand that past suffering ushers you into higher vibrations of being that are more interesting, fresh and optimal than what you are leaving behind. You are Spirit. You are floating upon the waters of this dream life, dreaming in this dream. Remember it's all a dream, as you float beneath on the ocean's floor in the stillness of truth. In this space, allow your creative mind to link with your heart as you overflow with passion, purpose and power. Open to receive your blessings of knowledge, courage and wisdom to reap the harvest of a fruitful, and conscious life.

As the setting sun in the west retires, it is time for you to rest. Relax in the waters of the truth of your existence, your eternal oneness with your Creator. Completely let go of all mental worries, concerns or suffering. Allow the energy of the sunset to absorb them. Allow your mind, body and spirit to rest into the presence of the now. You are resting on the waters of peace as you trust and flow with Spirit.

When you return from your journey, take a deep breath and reflect on the insights you received. Smile inwardly into your heart and thank your Godly self for the work you have done to accept life, yourself and others. Record any insights or awakenings in your copy of the *Reawakening the Soul Vision Quest Workbook*.

Introspection

Am I willing to let go of all pain and suffering from my past?

Can I celebrate my accomplishments without any judgment?

Am I willing to become a responsible, mature being in order to take others by the hand and lead them towards wisdom?

EFT/Tapping

KC: Even though I don't feel like I'm flowing in life, I deeply and completely accept the way I feel.

KC: Even though I don't feel like life is flowing my way, I accept the way I feel.

KC: Even though emotions flood my mind, I deeply and completely love myself.

EB: All these emotions.
SE: All my thoughts.
UE: I have so much activity going on.
UN: It's constantly roaring.
CP: Sometimes it feels like crashing waves.
CB: It drives me crazy.
UA: I don't like to feel all this foolishness.
TH: I know is caused by my mind.

EB: They make me nauseous.
SE: Many of these thoughts are from the past.
UE: Actually, all of them are.
UN: Because there's only the present.
CP: I want to flow more harmoniously with life.
CB: I want to flow more harmoniously in life.
UA: This feels good.
TH: What would I have to release to accomplish this?

EB: I would need to let go of my racing mind.
SE: Can I do this?

EFT
Audio Available
to create
Peace & Flow
in Your Life!!

UE: Yes, I can.
UN: I choose to let it go.
CP: Let it all go.
CB: My mind is calm, still and peaceful.
UA: I breathe in peace.
TH: What else do I have to release?

EB: I would also have to let go of expectations.
SE: I'm always expecting.
UE: And I feel disappointed when it doesn't happen.
UN: Can I really let go of expectations?
CP: This feels difficult.
CB: But I'm ready to give it a try.
UA: As I tap, I let go of all expectations.
TH: And allow myself to feel free.

EB: No expectations.
SE: I have no expectations.
UE: I trust my Creator.
UN: And I flow with Spirit.
CP: I flow in the waters of this dream world.
CB: I am the dreamer.
UA: I am dreaming this dream called life.
TH: Life flows peacefully.

EB: My body is mostly water.
SE: The earth is mostly water.
UE: The earth and I flow as One.
UN: One Universal Truth.
CP: Everything is Spirit.
CB: I am Spirit.
UA: I flow effortlessly in life.
TH: Life flows perfectly for me.

Fire

The limitless light and will of Spirit.

"The fire, which enlightens
is the same fire, which consumes."
~ Henri Frederic Amiel

Affirmation

I allow fire to energize my dreams and visions.

Card Message

There is a lot of passion, desire and action burning within you. Now is a great time to utilize this incredible force of fire energy to make things happen. Allow this force to channel through you to create your dreams, desires and passions. Now is the time to take action! This cosmic flame fuels the vision of your soul. Allow it to burn and produce the desired outcome of your intentions. Allow the healing sun to penetrate your body and fill you with vitality and rays of nourishment. Make a conscious effort to receive the sun's life force every day by taking 15 minutes to consciously receive the healing sun's light magic.

Your body consists of approximately 4% of the fire element. Elemental Fire is ruled by the direction of the South, the summer in the year. The South's energy amplifies and disperses currents of heat, acting as a magnifier. This powerful burst is a great energizer supporting you to take action for a greater purpose. South is the place of passion, creation and inspiration, whose warm breath ignites your heart with love. Fire Element governs the future. Whatever thoughts you generate in the present moment while uniting mental power with personal action will create your future. Be conscious and present as fire is raw energy and will support you in taking action.

Card Symbology

The central figure holds the southern flames that burn away limiting beliefs along with fueling our zeal for life. This is the fire generating our inner joy to accomplish our individual divine missions. This passion is always burning. By connecting and utilizing this fervor, we manifest our desired outcome, therefore living the life we were destined to live. Passion and action creates our future outcome.

The six-pointed star (hexagram) symbolizes the perfect meditative state of balance achieved between Man and God. When this balance is maintained, results in nirvana are obtained, releasing us from the bonds of the earthly world and its material trappings. This shape consists of two triangles—one pointed up and the other down—locked in harmonious embrace, symbolizing man's position between earth and sky. The downward triangle symbolizes the sacred embodiment of femininity, and the upward triangle represents the focused aspects of masculinity. The mystical union of the two triangles represents Creation, occurring through the divine union of male and female.

32

The solar plexus chakra governs our power center. It is the generous life force igniting our ability to take action with strong conviction. When this chakra is aligned to its Source through clear, open channels, its power is magnetized producing superhuman affects.

The figure sits upon the lotus flower; the flower represents purity and beauty as it grows out of the murky darkness of the water. The flower is a reflection of our own purity and wisdom that progresses from the lowest to highest states of consciousness. The lotus flower inspires us to continue to grow through the trials of our life so we can bloom and reach our highest potential. This spiritual unfolding can be achieved by fully surrendering to our Creator. The lotus flower reminds us that there is beauty in every aspect of life.

Journey

Experience the Transcendental Video & Audio Journey on my Website to Ignite your Passion!

Find a quiet place where you can relax undisturbed. Sit comfortably with your spine straight. Take a deep breath in, tensing your body from your feet to your head. Bring awareness to each body part, as you tense each muscle one by one, within the same inhale. As your entire body is tensed with energy, hold your breath until you are ready to exhale and release. As you exhale, make any audible sounds to expel all tension from your body. Repeat this exercise three times or until you feel relaxed. Gently begin allowing your natural breath to move in and out. With each inhale, silently chant: "I breathe in passion." With each exhale, chant: "I breathe out fire." Repeat this chant several times as you naturally breathe in and out. Remain in this state for as long as needed, feeling all distracting thoughts subside.

You are now being charged as you travel the portal of fire, passion and desire. As you swirl into the spiraling flames, you feel this blaze consume your being, igniting your soul. You are open to receive and utilize this incredible force of energy. Open your consciousness and feel this life force stimulating you with excitement, determination, and motivation, giving you the gift to take action. This energy is directed through your will power.

You are now being transported into the solar plexus chakra located in the center of your belly. As you draw upon the fire energy, allow the healing light to penetrate your power center. This chakra is harmoniously aligned to your Creator. Allow it to activate and release your superhuman powers. You feel your power center being activated from the magnetic forces firing from the south emanating light into your core. Receive the electrifying spinning wheel of light energy, and allow it to clear and balance your solar plexus. Welcome the fire for your personal transformation. Allow it to burn, devour and destroy old patterns, beliefs and habits. While fire consumes, it also creates new life. Now, your center is balanced, and you feel divinely connected to your Source. You are united with your Creator as you use the force of Spirit to co-create together.

Now look deep within your soul. Allow yourself to clearly feel and see your deepest dreams. With heightened imagination, you see all your wildest dreams being created. You feel this incredible supporting energy of light aiding you, and offering you all your dearest wishes. You have extreme faith in knowing that all your dreams, desires and passions are now in stages of manifestation. Allow this cosmic flame to ignite, and forever burn away any false beliefs holding you from your soul's vision. You are free to produce the desired outcome of your dreams. You are energized with grand support to take action now for your greater purpose and to live your dreams. The action you take now produces your future. You are now charged with the generating power of your inner desire to accomplish your divine mission. With enthusiasm consuming your being, you interact with these flames as you make manifest the desired outcome of your dreams. You are now living the life you were destined to live.

Sit in the lotus flower of wisdom, and merge your thoughts with the present moment where God resides. Receive your blessed gifts from this act of awareness. Act upon opportunities you receive as gifts from Spirit. Use your dynamic will and take immediate action. This creates your magical future.

The six-pointed star appears before you. You feel it as the reflection of your own halo. The first triangle, pointing downward appears before you. You feel the sacred embodiment of your femininity. You honor the compassionate, nurturing and unconditional loving aspects of your being. You feel gratitude for your ability to forgive within this soft light. Take a moment to reflect upon the generous feminine energy pulsating within your heart. Now, the upward facing triangle appears before you. It penetrates you with the awareness of your masculinity; the strong, confident characters of your soul. You feel your ability to live with great strength, power and reason. You feel completely supported and protected in this cosmic intelligence. The triangles meld in a mystical union of divine love, as you feel yourself merge with all of creation. You are in a perfect meditative state of balance. You feel your earthly world and all your creations being energized with Spirit from the heavens. Your entire body is now filled with light of vibrating intelligent energy. You have entered nirvana, the truth of your essence. Melt in the flames of this sacred union.

The fire element in your body has a generous life force that ignites your ability to take action with a strong conviction. You are here to utilize the energy of fire towards a greater humanity, and a healthier world. You invite the raw energy of fire into your life as you feel your inward flames growing stronger and burning brighter. Affirm over and over: I am light. I am power. I am the burning flame of Spirit. I am Love. I am creative energy. Now, you have the ability to light the fire of your devotion, and transform all darkness into light!

When you return from your journey, take a deep breath and reflect on the insights you received. Smile inwardly into your heart and thank your Godly self for the work you have done to accept life, yourself and others. Record any insights or awakenings in your copy of the *Reawakening the Soul Vision Quest Workbook*.

Introspection

Am I utilizing the energy of fire to make my dreams a reality?

Am I willing to use fire to destroy old patterns and beliefs?

How can I receive more creative and passionate energy from the wisdom of the South?

EFT/Tapping

KC: Even though I feel like I don't have a lot of passion, I deeply and completely accept the way I feel.
KC: Even though I don't feel as passionate as I would like too, I completely love myself.
KC: Even though I don't feel like taking action, I completely accept the way I feel.

EB: What am I passionate about?
SE: What would light my fire?
UE: What excites me?
UN: What are my dreams?
CP: I want to feel passion.
CB: I want to take action.
UA: I want to move forward with my dreams.
TH: I desire more fire in my life.

EB: I allow myself to dream.
SE: I allow myself to create.
UE: I allow myself to receive the fire element,
UN: And take action towards my dreams!
CP: Just thinking about this, seems exciting.
CB: This action will result in my future.
UA: My passion is the fire.
TH: I reclaim my power center.

EB: My solar plexus is strong and grounded.
SE: Full of strength and fire.
UE: And connected to my creator.
UN: I feel this connection.
CP: And I feel strong.
CB: I feel Almighty.
UA: And my flames of love,
TH: Will burn brightly in the world.

EB: Spreading light.
SE: Spreading hope.
UE: Spreading wisdom.
UN: Spreading happiness.
CP: This is the flame of my love.
CB: I am this flame.
UA: I am Almighty.
TH: I am the almighty flame of God.

EFT Audio Available to Activate More Action!

Air

Air is waking consciousness.

"All things share the same breath—the beast, the tree, the man . . . the air shares its spirit with all the life it supports."

~ Chief Seattle

Affirmation

I am free like the air.

Card Message

Air pervades everything on earth and loves freedom, as it is nearly always free. Because it loves its freedom, if captured, it will escape at any given opportunity.

Air is associated with language, logic, and communication. Air governs your mind, thought, reason, ideas and intellect. You may find yourself dreaming, thinking, and planning, but not applying. Utilize this energy to be reflective and think things through logically before you implement your ideas. Your body is made up of approximately 6% air. Elemental Air is your most basic connection to life, as each breath is important to your body's survival. Remember that you receive powerful, cosmic energy through the air. When your Air Element is balanced and under control, your mind is peaceful and calm. By mastering your mind, you gain the capacity to handle all the other elements and use those energies to your best advantage. Controlling your thoughts is the most difficult thing to achieve and yet the most important, for your well-being.

Elemental Air is ruled by the direction of the East, where the sun rises each morning. East is the birth of a new day, the spring of the year, and the youth of life. East is the beginning of all life, where spirit is conceived and gifted to the womb of the mother-to-be. It represents the beginning of understanding, as light helps you see things from a clear perspective. East is the place of vision, inspiration, and new, fresh starts. It represents the vision as seen clearly from your soul. Like the eye of the eagle able to see the grand picture from afar in a way that is clear, and at the same time not attached to any specific outcome. On the path through air, you begin to dream, conceive and receive insights. Ponder on all the aspects of new beginnings from East that are currently showing up in your life. What are you beginning? What have you just begun to figure out? What visions, plans or dreams do you wish to create? You are the rainbow of truth and it's your time to take the knowledge from Spirit Above and make it manifest here in the physical world.

Spirit Above, Father Sky is consistent, reliable and predictable. The good masculine energies of Father Sky are stable, strong and protective. Call upon Father Sky for help with order, reason and discipline in your life.

Card Symbology

The figure sits gracefully on the lotus flower of fresh new beginnings, filled with the Spirit of Air, and feeling extreme freedom from being full of cosmic energy. The image reflects our waking consciousness birthed from thoughts, ideas and intellect. The vibrant rainbow is a natural phenomenon of beauty representing the bridge from heaven to earth. The rainbow takes the knowledge from Spirit Above and co-creates with the creative aspect of the mind while making it manifest in the physical world. The personification of the rainbow is a messenger linking the gods to humanity. For Buddhists, the rainbow is "the highest state achievable before attaining Nirvana, where individual desire and consciousness are extinguished." Eagle symbolizes our ability to be directed by our soul to see clearly the bigger picture of life, without any attachments. The eagle soars effortlessly in trust towards conscious leadership, reminding of your individual leadership skills.

Experience the Transcendental Video & Audio Journey on my Website to Soar Into New Beginnings!

Journey

Find a quiet place where you can relax undisturbed. Sit comfortably with your spine straight. Take a deep breath in, tensing your body from your feet to your head. Bring awareness to each body part, as you tense each muscle one by one, within the same inhale. As your entire body is tensed with energy, hold your breath until you are ready to exhale and release. As you exhale, make any audible sounds to expel all tension from your body. Repeat this exercise three times or until you feel relaxed. Gently begin allowing your natural breath to move in and out. With each inhale, silently chant: "I breathe in Spirit Air." With each exhale, chant: "I breathe out Spirit Air." Repeat this chant several times as you naturally breathe in and out. Remain in this state for as long as needed, feeling all distracting thoughts subside.

You are sitting upon a lotus floating through the portal of Air. As you travel, you feel yourself as the free and flowing air in the clouds of space. Your breath shares the same breath as everything in the world: the trees, animals, plants and all humans. You experience the cosmic motion of air flowing through everything as you sense your own breath. You are breathing in the same air from all the great masters that ever existed. As you breathe, you fill yourself with the high vibration of the only reality - Spirit. Your inner spirit expands wider and broader until you become completely free, flowing in the oneness of your pure essence as Spirit. You are now completely free from all limitations. You fully realize that you are ever-existing consciousness. This powerful cosmic energy of air continuously flows through you and all existing creatures. You are connected to Spirit Above, your Father Sky. You feel the solid, grounding masculine energy from your Heavenly Father. You feel stable, strong, safe and protected. This energy is consistent, reliable and predictable. Call upon Father Sky for help with reasoning, order and discipline in your life. Whatever confronts you, ask him for help and know with firm conviction that you now receive all of your requests.

The glorious rising sun waking from the horizon of the Eastern sky shines its morning light before you, as you celebrate the dawn of a fresh new day. You find yourself loaded with inspiration as excitement fills your diamond soul with a fresh new start. Your creativity is sparked as you now co-create through conscious awareness. You feel motivated as new beginnings are unfolding in your life. You are free to dream and create as you wish. You are the creator who produces anything you dream – anything! You notice a ravishing bald eagle gliding through the clouds. He reminds you to follow your heart and soul towards your vision in life. He activates you with magic to trust your intuition and higher mind towards moving forward on your goals and aspirations. With fresh new awareness, you are able to see the magnificent big picture of your life. You take immediate action from this impulse and begin to apply it in your life. Your thoughts and visions create your reality. A splendid rainbow reaching across the skies of heaven penetrates your being. This natural phenomenon of beauty represents the bridge from heaven to earth. You have reached the highest state achievable and your consciousness is united with your Creator. It is your time to bring your spiritual awareness from the heavens and make them manifest here on earth. Your heart center explodes with enthusiasm because you know exactly what you must do. You have a mission here on earth to accomplish, and you have moved beyond all limitations holding you back. You are limitless; you are unstoppable and you are almighty. Only you have the unique gifts bestowed by your Great Creator. Now go shine your diamond light and create for the goodness and freedom for all!

When you return from your journey, take a deep breath and reflect on the insights you received. Smile inwardly into your heart and thank your Godly self for the work you have done to accept life, yourself and others. Record any insights or awakenings in your copy of the *Reawakening the Soul Vision Quest Workbook*.

Introspection

Am I willing to see things clearly with the help of the wisdom of the East?

What are my visions and goals?

What new, fresh start do I wish to create?

EFT/Tapping

KC: Even though I don't feel free, I'm open to explore how to free myself.

KC: Even though I don't dream enough, I completely love myself.

KC: Even though I feel my dreams aren't important, I'm ready to begin to create them.

EB: What are my dreams?
SE: What are my visions?
UE: Do I give them the energy they deserve?
UN: They are important to me.
CP: But I'm always putting them last.
CB: I do want to create them.
UA: But I never seem to have the time.
TH: I just don't feel supported.

EB: Where does support come from?
SE: Is this only an excuse?
UE: I do want to open up to the spirit of Air.
UN: And trust in my Heavenly Father Sky.
CP: I call forth my dreams to be birthed.
CB: This excites me.
UA: Then why don't I do it?
TH: I guess I don't trust myself.

EB: I feel that my dreams aren't real.
SE: They're only dreams.
UE: But I do want to create them.
UN: And I'm choosing to make different choices.

CP: I'm ready to take action.
CB: I'm ready to follow my higher mind.
UA: And trust in my higher self.
TH: I feel trapped.

EFT Audio Available to Activate Your Divine Safety Net!

EB: I'm so caught up with other work.
SE: And this takes all of my time.
UE: I'm ready to feel free.
UN: I'm ready to free myself.
CP: I am committed to achieving this.
CB: It all begins with taking the first step.
UA: I am now willing to take the first step.
TH: I commit to taking one small action every day towards my dreams.

EB: This already feels good.
SE: I feel excited to begin.
UE: I feel the breathe of spirit within me.
UN: Guiding me towards my vision.
CP: I feel a new beginning happening.
CB: And every morning, I will allow myself to dream.
UA: And I promise to take action towards my dreams.
TH: I call in Spirit Air to guide me.

EB: I open to Father Sky for support.
SE: I trust Him.
UE: I trust Spirit.
UN: I am not separate from them.
CP: I am Spirit.
CB: I am co-creating with Spirit.
UA: I am free.
TH: I am unique.

Ether

Ether is the subtle element of vibration.

"I am convinced that there are universal currents of Divine Thought vibrating the ether everywhere and that any who can feel these vibrations is inspired."

~ Richard Wagner

Affirmation

I am Universal Cosmic Consciousness.

Card Message

Ether is the vibratory space in which creation is displayed. Your body is made up of approximately 6% Ether. Ether is the background on which Spirit projects finite creation. The energy of Ether is calling you towards deeper states of awareness. In order to align with this cosmic vibration, you must be aware of your present state of consciousness. When your energy centers are balanced, and your mind is still, calm and present, you become centered and aware of the etheric realm. You are awake to the fact that you are consciously vibrating as the substance of the creative life force; the same energy permeating all of creation. There is no separation between you and all that exists. You are vibrating energy manifested from all the elements of earth, water, fire and air, appearing as a physical form onto the etheric screen of life.

Call in the energies of your own essence. Feel yourself filled with divine conscious energy vibrating within the universe. Connect to the energies of your own uniqueness, your song and your gifts. Honor your own personal, energetic energy and feel fulfillment in who you are.

Card Symbology

The figure sits gracefully on the lotus flower filled with cosmic energy. The patterns within the image are the Sri Yantra. The Sri Yantra mandala permeates as the holy symbol formed from the mantric sound pattern of Aum (Om, Amen.) This vibration is the structure behind all creation. Its sacred geometry symbolizes the feminine creative aspect of sacred sound, which creates patterns of light that mirror many manifestations of divinity. We are all a part of this light. It is one of the most powerful, positive energy symbols.

The image reflects waking consciousness birthed from being centered and grounded in the present moment. The color magenta is one of universal harmony and emotional balance.

44

Experience the
Transcendental
Video & Audio Journey
on my Website to
Expand Your
Consciousness!

Journey

Find a quiet place where you can relax undisturbed. Sit comfortably
with your spine straight. Take a deep breath in, tensing your body from
your feet to your head. Bring awareness to each body part, as you tense
each muscle one by one, within the same inhale. As your entire body
is tensed with energy, hold your breath until you are ready to exhale
and release. As you exhale, make any audible sounds to expel all tension from your body. Repeat this exercise three times or until you feel
relaxed. Gently begin allowing your natural breath to move in and out.
With each inhale, silently chant: "I am Spirit." With each exhale, chant:
"Spirit has become me." Remain in this state for as long as needed,
feeling all distracting thoughts subside.

You are traveling into the portal of cosmic consciousness. You feel yourself as intelligent Cosmic Vibration, or Aum. This vibration structures all
of creation, including your physical body as the substance of the combined elements: earth, water, fire, air, and ether. These structural forces
are intelligent and vibrating in nature. You journey into your soul deep
within the layers of spirit, into the place of union, love and self-respect.
You honor the creative life force that pulsates within your own physical being. Gratitude pours out like a fountain of light guiding you to the
truth that you are vibrating spirit. Your entire being is now saturated with
the realization of truth. Call in the energies of your own essence. Call
yourself in by your name. Feel into your core, inside the particles of the
universe that is only and totally filled with you. Honor the energies of
your own uniqueness, your song and your gifts. All these vibrating energies make you unique and special. You are a brilliant diamond, flawless
and dazzling. Fill yourself with deep gratitude for your personal, energetic signature that is taking form within you. Remain in this space and
admire your own personal energies. Witness how pleasing it is to share
these gifts. Feel how exciting it is to create with the fuel of passion burning from your heart. It is natural for you to deliver the message of truth
through the channel of your throat. You are authentic. You float amongst
the swirling energies being projected on the screen of the cosmic motion picture of creation.

You are awake, present and centered, completely aware that you are
conscious vibration as the creative force.

Repeat and affirm:

> "Oh vibrating spirit of my soul, where perfection abounds, I give deep reverence for your creative energy that makes up my material existence. I am universal cosmic consciousness, vibrating with all of creation. I vibrate in the Etheric realm where all Spirit is projected. My spark is unique and talented, infused with my own personal energetic signature. The intelligence of God is the spark that activates and energizes all of creation. This spark created me. I am creative cosmic vibration, filled with transcendental energy. I am here to create and co-create in this synergistic energy of love."

When you return from your journey, take a deep breath and reflect on the insights you received. Smile inwardly into your heart and thank your Godly self for the work you have done to accept life, yourself and others. Record any insights or awakenings in your copy of the *Reawakening the Soul Vision Quest Workbook*.

Introspection

Do I acknowledge my own essential Spirit?

Am I connected to my Divine Source?

Am I aware of the subtle energy that sustains me?

EFT/Tapping

KC: Even though I don't feel like I'm vibrating energy, I completely accept the way I feel.
KC: Even though it's hard for me to comprehend vibration, I am open to exploring it.
KC: Even though I forget to honor my own unique energy, I deeply love myself.

EB: What is vibration?
SE: Do I really consist of all the elements?
UE: I never gave much thought to this.

UN: But it feels interesting.
CP: Parts of me are earth.
CB: Parts of me are water.
UA: Parts of me are fire.
TH: Parts of me are Air.

EB: Parts of me are Ether.
SE: I am vibrating energy.
UE: Existing in all of creation.
UN: What is unique about my vibration?
CP: How am I different from others?
CB: These differences are my gifts.
UA: What am I passionate about?
TH: These passions are the consciousness that makes me unique.

EB: I am ready to remember the spark of God that I am.
SE: I want to feel connected.
UE: I am willing to learn how to quiet my mind.
UN: To be in the present moment.
CP: This feels good.
CB: I just have to breathe.
UA: And breathe even deeper.
TH: As I release my mind through my breath.

EB: I feel my creative life force.
SE: My life force wants to expand.
UE: And spread throughout eternity.
UN: I am floating in the space of ether.
CP: As my consciousness expands.
CB: I feel myself as energy.
UA: I know myself as Spirit.
TH: I am vibrating energy.

EFT
Audio Available
to Activate
Your
Spirit!

"The only source of knowledge
is experience."

~ Albert Einstein

Abundance

Accumulate the wealth of wisdom acquired through God realization.

Abundance

"Doing what you love is the cornerstone of having abundance in your life."

~ Wayne Dyer

Affirmation

I am one with Spirit. I am abundant.

Card Message

Abundance, in all it's forms, is broad and expansive. The amount of abundance available to experience depends upon the amount of awareness one has gained through wisdom. Explore and feel the richness of this truth by developing a relationship with your Creator. In this place of connection, you will obtain and enjoy genuine wealth. See beyond ordinary states of being and reawaken the conscious realization of truth within yourself. You are Spirit manifested into human form. In reality, you are immortal!

Developing a relationship with yourself goes hand in hand with developing a relationship with God. When you love yourself, you naturally begin to feel God's love for you, which fuels your desire to love God. When you know and acknowledge the Divine Source supporting you in all your daily activities, your only desire will be to please God. The more consciously aware you become, the stronger your union with Spirit will be.

By gaining wisdom through experience, you cultivate awareness of the Divine energy that sustains your very existence. Through this wisdom, you are able to fully love and serve others by shining your light into their hearts. The more you shine in this generous manner, the more abundant you are. Pay attention to any emotions or situations in your life that may be taking your valuable time and blocking your flow. Empty yourself of all negative energies that stop you from giving and receiving. Let go of old patterns, beliefs and judgments that no longer serve you. Free up more space by forgiving everyone in your life, including yourself. (See Forgiveness) The more layers of ego you shed, the more expansive you become as a "container" of all good things. With this clearing, you will have the extra space to welcome Divine love, financial wealth, health, wellness and peace of mind.

Abundance is measured by your capacity to love. You are able to feel abundance in proportion to the size of your container, which is the amount of space you have available to love. When you feel the over flowing, all-powerful love of God, your consciousness expands and your capacity to love magnifies. The more you love and allow yourself to be loved, the more you feel Spirit moving through you. When you remain connected to this Divine flow, which is universal law, your life will change. Staying in this natural rhythm creates a harmonious, happy, healthy and prosperous life. This is true abundance!

Card Symbology

The Sri Yantra mandala is the holy symbol formed from the mantric sound pattern of Aum (Om, Amen). This vibration is the structure that forms all creation. This sacred geometry symbolizes the feminine creative aspect of sound, which creates patterns of light that mirror many manifestations of Divinity. We are all a part of this light. The Sri Yantra is one of the most powerful and positive energy symbols in existence.

This symbol is formed by nine triangles surrounding and radiating out from the central point. This center is the junction point between the physical universe and it's unmanifest potential. The four triangles pointing up represent masculine energy. The five triangles pointing down symbolize feminine energy. The combination of these triangles represents the union of the masculine and feminine Divine. The Sri Yantra is enclosed by two rows of (8 and 16) petals, representing the lotus of creation and reproductive vital force. Triangles also represents good, evil, and activating qualities that make up character. All the life currents have to have three qualities to create our physical body. When our existence becomes pure, free from these three energies, then we are in Spirit. The sphere containing the triangles represents Eternity. There are two forces of Spirt, one projecting, creating finite forms and one attracting, withdrawing energy into the Infinite.

Journey

Find a quiet place where you can relax undisturbed. Sit comfortably with your spine straight. Take a deep breath in, tensing your body from your feet to your head. Bring awareness to each body part, as you tense each muscle one by one, within the same inhale. As your entire body is tensed with energy, hold your breath until you are ready to exhale and release. As you exhale, make any audible sounds to expel all tension from your body. Repeat this exercise three times or until you feel relaxed. Gently begin allowing your natural breath to move in and out. With each inhale, silently chant: "Abundance flows naturally." With each exhale, chant: "I am abundant." Remain in this state for as long as needed, feeling all distracting thoughts subside.

Radiant colors swirl all around you. As you breathe in this rainbow array of colors, you feel your internal body being cleansed. The color vibrations penetrate your light body, washing away the debris of limiting beliefs. These old beliefs have cluttered your energetic space. You are

Experience the Transcendental Video & Audio Journey on my Website to Create Absolute Abundance!!

aware that you are a vessel and you welcome abundance to pour into you. This healing rainbow light is like a magnet, pulling all the negativity out of your energy field. You easily allow and trust this transmission to clear and open your field, adjusting your point of attraction. You now feel still and powerfully magnetic, in a profound state of deep peace.

You are now transported into a portal of Divine energy. You feel expansive, like a wide-open receptive channel. You are ready and willing to shift your energy through awareness as you welcome the flow of increased abundance to enter into your rainbow body. As you begin your quest into this portal, you feel safe, confident and ready to be activated and initiated with Divine love. All the channels in your energetic field are now open as you receive this magical burst of light. Your heart is expanded, as it intuitively knows the language of love. Feel this love pulsating through your vital body, for this is the source of your existence. Your physical body is made up of light with the energy of love. Be still and receive this sacred attunement. With this transmission, you now know and feel the true meaning of love. With your openness, you experience unconditional love. So much love pours out through you, that there is no room for conditions. You are able to love for the sake of love itself. No more attachments or conditions inhibit you from loving. Just bask in this and feel how much love you have to give. You are able to share this love open-heartily because you now experience how loved you are by your great Creator. In this fullness, you can unite your soul back to Spirit. You know this is the highest form of abundance. You are aware that abundance is more than material riches. You feel yourself as essential love and you know this is God, This is Eternal Abundance, The Absolute, the Almighty and you are a part of this vibrant life force. You are not separated; you are One with this energy.

The Sri Yantra is the abundant everlasting consciousness permeating within everything and every being. This sacred geometry is the universal pulse that emanates out from Creation – God, Cosmic Intelligence, the Absolute . . . manifested in the material realm. The Sri Yantra is formed by the sacred sound vibration of Aum (Om, Amen) containing the frequency of spiritual harmony. Your soul is attuned to this harmonic vibration. You feel, hear and experience yourself as the essential Oneness of Om, resonating it's rhythm within your heartbeat. This is the pulse of the Divine Mother. You breathe, live and are sustained by this vibration, the essence of eternity. Merge into the vibration of Om and free yourself!

This holy light has activated you. With a wide-open heart you receive the unlimited blessings now pouring forth into your life. Welcome all the gifts of opportunity and glorious surprises. Feel the expansive amount of financial wealth entering into your life. Open and receive, for you are Spirit in a physical body. This burst of realization reminds you that you are healthy and whole, free from any illness or disease. You are a luminous spark of the Divine with profuse wisdom. You are free to create and live with passion, purpose and power. Envision yourself living every day of your life engaging in only the things that you love to do. Feel the achievement and success in living an authentic spirited life. The highest form of abundance is to live with the freedom found in remembering your true nature. You are Spirit and you are free to create. The whole universe moves in unison with your breath in an eternal cosmic rhythm. Every cell of your body beats with the cadence of oneness. You are immortal and true abundance is your inheritance!

When you return from your journey, take a deep breath and reflect on the insights you received. Smile inwardly into your heart and thank your Godly self for the work you have done to accept life, yourself and others. Record any insights or awakenings in your copy of the *Reawakening the Soul Vision Quest Workbook.*

Introspection

What does abundance mean to me?

How can I feel more abundant?

Can I allow myself to feel that I am a success exactly as I am in this moment?

EFT/Tapping

KC: Even though I don't feel as abundant as I would like, I accept the way I feel.

KC: Even though I am open to bringing forth more abundance in my life, I am content to where I am at this moment.

KC: Even though I know there is more abundance than I can comprehend, I am excited to explore new ways of receiving.

EB: What is abundance?
SE: What does it feel like to be abundant?
UE: When do I feel the most abundance?
UN: As I tap, I feel what abundance means to me.
CP: As I tap, I ask to experience true wealth.
CB: I ask to receive true health.
UA: And to experience spiritual vitality.
TH: And absolute truth.

EB: And peace and calmness.
SE: This is abundance.
UE: I know that I am abundant.
UN: Even though I want to be more abundant.
CP: I'm always wanting more.
CB: Maybe it's not having more.
UA: Maybe it's appreciating all that I have right now.
TH: Just by feeling this, I feel more expansive.

EB: I feel more abundant at this moment.
SE: I choose to let go of chasing after rainbows.
UE: And open to remember how abundant I am right now.
UN: My soul is flourishing with the essence of God.
CP: I am open to vibrant health.
CB: I am open to an abundance of wealth.
UA: I am prosperous.
TH: Because I know my oneness with Spirit.

EB: And I know my power.
SE: Spirit governs my power.
UE: And through this power is love.
UN: And love sustains me.
CP: And loving others feeds my soul.
CB: I love myself.
UA: As I love myself, and honor and give myself what I need.
TH: I open up to more abundance.

EB: By becoming better every day.
SE: And recognizing my faults without judging.
UE: I strive to do better.

EFT
Audio Available
to Clear Limiting
Blocks around
Abundance!

UN: And I become more abundant.
CP: I become more expansive.
CB: I'm willing to release old patterns.
UA: So that I have the space to love.
TH: And to be loved.

EB: I have the capacity to love whole heartily,
SE: Unconditionally.
UE: I feel abundance unfolding before me.
UN: I welcome and accept all this divine abundance.
CP: In this divine abundance,
CB: I know that health, wealth, wisdom and prosperity
UA: Is granted upon me.
TH: Abundance begins by being grateful.

EB: For everything in my life at this moment.
SE: Everything!
UE: I create my reality from my thoughts.
UN: I am so grateful.
CP: Because I feel the true meaning of abundance.
CB: My heart feels enlarged.
UA: I feel whole and complete.
TH: I am abundant.

"When you focus on being a blessing,
God makes sure that you are always
blessed in abundance."

~Joel Osteen

Acceptance

Embrace and be at peace with everything in your life.

Acceptance

"The good or bad is not in the circumstance, but only in the mind of him that encounters it."

~ James Allen ~

Affirmation

I embrace and accept everyone and myself.
I thank every situation in my life.

Card Message

The spirit of deer is gentle and innocent, reminding you to reflect on the calm peace residing deep within your soul. This card shares the message of the need for gentleness in your relationships with others as well as the importance of being gentle with yourself. To fully love others, you must first love yourself. Condition your mind to send sweet messages to yourself throughout the day. When you catch yourself thinking negative thoughts, replace them with encouraging and affirming ones.

It is important to open your heart to receive the universal love that permeates within and around your being. The deer remind you how love connects your mind with your soul. You achieve this connection by loving and accepting yourself exactly as you are in this very moment. When you learn to fully accept everything and everyone in your current life experience, you feel complete. Accept that you already have everything you need. By loving and accepting everything, you experience your true essence, which is Divinity. By allowing the perfection of what is, you become the expression of your higher self.

Card Symbology

The male and female deer in this card represent the ability to accept and appreciate the beauty of balance. Deer totem symbols represent: gentleness, kindness, compassion, innocence, grace, femininity, acceptance, renewal and connection to Spirit. The union of the red and orange colors that surround the deer bring vitality, courage, self respect and self confidence to support your place on this earth. As the colors blend from red to orange, they encourage you to cultivate the stability and survival skills needed to move into your own self interests, thereby strengthening your appetite for life. The color blue at the top of the card depicts self expression, knowledge and acceptance. The dream catcher in the center reminds you to view this life as only a dream. Stay clear of drama so that you do not forget to receive all the goodness that Spirit has to offer.

Journey

Find a quiet place where you can relax undisturbed. Sit comfortably with your spine straight. Take a deep breath in, tensing your body from your

58

Experience the
Transcendental
Video & Audio Journey
on Website to
Embrace Life
More Deeply!

feet to your head. Bring awareness to each body part, as you tense each muscle one by one, within the same inhale. As your entire body is tensed with energy, hold your breath until you are ready to exhale and release. As you exhale, make any audible sounds to expel all tension from your body. Repeat this exercise three times or until you feel relaxed. Gently begin allowing your natural breath to move in and out. With each inhale, silently chant: "I accept myself." With each exhale, chant: "I accept others." Remain in this state for as long as needed, feeling all distracting thoughts subside.

Find yourself sitting peacefully in a beautiful field at dusk. As your body relaxes into the peace of the wilderness, you notice that two beautiful deer, a male and female, have joined you in this beautiful field. As twilight approaches, fireflies illuminate this beautiful setting before you. As you gaze with admiration at the deer, they gently send their spirit blessings into your heart. Breathe in their gifts of gentleness, kindness, compassion, innocence, peace, awareness and acceptance. Inwardly recognize your own reflections of these characteristics. As you continue to breathe deeply, unify yourself with the essence of your Spirit and acknowledge your own unique gifts. Thank yourself for being able to embrace these precious attributes. Feel the presence of deer medicine invigorating your ability to move through life's obstacles with grace. Recognize the innocence of your inner child and embrace that special part of your self.

As the deer slowly walk away, you receive deep messages from them that will stay with you forever. You are now embraced with vibrant, swirling variations of the color orange. You feel radiant warmth embracing you with happiness. You experience such contentment and relaxation as you absorb the vibration that shines from this color. Bring any uncomfortable situations you are now facing into your awareness. Look deeply within as you ask yourself: "Am I embracing each and every circumstance?" "Am I feeling any resistance?" Fully accept everything in your life exactly as it appears before you, knowing that you have created these situations with your thoughts. Find peace in every scenario and search for a way to be grateful for every manifestation that helps you grow spiritually. Through the deer medicine spirit, you are now able to see the changes that need to be made in your life. Visualize these changes and take action to create your new reality.

You are now ready to see how you perceive others in your life. Inwardly ask yourself a few questions: "Do I find harmony in all my relationships?" "Can I fully love everyone exactly as they are without trying to change them?" "Do I find myself judging anyone?" As these answers become clear in your mind, release any expectations you have around how you feel another should behave. Each individual is perfect just as they are. Hold this perfection in your heart as you love them flawlessly. Bring serenity into your energy field and free everyone from any judgments you have about them. As you free them, you will feel your soul expanding.

Now it's time to look within your own heart and ask yourself: "Do I accept myself exactly as I am in this very moment?" "How can I love myself more deeply?" Feel any emotions that arise and breathe in your answers. Now ask: "How can I accept myself completely?" Find compassion for yourself. Embrace the beautiful, gentle deer energy that lives within you and has no judgments, blame or faults. Love yourself in this precious moment of the "now." Because of the impeccable nature of the divine law, you are flawless and your life is perfect. Accept and embrace the fullness of all that is and give thanks!

When you return from your journey, take a deep breath and reflect on the insights you received. Smile inwardly into your heart and thank your Godly self for the work you have done to accept life, yourself and others. Record any insights or awakenings in your copy of the *Reawakening the Soul Vision Quest Workbook.*

Introspection

Am I willing to learn to love myself?

Am I gentle to myself?

Am I open to allow myself to receive unconditional love from God?

How would I feel if I were to accept everything about my life situations?

EFT/Tapping

KC: Even though it's hard for me to fully tolerate this situation, I deeply and completely accept myself.

KC: Even though it's hard for me to completely accept myself, I deeply and completely love myself.

KC: Even though it's hard for me to completely embrace myself, and all the situations in my life, I deeply and completely love myself.

EB: I accept everything in my life.
SE: I accept what appears to be happening before me.
UE: I welcome all situations in my life.
UN: Because I embrace myself.
CP: Even though I judge myself.
CB: I'm constantly judging myself.
UA: I have a critical voice.
TH: I don't know how to silence it.

EB: How do I silence it?
SE: It's been a part of me for so long.
UE: This critical voice.
UN: It's in my head.
CP: Why do I criticize myself so much?
CB: My mind and my thoughts are full of self-judgments.
UA: What if I'm not good enough?
TH: Can I be better?

EB: All these judgments.
SE: Are they serving me?
UE: Why am I doing this?
UN: How can I stop?
CP: How can I be easier on myself?
CB: These judgments only create worry.
UA: And create stress in my life.
TH: How would I feel without any judgments?

EB: No judgments whatsoever.
SE: How would I behave differently?
UE: Can I really love and accept myself for exactly who I am?
UN: Without always judging myself?
CP: Without always trying to be better?

EFT
Audio Available
to Fully
Accept Life!

CB: Can I fully love and embrace myself?
UA: How can I forgive myself?
TH: Maybe I can take a deep breath.

EB: And forgive myself.
SE: I'm not perfect,
UE: And neither is anyone else.
UN: Releasing this need to be perfect.
CP: Forgiving myself.
CB: Accepting myself.
UA: And quieting this critical voice.
TH: It's time to quiet this critical voice.

EB: I thank this critical voice.
SE: Because this voice has been trying to help me.
UE: But now it's time to move on.
UN: It is safe to embrace myself.
CP: It is safe to love myself.
CB: My spiritual essence is love.
UA: My spiritual essence is LOVE.
TH: Every fiber of my being is made up of this essence.

EB: I fully accept this.
SE: I am willing to embrace this love.
UE: I open my heart and release the thought preventing
       me from receiving love.
UN: I let go of all self-judgment.
CP: Because it's all made up from my mind.
CB: I am love.
UA: And I accept the love that I am.
TH: I fully accept myself.

Awareness

Know and understand what is happening in your created world.

Awareness

*"The first step toward change is awareness.
The second step is acceptance."*

~ Nathaniel Branden

Affirmation

I am aware that I am Spirit.

Card Message

Stop. Take a moment and breathe. Begin to fill yourself with the breath of silence. Allow your body to melt into the Universe. You are grounded, mindful and fully present. You feel Spirit occupying every cell of your being.

You observe the world around you with a watchful, open heart. You are consciously aware that your thoughts create everything you experience. You are seeing through the eyes of God. Pause and take note of the life you have uniquely created. There is no space for judgment. You accept everything in your life because you know it's all perfect.

You witness every earthly experience as an opportunity to remember your Divine essence. You welcome whatever comes your way because you are in tune with your Great Creator. You trust life deeply because you know that everything is happening in harmony with nature. Your thoughts are in alignment with truth and you live a completely authentic life. Now is the time to burn away the past, spread your wings and soar!

Card Symbology

The white birds that fly free represent the purity of your soul. They reflect the inner awareness of your truth. In this truth within your soul is the passion required to soar towards your dreams. You are one with Spirit and have never been separated. The fanciful bouncing spheres represent the inner child who is part of each of us, full of wonder, play and innocence. The energy of the child contains the freedom to create with enthusiasm.

The center of the mandala holds the flames that burn away limiting beliefs. Flames also represent our inner passion to accomplish our individual divine missions. This passion is always burning and by connecting and interacting with burning passion you will manifest the desired outcome, the life that you were destined to live.

The star has many meanings. It is a symbol of the spiritual eye that can be seen when you fix your whole attention at the point between the eyebrows. This is the Christ Consciousness center, the seat of the single eye spoken of by Jesus, "The light of the body is the eye: if therefore thine eye be single, thy whole body shall be full of light" (Matthew 6:22). The star is also a symbol of faith. The six pointed star signifies balance and protection. It connects the heart chakra and the mind, the mental plane and produces powerful healing aspects. Each star point represents an individual aspect: Spiritual Will/Purpose; Emotional; Rational Mind; Higher Mind; Universal Love; and Physical Body.

Journey

Find a quiet place where you can relax undisturbed. Sit comfortably with your spine straight. Take a deep breath in, tensing your body from your feet to your head. Bring awareness to each body part, as you tense each muscle one by one, within the same inhale. As your entire body is tensed with energy, hold your breath until you are ready to exhale and release. As you exhale, make any audible sounds to expel all tension from your body. Repeat this exercise three times or until you feel relaxed. Gently begin allowing your natural breath to move in and out. With each inhale, silently chant: "I breathe in silence." With each exhale, chant: "I breathe out peace." Remain in this state for as long as needed, feeling all distracting thoughts subside.

You are embarking on a journey into a vortex of consciousness where the seed of awareness is planted. You are traveling to another dimension, and another place and time. Flying inward towards the center of your soul, you embrace this breathtaking voyage to bliss. You relinquish all your senses and allow them to float away as they merge with the omnipresent vibration of Spirit. You are now an electromagnetic wave, and you feel yourself as pure cosmic consciousness, fully alive and vibrating with the energy of spirit. You feel the grand expansion of this Holy Spirit rippling out from within you and feel it residing in everything and everyone.

As you travel through this holy and sacred light, you feel yourself letting go of all bodily attachment. You begin to feel lighter and completely free. You are now free from all sensory attachments entering into the zone of absolute awareness. You are no longer attached to the material world. You are free from emotions that create your karmic destiny. In this state, your will is aligned with God's will.

Experience the Transcendental Video & Audio Journey on my Website to Gain Deeper Awareness!

Appearing before you is a star ignited with flames and bursting with force. You feel these flames representing your own inner passion to accomplish your divine mission. The flames ignite the passion of your soul, endowing you with enthusiasm. You allow these flames to open the eyes of your heart and direct you forward on your earthly mission, into the life that you were destined to live.

The star represents the balance of the masculine and feminine energies in your energetic field. You take a moment as you notice all of your feminine qualities. Notice how compassionate, loving, nurturing, and giving you are. Now notice all of your masculine qualities reflected out of this sacred geometry. Energies of will power, safety, security, and the ability to reason.

Become aware of any areas hindering you from achieving perfect balance, for example; Are you giving too much? Are you allowing yourself to receive? Are you too sensitive or emotional? Are you repressing emotions? Do you always feel the need to be in control? Whatever these may be, look into the areas where you don't feel balanced. What limiting beliefs are you holding onto that are keeping you from living your passion? Which of your dreams may be suffocating due to fear? Release all the energies that are no longer serving you into the fire. Allow the glowing cosmic heat to align your energetic field as it charges you with perfect harmonious balance.

You are now floating on the bosom of the cosmic mother. As you gaze at the birds, feel yourself becoming part of the flock, flying free without any resistance towards your dreams and goals. Feel the innocence of your inner child having fun, playing and feeling full of joy. Your creation is a gift to yourself and to the world. This gift is completely unique and one only you possess.

What are you deeply passionate about? Maybe there's some secret passion hidden in your soul that wants to speak. Take time to listen to the voice of your soul. By listening and acting, you've freed the karmic bondage holding you back from creating your dreams. You see all your dreams with crystal clarity. You will never stop dreaming, nor will you allow anything or anyone to hold you back. You are fully awake and aware of your vision. Keep dreaming because you can create anything. Spread your wings wide open like the bird soaring through the sky.

Repeat the following:

"I have broken all the bonds holding me back from flying towards my dreams. I now fly, fully awake and aware. I am absolute Spirit. I am God's little child here on earth playing and creating.

I am vibrating intelligent consciousness. I am consciously aware that my thoughts create everything in my experience. I know that everything is harmoniously occurring according to the nature of my thoughts. My thoughts are in alignment with the truth that I am Spirit.

I trust life because I trust myself. I am authentic. I now understand my created world, and how I contribute to its creation. I have returned to earth to break away from my limiting mortal delusion, and to live as an immortal child of God.

I am aware that all my dreams are possible, and all my goals are achievable. I now see through the eyes of God. I welcome whatever comes my way, because I am in tune with my great Creator. I am fully awake and aware.

I spread my wings and soar in the open skies of grace!"

When you return from your journey, take a deep breath and reflect on the insights you received. Smile inwardly into your heart and thank your Godly self for the work you have done to accept life, yourself and others. Record any insights or awakenings in your copy of the *Reawakening the Soul Vision Quest Workbook*.

Introspection

Am I completely authentic?

Am I living in the present moment?

Can I love and embrace the perfection of my life exactly as it appears in this moment?

EFT/Tapping

KC: Even though I think I'm aware, I'm willing to explore becoming more aware.

KC: Even though I get caught up in the world, and I forget my spiritual nature, I except the way I feel.

KC: Even though I don't feel present and grounded, I deeply love myself

EB: What exactly does it mean to be aware?
SE: I know at times I'm caught up in the world.
UE: My mind seems to constantly ramble.
UN: Can I bring myself back to the present moment?
CP: And become completely aware.
CB: Conscious of what I'm thinking.
UA: Fully aware that I am a soul.
TH: Living in this space seems nice.

EB: And feels peaceful.
SE: It feels content.
UE: Ah, Just being here now.
UN: And being conscious of the now.
CP: It feels liberating.
CB: I choose to breathe deeply.
UA: And fully awaken to the spirit that I am.
TH: This feels good.

EB: This makes me feel alive.
SE: This makes me feel powerful.
UE: Knowing that I am spirit.
UN: I am all that exists.
CP: I am vibration.
CB: My consciousness comes from God.
UA: I feel alive.
TH: I feel more content.

EFT
Audio Available
to Activate
Higher
Awareness!

EB: I am electromagnetic waves.
SE: And I am aware of my power.
UE: I now reclaim my power.
UN: At times, my soul feels trapped.
CP: But I'm willing to explore how to let it out.
CB: Because I want my soul to fly free.
UA: My soul wants to be free.
TH: And I now choose to free my soul.

EB: I can do this by letting go of my mind.
SE: My busy mind.
UE: And choose to stay focused on the holy presence within.
UN: I am excited to free my soul.
CP: I fly into the awareness of spirit.
CB: And I release my soul once and for all.
UA: I am aware that I am a soul.
TH: I am immortal.

"The key to growth is the
introduction of higher dimensions of
consciousness into our awareness."

~ Lao Tzu

Balance

Bring harmonious equilibrium into your life.

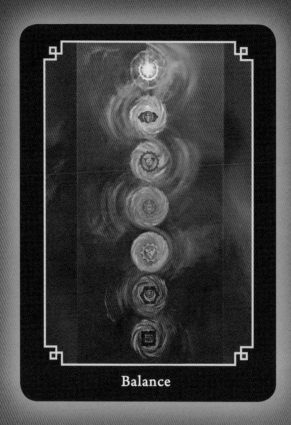

Balance

"Happiness is not a matter of intensity but of balance, order, rhythm and harmony."

~ Thomas Merton

Affirmation

I now experience perfect balance in my life.

Card Message

Achieving balance and harmony requires focusing on the physical aspects of your life while taking time to spiritually nourish your soul. Balance is necessary for well being as it connects you to your source. Paramahansa Yogananda says "Life is expressed in a threefold way: through thoughts, desires, and actions. Rightly guide all three forms of expression and they will lead you to a higher state of consciousness. In your activities you are the creator, the preserver, the transformer: your will is the director." Perfect balance is only living in the present instead of living in the past and in the future at the same time.

When you attain balance in your mental, physical, emotional and spiritual life, you will flow effortlessly through circumstances and situations. You begin to feel calm, intuitive, peaceful, joyous and centered in your being. When you are in balance, your body feels light and connected to the universe yet grounded and without physical discomfort. When you feel excited about life and look forward to the magic found in every moment, you have found harmony.

When your mental, physical, emotional and spiritual life is out of balance, you may experience emotions such as anxiety, nervousness, sadness, depression and anger. Without balance, you may lack a sense of purpose or belonging. You may blame others for your discomfort and mistrust the world. Your body may feel fatigued and lack energy because you have disconnected from the natural flow of life force.

Take a look inward and see how balanced you feel right now. Pay attention to any adjustments needed in order to bring yourself back to your center. Challenge yourself to take a step back and witness how you are currently spending your days. As you allow yourself to process this information, pay attention to how your body responds. You will know instantly if you are living your life in alignment with your soul's purpose by how your body feels. The wisdom of your body sends messages alerting you to what areas of your life are out of balance; all that is required is taking time to stop and listen to the body's wisdom. If you feel out of balance, make any necessary changes that will bring you back into alignment.

Balance is also found when you allow yourself to equally give and receive. Observe these areas in your life and see how you currently handle giving and receiving. Are you giving too much of yourself to the external world physically, energetically and emotionally? Are you able to receive equally in these same areas? When you harmonize with your inner being, you will feel the ease of giving with love and receiving with an open heart.

Your body is made up of energy centers known as chakras. Chakras are spirals of spinning energy that are closely associated with specific organs and joints in the body. These living energy centers spin individually along a vertical power current that runs up and down your body. Even though each center moves and functions independently, together they create a unified system. When one of the centers is not spinning in harmony, it will cause imbalances within your physical, emotional, spiritual, intellectual and physical journey. Every life experience has an affect on your energy body; some experiences will be perceived as positive and some will feel negative. The perception of negative experiences over time can manifest physically as disease. When illness or disease is indicated, the body is communicating to you that your way of thinking is out of alignment with your highest good. Illness indicates the need to change your belief system and lets you know that you have reached your physical and psychological limits. You are Spirit in a physical body and your goal is to find harmony within yourself midst the disharmony.

Card Symbology

Painted on this card are the seven main energy centers (chakras) of the body. "Chakras" are energy centers where life force flows into and out of our being. The word chakra comes from the Sanskrit, meaning "wheel" or "disk." These spinning vortexes of energy are part of the subtle energy system from the teachings of many ancient cultures. These centers are a basic part of our energetic anatomy. When we are healthy, these centers are in perfect alignment with the universal flow of life. Chakras move individually in balance and interdependently with one another, like an orchestra of energy. Chakras correspond to the colors of the spectrum; and each center resonates with it's own musical note. Depending on what energy we take in from our environment and how easily we release old, stuck energetic residue, we can either be invigorated or restrained by our chakra centers. It is important to replenish your chakras if they have become depleted of energy. This can be done with light therapy and visualization along with taking necessary action to change the behaviors that caused the imbalance in the first place.

Beginning at the bottom of the painting and moving upward, each chakra will briefly be explained.

Root Chakra:
Root Chakra: The first chakra is the foundation of the entire chakra system. The Root Chakra is related with physical needs and basic human survival. This chakra records and stores your earliest experiences in infancy and how your basic needs were met or not.

Location: Base of spine, coccygeal plexus, perineum.

Color: Red.

Purpose: Foundation, survival, stability, grounding, self-preservation and self-awareness.

Issues: Home, family, health, work, finances, trust, security, nourishment.

Painted symbol: The Root Chakra is depicted as a four-petalled lotus flower encompassing a downward-pointing triangle and is set within a square. The square represents the element Earth, or yantra, and the inverted triangle denotes downward movement of energy that keeps us grounded and connected to the Earth. The four lotus petals symbolize the four elements.

Unbalanced characteristics: Lack of energy, restlessness, volatile emotions, selfishness, insecurity, fear, self-pity, aggression, jealousy, resentment, poverty, low self-esteem, anxiety, fear, anger and frustration.

Balanced characteristics: Groundedness, physical health, prosperity, feeling comfortable in your body, a sense of safety and security, stability and solidity, ability to be still, presence in the here and now.

Sacral Chakra:
Sacral Chakra: The Sacral Chakra leads us from basic existence and survival upward to the "pleasure principle" to help embrace what makes life sweet and worth living. It is linked with your inner child, creativity and spontaneity.

Location: Sacral area, lower abdomen, between navel and genitals, hips, low back.

Color: Orange.

Purpose: Movement and flow, change, passion, creativity and pleasure.

Issues: Emotions, sexuality, nurture and receptivity.

Painted Symbol: A six-petalled lotus containing a white circle that symbolizes the element of water and a crescent moon. The moon relates to creativity, the energy that shifts humankind from survival to nourishing the soul. The moon is crescent because there is duality in this chakra representing visible light and darkness. This tribal energy of the Root split into yin/yang, suggesting the need to evolve beyond the group to establish your "self."

Unbalanced characteristics: Rigidity in your body, beliefs, or behavior, fear of change, lack of desire, passion or excitement, poor social skills, fear of sexuality, avoidance of pleasure, emotional numbness or insensitivity, boredom, poor boundaries, instability, feelings of guilt, emotional imbalances, addictions.

Balanced characteristics: Passion, trust, expression, attuned to your own feelings, creativity, emotional intelligence, ability to embrace change, nurturance of self and others, healthy boundaries, ability to enjoy pleasure, sexual satisfaction.

Solar Plexus Chakra: With your body grounded and your emotions flowing, you can now generate energy. As it rises into this third chakra, your energy has the potential to become power. The Solar Plexus Chakra involves transforming the Self into a being of power and self-will.

Location: Solar Plexus.

Color: Yellow.

Purpose: Energy, will.

Issues: Personal power, strength of will, self-esteem, self-mastery, individuation.

Painted Symbol: A ten-petalled lotus flower with a downward-pointing triangle surrounded by three T-shaped svastikas (Hindu symbols of fire.)

Unbalanced characteristics: Dominance, passivity, lack of energy, blame, low self-esteem, lack of confidence, weak will, poor self-discipline, anger, insecurity, stubbornness.

Balanced characteristics: Responsible, reliable, confident, warm, energetic, spontaneous, playful, humorous, disciplined, able to take risks, personal power, respect for self and others.

Heart Chakra: From awakening the fires of your will, you now enter the sacred realm of the heart. The Heart Chakra intercedes between the worlds of spirit and matter. This is the central chakra within the sevenfold system—the heart of your journey. This is the chamber from which you give and receive love—the heart of your being.

Location: Chest, cardiac plexus.

Color: Green.

Purpose: Love, relationship, compassion.

Issues: Self-love, balance, relationship.

Painted Symbol: The symbol for this chakra is a twelve petaled lotus that contains two intersecting triangles that make up a six-pointed star. This star demonstrates the perfect balance between the downward-pointing spirit descending toward matter and the upward-pointing matter rising toward spirit.

Unbalanced characteristics: Loneliness, isolation, criticism, withdrawal, antisocial, lack of empathy, fear of intimacy, self-pity, conditional love, unworthiness to receive love.

Balanced characteristics: Caring, acceptance, compassion, self-love, peace, contentment, feeling centered, unconditional love, nurturing.

Throat Chakra: The Throat Chakra is the first of the higher centers. This fifth energy center is associated with sound, communication, vibration, rhythm and self-expression. It is about personal expression. As you successfully work through the lower four chakras, you can attain the purification necessary to open the Throat Chakra.

Location: Throat.

Color: Blue.

Purpose: Communication, creativity.

Issues: Self-Expression, speaking one's truth, listening.

Painted Symbol: 16 petaled lotus with a downward-pointing triangle symbolizing speech. Within the triangle is a circle representing the full moon.

Unbalanced characteristics: Fear of speaking, shyness, difficulty putting things into words, weak speech, difficulty being silent, lack of self-expression, unreliable.

Balanced characteristics: Clear communication with others, resonant voice quality, good communication with self, listening skills, artistic inspiration, sense of timing and rhythm.

Third Eye Chakra: The Third Eye Chakra is capable of seeing beyond the density of the physical world into the subtler realms of Spirit. By training your consciousness to be focused and directed, you can harness the gifts of your inner vision. This is the place where intuition becomes your insight. This sixth center is connected with the higher functions of consciousness and is used as a psychic tool.

Location: Above and between eyebrows.

Color: Indigo.

Purpose: Seeing, intuition, insight.

Issues: Intuition, clarity, imagination, vision.

Painted Symbol: The symbol is the two-petalled lotus, like wings on the side of a circle. Within the circle is a downward pointing triangle. The wings transcend physical limitations.

Unbalanced characteristics: Difficulty visualizing, lack of imagination, excessive skepticism, denial, insensitivity, difficulty concentrating, fear of success, highly logical.

Balanced characteristics: Strong intuition, charismatic, good memory, creative imagination, penetrating insight, lucid dreaming with recall, ability to visualize, clear vision for moving forward in life, non-attachment to the material world.

Crown Chakra: The crown Chakra represents the underlying consciousness that is the basic operating principle of the entire chakra system. Developing the other chakras is like a path that leads you to the ultimate goal – enlightenment, self-realization and ultimate freedom and fulfillment. This chakra assists you to free your consciousness from its usual distractions to experience and remember your own limitless, blissful nature. When you awaken the Crown Chakra you become aware of infinite possibilities with Divine wisdom and understanding.

Location: Crown/top of head.

Color: Violet or white.

Purpose: Pure awareness, understanding, unity with divine.

Issues: Spiritual connection, understanding, intelligence.

Painted Symbol: The Crown Chakra is a symbol of a halo with a thousand white petals associated with infinity, each petal is tuned to the highest states of consciousness.

Unbalanced characteristics: Spiritual cynicism, a closed mind, apathy, confusion, disconnection from spirit, learning difficulties, frustration, exhaustion, inability to make decisions.

Balanced characteristics: Spiritual connection, magnetic personality, wisdom and mastery, intelligence, presence, open-mindedness, ability to question, ability to assimilate and analyze information, peace.

Journey

Find a quiet place where you can relax undisturbed. Sit comfortably with your spine straight. Take a deep breath in, tensing your body from your feet to your head. Bring awareness to each body part, as you tense each muscle one by one, within the same inhale. As your entire body is tensed with energy, hold your breath until you are ready to exhale and release. As you exhale, make any audible sounds to expel all tension from your body. Repeat this exercise three times or until you feel relaxed. Gently begin allowing your natural breath to move in and out. With each inhale, silently chant: "My life is balanced." With each exhale, chant: "I am balanced." Remain in this state for as long as needed, feeling all distracting thoughts subside.

Move into the awareness of energy moving up and down your spine. Feel the spinning wheels of light that emanate from your spine that are giving you energy and will power. When your chakras are balanced, your state of being will reflect this balance and you will experience harmony in your life. This journey will allow you to draw in more light and help you release whatever stands in the way of your ability to receive light, love and well being. In this journey, you will begin at the root chakra and work up to the crown chakra, balancing each energy center as you go.

Experience the Transcendental Video & Audio Journe on my Website to Balance Your Energy Field!

Become aware of your root chakra located at the base of your spine. Visualize this center as a positive energy sphere. Inhale the color red; allow this vibrant color to penetrate light into your base center. The root chakra resonates with the note C. Begin to relax your entire pelvic floor. Release all tension from your coccyx, perineum and pelvic cavity. The foundation of your body is now completely relaxed. Visualize this energy center rooting deep into the earth. Imagine magnetic lines of energy coming from the earth's core, connecting with your root center. Allow this force of energy to rise from the earth and permeate your root chakra. You feel this force increasing its magnetic energy at the bottom of your spine. Allow this powerful energy of light to continue to flow into your body. You feel grounded, safe and protected. This nurturing energy connects you to your source. Release any fears of not feeling safe or supported in this world. Ask yourself, "How can I feel more support?" "How can I feel more grounded?" Discharge all blocks or residue into the vibrant red light and allow them to swirl away. This entire center is now fully open to receive healing light. Deeply breathe the radiant red colors into your core. Picture this light infusing you with grounded, supportive energy. You awaken and sense your connectedness to the physical world. You feel the universe fully assisting you with your dreams and desires. Now that you are connected to the earth's core, you feel grounded and complete. As you continue to breathe in the power of red, repeat these affirmations: "I feel safe." "I am completely supported." "I am grounded in Spirit." "I am always taken care of." Repeat as many times as needed until you feel totally confident and secure in the physical world.

Shift your awareness from your root center up to the sacral chakra, located just below your navel. Visualize this center as a positive energy sphere. Inhale the color orange, allowing the bright color to penetrate light into your sacral center and low back. This chakra resonates with the note D. Begin to relax your genital muscles. Release all tension from your buttocks, abdomen, hips, and pelvis. Release any energy blocks holding you from your ability to fully express yourself. Discharge all these blocks into the glowing orange light and watch them swirl away. This entire center is now fully open to receive healing light. Deeply breathe the warm, glowing orange color into your sexual center. Picture this light infusing you with creativity and spontaneity. Your inner child begins to awaken and you feel excited, alive and joyful. What is it that you love to create? What brings you joy? Bask in this light as you envision opening to express yourself in any way you wish. As you continue to breathe in the warmth, you draw forth the power of sexual energy. You feel passion and love invigorating your chakra. You begin to deeply love yourself as you draw in this healthy sexual stimulation. You feel yourself and your Beloved unite. You feel complete and whole in this perfect love. Now you ask yourself, "Are my relationships balanced?" View these relationships and see where they stand. When you are ready, draw in more light and envision your relationships harmoniously balanced. Repeat these affirmations: "I feel balanced in all my relationships." "I love myself." Repeat as many times as needed until you feel totally connected to your sexuality and creativity. You now are completely open to sensation, attraction and physical pleasure.

Shift your awareness from your sacral chakra up to the solar plexus chakra, located just below your heart and above your navel. Visualize this center as a positive energy sphere. Inhale the color yellow, allowing this energizing color to penetrate light into your solar plexus. This chakra resonates with the note E. Feel your abdominal muscles begin to relax. Release all tension from the organs of your stomach, intestines, kidneys, gall bladder and diaphragm. Release any energy blocks that have held you back from exerting your personal power. Ask yourself, "What am I afraid of?" Release all fears you may have of the outside world. These fears may make you feel vulnerable, afraid, defensive or aggressive. Discharge all negative energy into the glowing yellow light and allow them to swirl away. This entire center is now fully open to receive healing light. Deeply breathe the warm, glowing yellow color into your power center. Picture this light infusing you with self-esteem and personal power. You now awaken to your own power. You realize you no longer have any need to react to criticism. Your heart knows your truth and you don't need to please anyone. You feel powerful, brave and sure of your self. You are safe and secure. You feel heroic as if you can conquer the world. As you continue to breathe in the yellow flame, repeat these affirmations: "I am powerful." "I am brave." "I am safe." Repeat as many times as needed until you feel totally connected to your personal power.

Shift your awareness from your solar plexus chakra up to the heart chakra, located in the center of the chest. You have now reached the central chakra—the "heart" of your journey. The bridge of the heart intercedes between the worlds of spirit and matter, heaven and earth. Visualize this center as a positive energy sphere. Inhale the color green; allow this healing color to penetrate light into your heart. This chakra resonates with the note F. Begin to relax your chest muscles. Release all tension from your heart, lungs, thymus, and adrenals. Release any energy blocks preventing you from giving and receiving love. Ask yourself, "Am I able to receive love?" "Am I capable of loving others?" "Do I love myself?" Release all fears you may have around loving another and loving yourself. This light allows you to step into the act of forgiveness. Release everyone you need to forgive including yourself. Discharge any blocks around not being able to forgive. As you send these blocks into the nurturing, emerald green light, allow them to swirl away. This beautiful energy center is now fully open to receive healing light. Deeply breathe the expansive green light into your heart center and imagine your Beloved appearing before you. Feel the love coming in and out of your heart with each breath. Breathe in to receive soothing love and give it away every time you exhale. Picture this light infusing you with the capability to forgive and love unconditionally. Now allow your capacity of love to grow to include all the people you know. Gradually expand this love to all the people you don't know until your expanding love covers the world. You awaken and experience a new sense of freedom within. You feel such love as your heart bursts wide open with boundless compassion for all sentient beings. You are now able to love everyone unconditionally. You inwardly smile as you feel yourself as a kind, generous, loving being worthy of giving and receiving unconditional love that renews your soul. You love yourself, feeling complete and whole exactly as you are. You have a new acceptance of compassion and confidence for yourself. Maybe for the first time, you experience complete trust in your Creator. Celebrate this new gift of faith!

You feel such relief with a deep sense of inner peace and trust. Your inspiration and passion for life ignites a flame in your heart. You now embody earth and heaven within you, feeling a sense of the interconnectedness of all beings. With a wide-open heart, you now enjoy the qualities of goodwill, altruism, devotion and empathy. You have now arrived as a conscious participant in evolution. Every living being on earth is part of your family. You now choose to live and work for the benefit of the world. As you continue to breathe in the nurturing emerald green color, repeat these affirmations: "I am love." "I am loved." Repeat as many times as needed until you feel complete unconditional love for everyone and yourself.

Shift your awareness from your heart chakra up to the throat chakra, located at the base of the throat. Visualize this center as a positive energy sphere. Inhale the color blue; allow this soothing color to penetrate light into your heart. This chakra resonates with the note G. Begin to relax your throat muscles. Release all tension from your tongue, vocal cords, neck muscles, shoulders, arms and hands. With each exhalation, feel the radiant energy flow through your thyroid, at the base of your neck, and throughout your entire upper respiratory tract. Inhale the blue light and as you exhale, sigh out the sound, *Ahhh.* Repeat this several times until you feel your throat chakra begin to open. Release any energy blocks that have been holding you back from speaking and living your truth. Let go of anything inhibiting you from taking responsibility for your own needs. Discharge any blocks around not being able to express your personal creativity and soul-dreams.

Allow these blocks to swirl away into the blue spiral. This energy center is now fully open to receive healing light. Deeply breathe the healing blue light deep into your throat and neck. Picture this light infusing you with the capability to clearly communicate your ideas and needs and to fully express your creative self in the highest way possible. Breathe and allow yourself to fully surrender to Divine will. Inhale the healing blue light and feel how you can trust your Creator. You now awaken and experience a new sense of personal authority. Your throat feels completely open and your neck is soft and relaxed. You are able to easily express your thoughts. You are also able to express and create through sound. Your words are a creative union of thoughts and energy, filled with purpose and meaning. You clearly see your thoughts becoming ideas, concepts and manifestations in the material world. This is as a result of your intent, creation and skill. What you say is worthy of being heard. You are able to speak up for yourself. Your voice is strong and compelling as you speak from your heart. Continue to breathe in the vibrant blue and think of these words, "I want . . . I need . . . " What do you want? "What do you need? You have the right to ask for what you want and what you need. You have the right to have your demands heard. Repeat as many times as needed until you feel respected and validated. Know that your needs and wants are important. You have everything you need within you to meet these needs for yourself. By realizing this, you will find that others will support and honor your wishes as well.

Shift your awareness from your throat chakra to the brow chakra or third eye, located above and between the eyebrows. Visualize this center as a psychic energy sphere. Inhale the color indigo; allow the deep color to penetrate light into your third eye. This chakra resonates with the note A. Begin to relax deeply and imagine that each breath is opening this center in your head. Continue to open and allow the brilliant light directly into your third eye chakra. Feel your head becoming transparent and expansive. Picture a radiant, super-natural indigo colored light pouring in through your eyes and brain, illuminating your consciousness in every dimension. Your mind becomes completely still as the silent voice of intuition is activated. You glimpse the skies of quietness and taste the fountain of your joyous existence. With a deep inner knowing of absolute truth, you are now beyond the limits of your senses. You have risen above your personal identity altogether. You know yourself as essential truth and divine love. You have direct perception of the great unseen forces of eternity. Absolute selflessness enables you to see beyond the ordinary limits of time and space. You now enter the psychic dimension of your inner vision. You continue to let the light in through the window of your inner eye as the universal light dispels all darkness, dis-ease and doubt. You step into your spiritual nature as a highly evolved soul, reincarnating through this lifetime and other lives. You have entered a cosmic journey towards enlightenment. Your mission is to liberate yourself and free others from delusional suffering. You continue to absorb the indigo color as you begin to perceive your Divine connection. You stand in humility and grace as you rediscover your gifts of healing. You are connected to the power of pure consciousness. Bask in this interconnectedness.

Shift your awareness from your third eye to the crown chakra, located at the top of your head. Visualize this center as a thousand-petalled lotus opening upward from the top of your head. Inhale the luminous, supernatural violet color and brilliant white light of pure cosmic consciousness; allow this spiritual light to penetrate into the crown of your head. This chakra resonates with the note B. Begin to relax deeply and imagine that you are now connecting with your higher self. Each breath is allowing Divine wisdom to pour into your being. You have become a fountain of truth. Continue to open and allow the brilliant white light to permeate your chakra. Eternity pours into you from below, above, on the left and on the right, in front and behind, within and without. You perceive yourself as the cosmic center around which the sphere of omniscient, blissful eternity revolves. You feel the gentle breath of Spirit breathing universes into your body. You perceive luminous twinkles of creation sparkling on the waves of cosmic consciousness. You are guided and lead by Spirit. By reuniting with God, you have become a fountain of wisdom with radiant inspiration flowing through your soul. You feel love percolating through you heart and trickling out into the earth, through the sky and into all of creation. You become one with your Source as the eternal motion of joy. Trust that everything in your life is unfolding perfectly and for your highest good. You perceive on a soul level that everything is Divine, Infinite and Spiritual. . . including yourself! Bliss becomes the truth of your existence. Your home is the universe. As a perfect instrument of the great plan, you spiritually contribute to the evolution of humanity towards planetary enlightenment. As a godly spiritual being, you are fulfilling this destiny right now.

All the colors of your chakras merge together and become white. You feel this energy flowing up into your spinal center. An iridescent spring of pure, brilliant white energy billows up from the earth and fills your root chakra, stimulates your sexual organs, warms your belly with power, fills your heart with love, resonates in your voice, vibrates your inner eye and shoots out the top of your head! This glittering light is the essence of pure universal energy. It is shining from your head into the sky and into deep space beyond. You are infinite. You are spaceless and timeless—beyond body, thought, matter and mind. You know your True Self, as infinite, endless bliss!

When you return from your journey, take a deep breath and reflect on the insights you received. Smile inwardly into your heart and thank your Godly self for the work you have done to accept life, yourself and others. Record any insights or awakenings in your copy of the *Reawakening the Soul Vision Quest Workbook*.

Introspection

How would my life appear if it were perfectly balanced?

How would I feel to be evenly poised?

What is one action that I can take today in order to begin to experience more equilibrium?

EFT/Tapping

KC: Even though my life doesn't feel harmoniously balanced, I accept myself and the way I feel.

KC: Even though I don't feel grounded and balanced, I deeply and completely love myself.

KC: Even though I don't feel balanced in many areas of my life, I deeply and completely accept where I am.

EB: What does balance mean to me?
SE: Am I balanced?
UE: As I tap, I look within.
UN: And feel if I am balanced.
CP: Is my body healthy?
CB: Am I suffering from any illnesses?
UA: Am I happy?
TH: Do I feel complete?

EB: Do I feel at peace?
SE: Do I feel joyous?
UE: How would I feel if I were completely balanced?
UN: I would feel energetic.
CP: I would feel passionate.
CB: I would feel joy.
UA: I tap and I look within.
TH: As I tap, I feel any imbalance.

EB: I can make any changes necessary to feel balanced.
SE: It is all my choice.
UE: I am safe to make these changes.
UN: It is safe for me to bring balance in my life.
CP: No matter what changes need to be made.
CB: I am willing to make them.
UA: I am willing to take the next step.
TH: Into a balanced and happy life.

EB: My soul feels this happiness.
SE: The more I align with my soul.
UE: And my absolute truth.
UN: I move into a more balanced state.
CP: I am excited to move here.
CB: Here, I feel grounded.
UA: Supported.
TH: And I have all the courage.

EFT
Audio Available
to Bring
Your Life
into
Balance!

EB: To make these necessary changes.
SE: To bring balance into my life.
UE: I now step into my power.
UN: And I take action.
CP: In bringing passion back into my life.
CB: I feel energized.
UA: I am complete, whole and balanced.
TH: In every aspect of my mind.

EB: My mind is balanced.
SE: My spirit is balanced.
UE: My emotions are balanced.
UN: And my physical body reflects this balance.
CP: My body is healthy and whole.
CB: I reclaim the power of my will.
UA: And the wisdom of my soul.
TH: I move into a place of perfect balance.

Beauty

Your true nature is reflected from your soul.

Beauty

"Everything has beauty, but not everyone sees it."
~ Confucius

Affirmation

The beauty that radiates within me spreads
throughout the universe.

Card Message

You will experience the truest essence of beauty when you realize the perfection of your soul. Your soul is the complete reflection of Spirit, made in the image of God. It has however become identified with the physical body and mind, and has lost its true identity. Beauty is reborn when you experience your true nature again. Meditation is the way for you to achieve this. When you cast aside all of your thoughts and merge with the oneness of your soul, you will remember your divinity. Every soul holds this quality. When you achieve this truth, you will behold the unity of all souls. You will be illuminated by the beauty and perfection of everyone and everything.

When you examine nature and see the wondrous patterns of flowers, trees, soft blue sky, and hear the music from the birds, your heart naturally feels a deep sensation of pleasure. Look behind the landscape of the sensory world and know that the energy responsible for everything is birthed from Spirit. Everyone is part of this same beautiful Spirit.

With wisdom, you begin to know that there is beauty to be found in every occurrence life brings to you. When you look deeply into every circumstance, you will behold the beautiful gift that is uniquely created just for you. Through this awareness and acceptance, you awaken to the innate calm nature of who you are—a beautiful child of God.

Take some time to look within and recognize your unique gifts. Observe your personality, talents, physical appearance, and wisdom. Love and accept the beauty found in every trait that makes up who you are. Celebrate all these traits and find the goodness in all of them.

Card Symbology

The swans reflect the authentic beauty of Spirit found behind the essence of creation. When we realize ourselves as this expression, we experience the magic of beauty found in everything. Once this beauty is awakened, it spreads far and wide to beautify our world. The swan shows us how to see the inner truth within others and ourselves regardless of outer appearances. Swan is the totem of the child, the mystic, the poet and the dreamer. They are devoted parents and mates for life. Swan spirit helps us to remember our real parents, Divine Mother and Father God. We all have the same spiritual parents and we all come from the same source. When we feel the unconditional love and acceptance from our spiritual parents, our lives are forever transformed. The dream catcher is a symbol to remind us that we are dreaming our earthly experiences. When we learn to see the beauty in each dream experience, we easily enjoy the blessings that come from taking the time to reflect and process our experiences. The blessings are depicted in the painting by the exquisite lotus flower, gifting us with beauty as our souls bloom.

Experience the Transcendental Video & Audio Journey on my Website to Feel Your Divine Beauty!

Journey

Find a quiet place where you can relax undisturbed. Sit or lie comfortably with your spine straight. Take a deep breath in, tensing your body from your feet to your head. Bring awareness to each body part as you tense each muscle, one by one, within the same inhale. As your entire body is tensed with energy, hold your breath until you are ready to exhale and release. As you exhale, make any audible sounds to expel all tension from your body. Repeat this exercise three times or until you feel relaxed. Gently begin allowing your natural breath to move in and out. With each inhale, silently chant: "I breathe in beauty." With each exhale, chant: "I breathe out beauty." Remain in this state for as long as needed, feeling all distracting thoughts subside.

Imagine that you are like the swan, gracefully floating upon the water of life. Know that you have a choice of how you wish to experience the movement of the water. If your current life situation feels like rapids or waves, know that by changing your thoughts, your perspective of the water will reflect this change. It is time to create a gentler rhythm of movement in your life. Visualize the water being still and calm. Notice your thoughts becoming clear and tranquil. Spend some time witnessing how you have the ability to shift your awareness with your thoughts. Now in this place of peace, delve deeply into your quiet soul and direct your attention inward.

See yourself reflecting the beauty of the swan, for you are a beautiful individual, inside and out. Recognize your gifts and talents. Honor your disposition, intelligence and personality. Know that only you possess these special unique gifts. Your soul is beautiful and is an expression of how you choose to share in this world. Celebrate and bask in your divine beauty. Experience the calm nature of your being as the joyous rays of your soul are now illuminated. Enjoy the beautiful, peaceful scenery of the kingdom within your heart. In this place you realize the beauty of who you are.

Embrace all the beauty that you found within yourself. Emerge in your divinity and shine your Godly gifts into the world. Walk, breath and live in this joy, for you are truly beautiful!

When you return from your journey, take a deep breath and reflect on the insights you received. Smile inwardly into your heart and thank your Godly self for the work you have done to accept life, yourself and others. Record any insights or awakenings in your copy of the *Reawakening the Soul Vision Quest Workbook*.

Introspection

How would I act differently if I expressed myself as a God?

How can I make myself more spiritually beautiful?

How would I experience life differently if I recognized the beauty in every person and every situation?

EFT/Tapping

KC: Even though I don't feel beautiful right now, I deeply and completely love myself.
KC: Even though circumstances in my life don't feel beautiful right now, I completely accept myself.
KC: Even though I feel unworthy to experience beauty in my life, I deeply and completely accept myself.

EB: What does the quality of beauty mean to me?
SE: What does having beauty in my life appear like?
UE: Am I beautiful?
UN: Do I feel beautiful?
CP: Do others see me as beautiful?
CB: Do I see myself as beautiful?
UA: I am beautiful.
TH: Everything about me is wonderful.

EFT Audio Available to Feel Your Own Divine Beauty!

EB: I have so many unique talents and gifts to share.
SE: My gifts are beautiful.
UE: My passions are radiant.
UN: I have so much to share.

CP: I open up to my own inner beauty.
CB: And I accept my physical beauty.
UA: It is safe to feel beautiful.
TH: It is safe to express this beauty to the world.

EB: Because this is something that only I have.
SE: And no one else has it.
UE: Only I can give my unique gifts to the world.
UN: I am open to share my gifts.
CP: I remove any blocks allowing me from seeing my loveliness.
CB: I am like the alluring swan.
UA: And I swim gracefully in this world.
TH: I see beauty all around me.

EB: I understand that everything happening to me.
SE: Has something beautiful within it.
UE: Everything happening to me in this very moment.
UN: Has some beauty to shine in my life.
CP: I open and welcome all these divine gifts.
CB: I open to love myself.
UA: I open to love everyone around me.
TH: I love every situation.

EB: I am beautiful.
SE: I am willing to shine my beauty.
UE: I now shine my elegance.
UN: As my soul reawakens.
CP: I walk in this splendidness.
CB: My eyes behold the divine essence all around me.
UA: I am this essence.
TH: I am this goodness.

EB: When I acknowledge how beautiful I am.
SE: And see my innermost being.
UE: And the gifts that I give to the world.
UN: I float gracefully like the swan.
CP: My beauty spreads throughout the universe.
CB: I am divine.
UA: My soul is a diamond.
TH: And I allow myself to shine.

"Never lose an opportunity of seeing anything beautiful, for beauty is God's handwriting."

~ Ralph Waldo Emerson

Celebrate

Rejoice in the glory of who you are and what you do.

Celebrate

"If . . . I have lost every other friend on earth, I shall at least have one friend left, and that friend shall be down inside of me."

~ Abraham Lincoln

Affirmation

I celebrate all my individual characteristics and accomplishments. I rejoice in the truth that I am Spirit!

Card Message

Now is time to turn inward and celebrate your uniqueness. Acknowledge all your accomplishments and award yourself soothing repose. Take time to honor your unique characteristics, validating all the special gifts you offer to the world. Observe the beauty of your individual personality, opening your heart to celebrate the fact that you are very special! Every gift you possess is a reflection of Spirit. The sharing of your wisdom, laughter and love is Spirit expressed in the highest form. Reminisce and bask in your holiness. Exalt in your Divinity and hail the beautiful soul you are! Celebrate life to the fullest, for you have created this life to enjoy!

It's easy to get caught up in always wanting to do more and be more. You have forgotten to take inventory of all that you've already done. You have overlooked your accomplishments and feel as though you have not contributed enough. This card reminds you to stop and pause for a moment to pat yourself on the back. You have grown so much spiritually, mentally and emotionally. You are constantly working to better yourself and your accomplishments need to be rewarded. The fact that you are engaging in this wisdom card deck means that you are striving to become a healthier and stronger spiritual being, which is cause for a great celebration. Every evening before you retire, pause for a moment to reflect and commend yourself for being special "you!"

Card Symbology

The passionflower on this card symbolizes faith and spirituality. This exotic flower contains sacred and blessed energy and it's purpose is to enhance our spiritual life.

The early Spanish conquistadors discovered passionflowers when they arrived in "New Spain." They saw symbols of their Catholic faith in this extraordinary flower and named it after the passion of Jesus. The geometric pattern of this flower reminded them of Christ's passion on the cross. The spiraled tendons of the plant became symbols of the lashes Christ endured; the five anthers represented his wounds; the 72 radial filaments were seen as the number of thorns on his crown; the three pistil stigmas signified the nails used in the crucifixion, as well as the holy Trinity; the ten outer petals refer to the ten apostles who did not betray or deny Christ. When the flowers draw inward after a day (the time Jesus spent on the cross), the petals do not drop-they re-close over the ovary. This symbolizes the hidden wisdom found in the mysteries of the cross, like the hidden wisdom of Jesus in the enclosed tomb.

Surrounding the passionflower is a six-circled mandala. Circles are universal symbols of the sacred Divine and the sphere with a central nucleus was the first vibration from God. These circles represent the Infinite nature of Spirit and the inclusivity of the universe. The five outer circles of the flower contain these symbolic keywords: wholeness, cycles, centering, initiation and completion. The inner circle that joins them together represents the perfection of God in the form of absolute truth, infinity, and unity. "God is a circle whose center is everywhere, and whose circumference is nowhere." ~ Hermes Trismegistus

Journey

Find a quiet place where you can relax undisturbed. Sit comfortably with your spine straight. Take a deep breath in, tensing your body from your feet to your head. Bring awareness to each body part, as you tense each muscle one by one, within the same inhale. As your entire body is tensed with energy, hold your breath until you are ready to exhale and release. As you exhale, make any audible sounds to expel all tension from your body. Repeat this exercise three times or until you feel relaxed. Gently begin allowing your natural breath to move in and out. With each inhale, silently chant: "I am Divine." With each exhale, chant: "I celebrate my Divinity." Repeat this chant several times as you naturally breathe in and out. Remain in this state for as long as needed, feeling all distracting thoughts subside.

Visualize yourself sitting in soft, plush grass under the brightly shining sun. Feel the warmth of the sun permeating every cell of your body. Breathe in the sun's rays as you fill your heart with radiant light. This solar light nurtures and sustains you. From the base of your spine, envision roots extending down into Mother Earth and connecting to her core. Your roots are planted in the fertile soil of the precious earth. Your spine becomes the stem of a flower as you draw upon the nourishment of this holy dirt. Your limbs and all your surrounding energy become vines and leaves that intertwine with the material world. Feeling fortified with nourishment from nature, you begin to emerge into a beautiful bud that represents your sacredness and spirituality. Continue to breathe in the

Experience the Transcendental Video & Audio Journey on my Website to Celebrate All of Life!

energy of the sun and soak up the nutrients from the soil beneath you. This fertile soil is the fortifying food that sustains your life. You experience tingles of life force energy stirring throughout your body. You feel this vibrating essence is pure Spirit and know you are safe. You have absolutely no needs or wants, feeling satisfied that all your needs are met. In this place of peace, you never have to think about money, work, food or any other responsibilities. You are a wild flower, living freely in the present moment. Remain in this freedom as you inhale sunlight and exhale through your roots into the ground. Continue inhaling the sunlight and exhaling into the earth for several breathes, feeling contentment in this space. Now you are filled with the remembrance of your holy substance; this is the Spirit that your soul is made of.

As you relish in the contentment of your soul, you begin to mature into a magical passionflower. Each one of your fingers becomes one of the ten green outer petals of the flower. Bask in this sensation as one finger at a time now opens, revealing each new petal. As you spread open each finger, feel the energy of life force awakening within you. You begin to feel your soul expanding, becoming the vibrant center of the exotic passionflower. You now experience a shower of radiant colors as you continue to grow. You feel warm shades of green, comforting hues of purple, brilliant variations of magenta and the purity of a white halo acting as the gateway to the center of your soul. The rich orange background color stimulates your creativity and passion. Float in peace and fill yourself with the magic born from the passionflower of your soul.

As you enjoy this magical feeling, you become aware of a sacred circle that forms around your energy field. This is the circle of wholeness. Allow yourself to experience all the areas in which you feel whole. Gradually, a second circle representing cycles appears. This circle reminds you to witness all the patterns that continually cycle in your life. Slowly, the third circle of centering unfolds, asking you to ground and remain focused. The fourth circle of initiation materializes and infuses you with the energy to take action and achieve your dreams. Then, the fifth circle of completion emerges, reminding you to celebrate all that you have created. Lastly, the sixth circle of God appears, intertwining all the circles. Without this last circle, none of the other circles could exist. Envision the circles expanding, growing larger and larger, until they encompass the entire space of the universe. The power of the circles is the infinite nature of spirit and the inclusivity of the universe. Now that all of the circles have enveloped you, feel your oneness with every cell and molecule of creation. Bask in the embodiment of your Christ intelligence. In this oneness with God, you are now ready to reclaim your Godly power and nothing of the world can touch you. Feel your soul as infinite Spirit.

Continue to celebrate your unique gifts and contributions to the world because no one has what you have to offer! Applaud yourself for all your accomplishments. Smell the fragrant aroma pervading from your soul, a fragrance that is only produced by you. Worship every aspect that makes you who you are. Rejoice in all the ways you have contributed while here on earth. Cheer yourself for the gifts you have given to the world: joy, compassion, smiles and acts of kindness. Praise your personality and bask in your beauty in every creative way you can imagine! Celebrate yourself- for you are Divine!

When you return from your journey, take a deep breath and reflect on the insights you received. Smile inwardly into your heart and thank your Godly self for the work you have done to accept life, yourself and others. Record any insights or awakenings in your copy of the *Reawakening the Soul Vision Quest Workbook*.

Introspection

Is it challenging for me to acknowledge my good qualities?

What are my accomplishments?

What are my unique gifts?

What does my own personality actually look like to me?

How do others perceive me?

EFT/Tapping

KC: Even though I forget to remember all my good qualities, I choose to explore these deeper.

KC: Even though I forget to celebrate who I am, I now choose to remember my Divinity.

KC: Even though I tend to forget all the good that I have done, I deeply and completely accept myself.

EB: What have I accomplished?
SE: I know that I've accomplished a lot.
UE: As I tap, I look at all my accomplishments.
UN: I see all that I have done.
CP: Have I done enough?
CB: I know that I've done a lot.
UA: But sometimes I forget all that I do.
TH: I forget to praise myself.

EFT Audio Available to Celebrate the Whole Unique YOU!

EB: What good do I share in the world?
SE: How can I celebrate myself more?
UE: I am good.
UN: And I do a lot of great things.
CP: Even though I forget at times.
CB: Now, I'm going to remember.
UA: As I look back at all I did.
TH: I see that I've done a lot.

EB: I am unique.
SE: No one else can do what I have done.
UE: I share my creative gifts.
UN: I share who I am.
CP: I have a unique personality.
CB: And I applaud my personality.
UA: I now remember all that I do, everyday.
TH: And I remember to give myself.

EB: What I deserve.
SE: Whatever that may be for me.
UE: Or whatever that may look like.
UN: I honor myself.
CP: And I love myself.
CB: I give myself the time and space.
UA: To do what I love.
TH: I am grateful I have accomplished so much.

EB: Even though at times, I forget all I do.
SE: Now I take the time to remember.

UE: Everything that I do.
UN: And who I am.
CP: As I tap.
CB: I smile within.
UA: And I give myself recognition.
TH: For all the gifts I give.

EB: In whatever shape or form.
SE: My gifts are one of a kind.
UE: I celebrate the joy that I am.
UN: I celebrate the love that I am.
CP: I have given a lot.
CB: And I will continue to give a lot.
UA: I have done a lot.
TH: And I will continue to achieve many things.

EB: And I know that I shine.
SE: I will continue to shine.
UE: This is my innate presence.
UN: I remember the love that I am.
CP: I celebrate the love that I am.
CB: I am divine.
UA: I am love.
TH: I now celebrate my divinity.

"The more you praise and celebrate your life, the more there is in life to celebrate."
~ Oprah Winfrey

Courage

Have the faith to take action, knowing that all perceived obstacles are only opportunities.

Courage

"Obstacles will look large or small to you according to whether you are large or small."
~ Orison Swett Marden

Affirmation

I walk this journey with faith, strength and courage because I know that I am Spirit.

Card Message

Courage is born when you identify and confront your fears in order to take action and move forward. When you remember your true Divine self, your fears will disappear before your eyes. With absolute faith in your Creator and knowing that you are created as an image of God, fear cannot exist. Fears come in many sizes, shapes and forms. Remain authentic to your feelings and stand in your truth by honoring yourself at all times. Become comfortable saying the word "no" when healthy boundaries are needed. Remember that you do not have to explain yourself. Sometimes the phrase "I choose not to" or a simple "No" is the only statement necessary. When you reflect upon your current life situations and take action to make changes, it is natural for fears to arise. Changes are necessary to reduce the presence of conflict and bring your actions into alignment with your true purpose. For some individuals, just the thought of change can create fear. It is important that you are living a balanced, harmonious life. If you feel your life is out of balance, adjustments need to be made that may require courage.

Become aware of the deepest convictions burning in your heart. Take appropriate action to manifest these dreams into reality. These necessary actions are needed for the birth of your dreams. As you act powerfully, you will feel a constant flame of strength burning inside you. With each act of courage, the flame grows brighter. By listening to your heart, you are being guided to the truth. Even though the messages you receive may bring discomfort, having the courage to listen and act on your inner voice removes all barriers. Develop and strengthen your relationship with God and know that you are never alone. It is through faith that courage becomes a natural part of your being and dissolves all perceived obstructions.

You will often make your greatest spiritual progress when you are faced with tremendous obstacles. In challenging times, Spirit will force you to exercise your inner strength and courage to achieve your maximum potential. Align your personal will with Divine will and you can rise above any challenge. As you succeed, you strengthen your personal will power. Your success depends greatly upon how you perceive the experiences that come to you. Observe your experiences from a place of being a witness. Remain emotionally non-attached in order to respond consciously instead of reacting to situations that arise. This strategy brings you much peace. All incidences are created by your thoughts and are specifically designed for your own growth. Hold on tight to the loving hand of God, for you gain the strength and courage to withstand fear.

Have the courage to leap, knowing that a "net" will appear. Dare to dive into your dreams with strength and faith, letting go of all expectations as to how you envision the net. This symbolic net does not appear until you leap. If you wait for the assurance of the illusion of a safety net before leaping, you may find yourself never taking a chance or waiting longer than necessary to move forward. Sometimes you may leap and fall to the ground. The pain that you endure is serving it's purpose, as the ground may very well be the net. What is this net? The illusory net symbolizes whatever experiences are necessary to assist you in your spiritual growth. Know that however the net happens to appear, it will be perfect for you. It's better to leap than to stay stagnate. Do not allow your personal will to become paralyzed. Refuse to stand still or let anything stop you from taking the next step towards your dreams.

Card Symbology

The wolf has excellent hearing skills and auditory awareness. Wolf is a reminder to listen to your own inner thoughts and to trust your own insights. The wolf teaches you to know who you are in order to develop inner strength, confidence and surety. When you hold these qualities, you have nothing to prove. The one who has courage does not rely on the opinions of others. It doesn't matter who you are to the world, what matters most is the truth of your soul. The wolf shows you how to breathe new life into your daily rituals. Now is the time to find a new path, seek a new journey and take control of your life. You are the master of your life. When you create and direct your experience with harmony and discipline, you will know the true spirit of freedom.

Cougar reminds you to learn how to use your personal power and encourages you to be assertive. He also teaches you to respect your own boundaries and the boundaries of others. You must think with a calm state of mind before acting so you do not waste precious energy. Cougar reminds you to make space for solitude and remain focused on your goals. Share with others without allowing anyone to become too dependent on you. Be fully alive and playful in every moment.

The crow is a master of change and movement, mystery and illusion. Crow is fearless and acts as a guardian of things hidden and sacred. Crow is the interpreter of the unknown. There is a trickster quality about the crow, as he knows when to reveal his presence and when to remain hidden. Make peace with your shadow self to open the door to hidden opportunities. The crow is a magical symbol of creation and spiritual strength. Crow messengers are calling you to see the creation and magic within your world.

The dream catcher acts as a net to release any fears that may hold you bound to old, outdated structures. Guided by wisdom, remain in the dream of your conscious awareness to create your destiny. Life is a dream. Engage in this dream wide-awake with clear, open eyes.

Journey

Find a quiet place where you can relax undisturbed. Sit comfortably with your spine straight. Take a deep breath in, tensing your body from your feet to your head. Bring awareness to each body part, as you tense each muscle one by one, within the same inhale. As your entire body is tensed with energy, hold your breath until you are ready to exhale and release. As you exhale, make any audible sounds to expel all tension from your body. Repeat this exercise three times or until you feel relaxed. Gently begin allowing your natural breath to move in and out. With each inhale, silently chant: "I am fearless." With each exhale, chant: "I am limitless." Remain in this state for as long as needed, feeling all distracting thoughts subside.

Bring into your awareness any areas where you need more courage. These may include speaking your truth, choosing a different direction, healing your past or moving forward on a project. Whatever your fear may be, open your heart to see all situations as clearly as possible. Listen intently with your body, mind and spirit. Pay attention to any fears that arise when you think of taking action to resolve this situation. Feel any emotions attached to these obstacles or oppositions. Pay attention to the sensations in your body where these emotions are being expressed. Breathe deeply into any areas of your body where you feel discomfort and allow the emotions to release. Deep down inside, you know a change is needed. This change may feel uncomfortable, but know that you are safe.

You find yourself sitting on soft, green grass in a peaceful forest. The sun is shining it's warm rays across your body. You feel safe and at peace as you bathe in this warm light. As you look into the distance, you see a beautiful cougar slowly walking towards you. She approaches closer and closer until she stops right in front of you. Your eyes lock together as if you are in a hypnotic trance. You sense her gaze as a sensation of love, courage and power. Through this eye exchange, the piercing energy of power, strength and assertiveness is fused into the core of your being. You feel this transmission within your entire spirit. She has completely filled you with mastery of authority. Suddenly, you feel different. You notice that all your fear has been washed away. You feel bountiful, free and relieved from a heavy burden you previously carried. You realize how this energy has weighed you down for a long time. Even though you feel light as a feather, there is a powerful strength contained in this lightness. This strength has always existed within your soul and now you will actively carry this power forever. Asserting your personal power becomes second nature to you. Some people may not approve of your new strength. They may try to keep you in the bracket of their desires. But you know it is time to grow and step into your personal power. You have been gifted with the cougar's ability to leap at opportunities. You feel the power she has infused within you. She reminds you to remain focused on your goals and tells you to inwardly inquire as to your next step. You now possess the courage to begin your journey towards your dreams. Thank her for all the gracious gifts. The cougar is complete with her mission and now gently fades away.

As you continue sitting in the field with the cougar, you notice a crow flying towards you. He lands on a branch in the tree beside you. He looks down at you and begins to caw in a language you mysteriously understand. Through his voice, you remember your ability to create magic and spread it in the world. This wondrous magic is available to you every day. Many opportunities suddenly present themselves to you. You now can create and manifest the magic of life. As the crow continues to caw, receive any other messages he wishes to share with you. After delivering his gifts, the crow gracefully flies away.

You sit in the silence of nature for a moment, until you hear the sound of a wolf howling. You sense his true, wild spirit and feel the freedom and unspoiled splendor of the wilderness. As you take a deep breath of fresh air, you are ready to receive the medicine from the wolf. As he howls once again, you recognize his language and feel the truth of his message resonating in your soul. He reminds you to remember that you are not mortal, but pure, immortal Spirit. He charges you with the strength, confidence and conviction of your essential spiritual nature. You no longer feel a need to demonstrate and prove yourself to the world. His howling vibrates within your throat and you are now able to speak your truth freely, effortlessly and with ease. The howling begins to come closer and louder and you feel the force behind his voice. He is now very near to you and you are captivated by his appearance. You view his stance and notice his grace, beauty, and gentleness. You behold the radiant full moon behind him, reflecting your own fullness. He howls right before you and asks you to take a deep look at how you are currently living your life. Are you living in harmony? Do you feel free? He reminds you that true freedom requires courage and discipline. Look into his eyes and receive the gift of courage that he has to offer you. Gaze directly at him until you feel full from the medicine of the wolf. When you are done, silently thank him for his gifts and allow him to return on his journey. You can now clearly see exactly what steps are needed in order for you to feel empowered and balanced.

A beautiful dream catcher now appears before you. You are asked to release any concerns you are currently carrying. Let all of your cares go into the magic dream catcher until you feel clear and fearless. Now that you have completely washed away your fears, the dream catcher dissolves into thin air. Your energy field is now clean and strong.

You now have the courage to take action and create any changes you wish to experience. Visually see and feel yourself taking the course of action needed to change your situations. Envision yourself stepping into your power and taking the first step to create your desired outcome. You are now clear to speak your truth. You are brave and confident now that you live every moment with authenticity. You feel relieved and happy that you were able to have the courage needed to resolve this situation.

Take with you all the medicine from cougar, wolf and crow and reclaim your personal power once and for all!

When you return from your journey, take a deep breath and reflect on the insights you received. Smile inwardly into your heart and thank your Godly self for the work you have done to accept life, yourself and others. Record any insights or awakenings in your copy of the *Reawakening the Soul Vision Quest Workbook*.

Introspection

What am I afraid of?

What changes do I need to make in order to feel balanced?

What fears do I have around making changes?

What time in my life did I act braver than I ever dreamed I could?

What motivated me to take action? What did I gain from this?

How would my life look if I had the courage to make all necessary changes to live my dream?

EFT/Tapping

KC: Even though I am afraid to make some necessary changes, I choose to look deeper into this.

KC: Even though I feel frozen and scared, I deeply and completely accept the way I feel.

KC: Even though a part of me wants to move forward and I'm a bit scared, I choose to face my fears.

EB: I'm afraid to make changes.
SE: Changes feel so uncomfortable.
UE: It seems so hard.
UN: Part of me is scared.
CP: But part of me wants to move forward.
CB: It feels like its time to change.
UA: But I'm still nervous.
TH: I feel stuck.

EB: I feel bound.
SE: I feel helpless.
UE: It's safe to look at these issues.
UN: But part of me doesn't feel safe.
CP: I don't even know who I am.
CB: Who am I?
UA: Is it safe to be me?
TH: Why wouldn't it be safe?

EFT
Audio Available
to Give You
Instant
Faith &
Courage!

EB: What would happen if I stepped into my power?
SE: All these fears around having courage.
UE: All these fears.
UN: All these learned behaviors.
CP: What would it feel like if I were safe?
CB: What would it feel like if I were safe to express myself?
UA: I choose to feel safe.
TH: I choose to feel safe being in my power.

EB: I am safe in my body.
SE: I am safe being myself.
UE: It's time for change.
UN: I'm putting the time in.
CP: I'm open for change.
CB: I'm ready to step into my power.
UA: It's safe to express myself.
TH: I only need to focus on the next step.

EB: And then the following step will appear.
SE: I am ready to take the next step.
UE: I feel brave.
UN: I feel courageous.
CP: Nothing can hurt me.
CB: I am safe.
UA: I am spirit.
TH: This feels great.

EB: I see myself as the cougar.
SE: I call in this animal spirit.
UE: And I feel the power of the cougar within me.
UN: He is supporting me.
CP: I am always supported.
CB: I know this life is all a dream.
UA: In this dream, I have courage to be powerful.
TH: I get excited as I feel my growth.

EB: I feel my strength by being me.
SE: I am powerful.
UE: With my power, I am able to lead others.
UN: I am able to take responsibility.
CP: I am able to transform myself.
CB: And live free from fear.
UA: I now choose to completely free myself.
TH: I am brave.

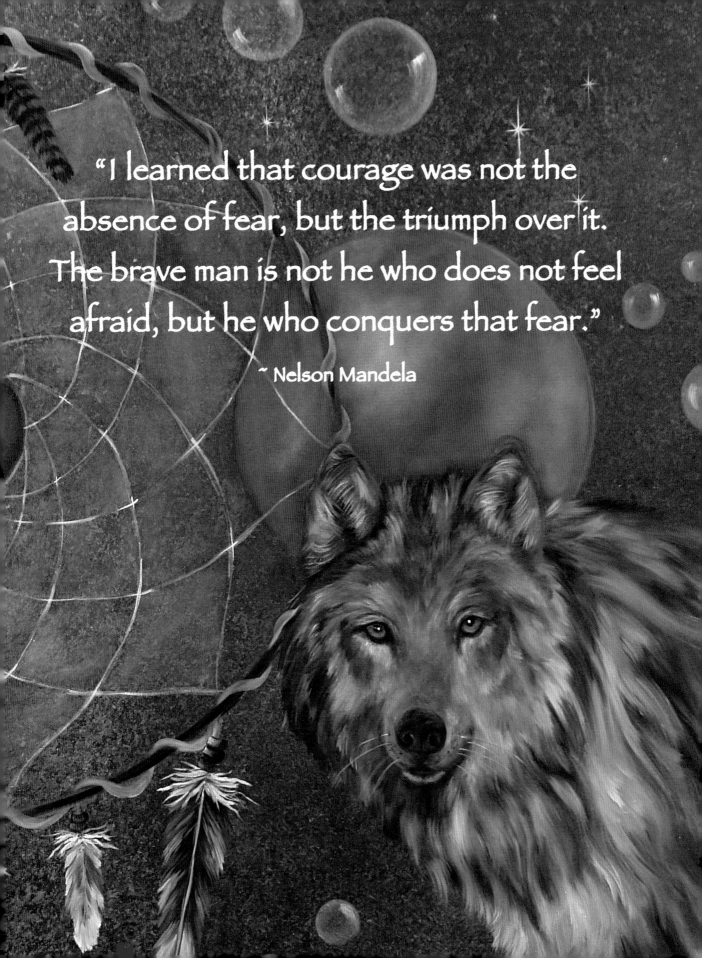

Dreams

Visionary creations are birthed from your imagination.

Dreams

"Cherish your visions and your dreams as they are the children of your soul; the blue prints of your ultimate achievements."

~ Napoleon Hill

Affirmation

I create my reality through my thoughts and dreams.

Card Message

This card reminds you to get in touch with your deepest dreams. Go within your heart and tap into your greatest desires, aspirations and goals. Take an inward journey and feel what beckons from your heart. Observe the passion within you that yearns to come forth in some creative form. Give yourself permission to call forth all your dreams as you smile inwardly.

Dare to dream without any limitations. Visualize and feel what makes you happy. Dance and rejoice in what brings you joy—you deserve it! You can manifest this happiness by consciously guiding your own personal will power. Know that your personal will is a reflection of Divine will. Acting upon this truth opens the doors to new opportunities allowing your dreams to take shape. Believe with conviction that everything is your own creation. Create what you dream about and live the life you deserve. This is the joy your soul is longing for. Look upon this world as God's dream. You began as God's thought; created within the cosmic dream. Know that He is dreaming through you and only wishes for you to have peace. As the dreamer, you get to decide for yourself what dream experiences you create during your lifetime. Realize that you have the choice to create nightmares or magical dreams while here on earth. Make a conscious decision to create dreams of happiness. When you leave your physical body at death, your consciousness will realize that it inhabited a dream-body. Hold on to this awareness and experience great freedom during your short time on earth.

Card Symbology

The wolf teaches you how to know yourself and understand others. Wolf is a pathfinder; bringing you new ideas. He shares skills that develop strength, confidence and wisdom in order to create your own reality. When you create a reality based on utilizing your passions, you are living life to the fullest. Wolf reminds you that you have a gift to share. As he howls at the moon, the wolf spirit asks you to listen to your inner desires and express them through your own song. The moon is a symbol of your psychic ability. The essence of the full moon contains the energy of action and creative expression. Tap into these powerful energies by taking action now. The raven is a bird of mysticism and magic. This bird shares a symbiotic relationship with the wolf and they often follow wolf packs. Ravens will fly ahead to a tree and wait for the wolves to pass. They repeat this pattern over and over again as they travel along with the wolves. Raven teaches you about birth and death, darkness and light. Raven encourages you to become the magician of your own life. She shows you how to bring your shadow self out of the dark and into the light. She delivers messages from the spirit realm and shows you how to shape shift your life. She instructs you how to take unformed energy and shape that energy into whatever form you wish. Raven may present you with tests to teach you how to see through illusions. If you pass these tests, she will become your guardian. Since the raven is considered an omen, stay open to any inner guidance you may receive from her.

The Native American dream catcher is a symbol to remind you that you are the creator, dreaming this dream we call life. Practice remembering your oneness with Spirit and you will know this life is a dream. The feathers represent the flight of magic you embark upon when you remember your native soul: a pure reflection of God. When you hold the truth of your soul close to your heart, you align your personal will with Divine will and alchemy is born! This painting reminds you to surrender to God and allow your life to unfold with the power of Spirit. When you practice the art of surrender, your dreams become reality. The bubbles reveal the illusion of time and space and the magic that is found in living your dreams.

Experience the Transcendental Video & Audio Journey on my Website to Begin Living Your Dreams NOW!

Journey

Find a quiet place where you can relax undisturbed. Sit comfortably with your spine straight. Take a deep breath in, tensing your body from your feet to your head. Bring awareness to each body part, as you tense each muscle one by one, within the same inhale. As your entire body is tensed with energy, hold your breath until you are ready to exhale and release. As you exhale, make any audible sounds to expel all tension from your body. Repeat this exercise three times or until you feel relaxed. Gently begin allowing your natural breath to move in and out. With each inhale, silently chant: "This life is a dream." With each exhale, chant: "I am free to dream." Repeat this chant several times as you naturally breathe in and out. Remain in this state for as long as needed, feeling all distracting thoughts subside.

Now that you are completely relaxed with your eyes closed, open your inner gaze and find yourself leaning against a tree in a peaceful forest.

The silence of the nighttime hours allows you to feel calm and safe. The deep, rich hues reflected by the light of the glowing moon captivate you. Surrounding trees glisten with light, revealing their secret wisdom. You become aware that the moon amplifies your psychic ability. You lift your gaze and notice patterns of woven tree branches. As you study the outline of intricately shaped branches, you feel their mystery. The only sound you hear is the subtle music of leaves dancing in the gentle wind. You relax and spend time in the gleaming forest; absorbing every detail of nature.

The energy seems to shift as you hear a rustling sound in the branches above you. As you look up, you see a raven sitting on a tree limb. You sense that this raven is an omen. Instinctively, you open to receive the gifts she wishes to share. You instantly become attuned to her presence and her wisdom merges with your soul. She asks you to bring forth any perception of darkness you are now experiencing. Take whatever time you need to bring the shadow side of any situation into your consciousness. As you sit before this dark experience, it feels different. You no longer have any attachment or any emotions connected to this darkness. It feels like you are witnessing this situation happening to someone else. This feels liberating to you and you now relax into the visual experience and see the whole scene with clarity. In the place of clear vision, you are now able to see the light of the situation. You know exactly why this situation is happening in your life. You take full responsibility of being the sole creator of this story, watching it play out in the movie of your life. You notice how your thoughts have created these scenes; keeping this story alive. You realize how this movie has played over and over again in your mind. Raven caws loudly three times showing you that you have the power to release this story since it no longer serves you. You suddenly burst with magic as you feel the power of being the magician. As you reclaim your power, you understand life's circumstances as being a test. Your higher self knows the way to pass this test. You choose to open your heart and shed the light of compassion onto the darkness. The energy of the situation that once appeared so dark is now beaming golden rays of light. You have shape shifted this experience and know that you are able to do this with any illusion of darkness. Feel your power and strength. Receive your gift of understanding and know that you are the magician!

Your attention is then redirected to a howling sound that seems very close. You glance to your right and behold a magnificent wolf that seems to have appeared out of nowhere. You can feel more magic in the air as the wolf's energy penetrates your field. With each howl, you become aware of your own heart's song stirring within your soul. You take a moment and listen to your unique soul song. The wolf's medicine brings you new ideas. You realize these ideas are your own creative expression. As you feel passion burning within your heart, you realize you want to share this expression with the world. These dreams are ready to be delivered. You know that you have a gift to share and you have confidence to deliver your gifts through wisdom and truth. Wolf shows you your unique life path and how it will help others gain knowledge and understanding. You discover your own wolf spirit within; seeing how you are an inspiration to all. As you sit under the full moon, you spend the necessary time acknowledging these great gifts of yours. You know these gifts are unique and only you possess them. Feel your personal power and excitement explode with the ability to manifest these dreams!

The raven caws one last time as if to say good-bye before she flies away into a faraway tree. The wolf howls at the moon and then turns back to you. He lets you know that you have been infused with his magical powers. As you sit completely unified with these totem animals, breathe deeply into your inner wisdom where your dreams exist. You are now free to dream without any limitations or judgments. Dream as big as you can; no dream is foolish! Be like the child who has the natural ability to step outside of the box and dream. What is your creative soul wishing to express? Allow yourself to take risks with this self-expression and all illusions of peril will dissolve. Begin to ask yourself: What is the function of my current job? Is it aligned with the expression of my dreams? What makes me the happiest? Embrace the joy that fills your heart until your entire being is fulfilled. Visualize yourself living in this bliss. Give yourself permission to have this gift every day of your life. Take the healing medicine of raven and wolf with you and reclaim your personal power once and for all! You are now free to live your dreams!

Take the healing medicine of raven and wolf with you and reclaim your personal power once and for all! You are now free to live your dreams!

When you return from your journey, take a deep breath and reflect on the insights you received. Smile inwardly into your heart and thank your

Godly self for the work you have done to accept life, yourself and others. Record any insights or awakenings in your copy of the *Reawakening the Soul Vision Quest Workbook.*

Introspection

How would it feel to live every moment of my life with excitement and enthusiasm?

Do I allow myself the permission to dream?

What are my dreams?

What were my dreams as a child?

How would it feel if I were living my dream?

EFT/Tapping

KC: Even though I don't give myself permission to dream, I am now ready to explore my dreams.
KC: Even though I was told dreaming was foolish, I now open up to new beliefs.
KC: Even though I don't fully believe in my dreams, I deeply and completely love myself.

EB: It doesn't feel safe for me to dream.
SE: Dreaming is foolish.
UE: I have to be realistic.
UN: I don't have time to dream.
CP: Do I even know what my dreams are?
CB: Am I denying myself from creating?
UA: I used to dream as a child.
TH: It was easy and natural then.

EB: I wonder what happened over time.
SE: What if I could dream again?

EFT
Audio Available
to Activate
Your
Dreams!

UE: I want to dream again.
UN: It would feel so good.
CP: What are my dreams?
CB: What do I feel passionate about?
UA: What do I wish to create?
TH: I am free to dream.

EB: I am now living my life as beautiful dream.
SE: I feel so empowered.
UE: I have so many gifts to share.
UN: I feel my passions.
CP: I create from this passion.
CB: I feel completely fulfilled.
UA: Dreaming is fun.
TH: I choose to visit my dreams every day.

EB: I am dreaming this dream called life.
SE: I am the dreamer
UE: And I create anything I wish to create.
UN: My dreams are important.
CP: My dreams are unique.
CB: I am excited to begin living my dreams.
UA: I am excited to share my dreams.
TH: Dreaming is easy and natural.

"Dream as if you'll live forever.
Live as if you'll die today."

~ James Dean

Duality

Embrace the truth of contrast in the three dimensional material world.

Duality

"This world is a world of duality: life is made up of pleasure and pain, health and sickness, heat and cold, love and hate, life and death. Man's goal is to take his consciousness beyond this law of duality, the veil of maya, and find the One who is present in all creation and beyond creation."

~ Sri Daya Mata

Affirmation

I now choose to see Spirit existing within all creation.

Card Message

Your mind interprets life as duality as it processes information by comparing and defining. You have been conditioned to experience the world through your senses and from the observations of those who have influenced you. You have learned to comprehend life in a certain manner. Now, you are opening to new understanding—a truth derived from wisdom. You are beginning to realize that your perceptions are illusions. You are now ready to see from the heart of wisdom and step into your truth as infinite Spirit.

Spirit is the essence behind all creation. Your entire being is made up of Spirit. When you focus your life, ideals and ambitions solely on worldly pursuits, the sense of accomplishment is only temporary. Your soul is seeking a higher goal—a direct experience of God. In order to attain this experience, you must quiet both body and mind and listen to your inner voice of intuition. This is accomplished through meditation. Meditation is a vital part of each day and is just as important as proper rest and nutrition. When you experience the joy found in spending time with God, you will realize that you are a soul. You have a body, but you are not the body. You have a mind, but you are not the mind. By living in this awareness, you will not be limited by the mundane experiences of daily life. When you wake up to absolute truth, you realize that your soul is held in the protective and loving arms of the Beloved. When you remember the divine link between your soul and God, you will gain the wisdom that duality doesn't exist in higher realms of consciousness.

Card Symbology

The woman in this painting wears a black and white mask with peacock feathers on each side. The colors depict the contrast of duality and the feathers symbolize the eyes of wisdom. She is aware that her physical eyes are masked with illusion. This woman is now able to open her inner eye of wisdom to reveal the truth of oneness. She knows that there is one life force responsible for all creation and this is termed God. She is aware that this same life force energy resides within her. By staying in this realization, she is not affected by any worldly contrasts. The energy that permeates all of life sustains her. The sun and moon on each side of her are symbols of the opposition that seems to exist between light and dark. The male and female deer on each side of the circle represent the masculine and feminine balance found in nature. The lotus flower between the woman's eyebrows represents an opening; an inner awakening. This flower is located where the spiritual eye resides. The sphere of light upon her chest symbolizes the soul's union with Spirit. This emblem located at the top of the circle is the Self-Realization Fellowship logo. This beautiful image depicts the light of Christ consciousness that is seen during meditative union with God. The flowers surrounding the circle portray the fragrant beauty found within yourself as you open to absolute truth. The six-pointed star on the bottom of the circle symbolizes the soul-infused personality. The star is a symbol of God's relationship with the physical world. This sacred geometry represents His desire and intention to infuse all of physical manifestation with the pure light of Spirit. This holy, sacred symbol is one of healing, redemption and transformation. The star has two overlapping triangles. One triangle points upward symbolizing matter rising into Spirit. The other triangle points downward representing Spirit descending into manifested form. Both triangles must be brought into balance in order to achieve enlightenment. The descending dove represents the Holy Spirit of God that blesses you when the inner eye of wisdom is opened. When you live with the awareness of your spiritual essence, you awaken to Christ consciousness. Dove is a spirit messenger that brings communication between the realms of the conscious and the unconscious. Dove is signaling that it is now time to go within and release emotional discord. She can assist you in releasing old memories of past trauma. The dove bestows healing on many levels. When you release inner turmoil, peace and prosperity become attainable. The goal of mastering duality is to bring into balance the various aspects of your existence such as male and female, light and shadow, mind and body, practicality and spirituality.

Journey

Find a quiet place where you can relax undisturbed. Sit comfortably with your spine straight. Take a deep breath in, tensing your body from your feet to your head. Bring awareness to each body part, as you tense each muscle one by one, within the same inhale. As your entire body is tensed with energy, hold your breath until you are ready to exhale and release. As you exhale, make any audible sounds to expel all tension from your body. Repeat this exercise three times or until you feel relaxed. Gently begin allowing your natural breath to move in and

Experience the Transcendental Video & Audio Journey on my Website to Dissolve Duality!

out. With each inhale, silently chant: "Everything is Spirit." With each exhale, chant: "I am Spirit." Remain in this state for as long as needed, feeling all distracting thoughts subside.

You find yourself in a beautiful field surrounded by nature. Up ahead, you notice a path and become curious as to where it will lead you. When you enter the path you immediately feel excitement, as if a mystical journey is about to begin. As you slowly and quietly walk on this path, you become aware of the many sounds beneath your feet. The softly crunching leaves, rocks, twigs and soil seem to be singing a song to you. Bordering the pathway are freshly blooming flowers. The floral fragrance lightly fills the air and you pause for a moment to breathe in their essence. The wind is lightly blowing and you feel the whispering air float across your body. You notice how the temperature is absolutely perfect on this glorious day. As you continue to walk, you see something blowing and tumbling on the path in front of you. You come nearer to the object and bend down to pick it up. In your hands you hold a beautiful, sparkling mask. You admire the mask's black and white checkerboard pattern and lovely peacock feathers dancing in the wind. You sense that these feathers have eyes of wisdom guiding you towards something new. You're a bit curious as to why this magical mask would be floating around, but you know this is a special gift for you.

You are drawn to place the mask on your face. You feel as though the mask was made for you since it fits perfectly and feels so comfortable. When you open your eyes, you are surprised that everything around you looks and feels different. All the colors surrounding you are more vibrant. There are millions of colors that you have never seen before! You never imagined so many colors could even exist. As you inhale, the fragrant aroma of the flowers is magnified and captivates your senses. The floral perfume fills you with ecstasy. As you glance up into the open sky, you notice the various shades of blues and purples. You are awestruck at the fluffiness of the clouds as they gently move across the heavens. The world around you appears flawless. Everything is vibrating energy; you can even see energy in motion. You notice you are also vibrating with spiritual energy and you feel entirely different. The way you view the world has shifted and your awareness is heightened. You no longer identify the tree as being a tree or the flower as a flower or the sky to be separate from anything else. You discover that everything is a part of yourself. Every spark of life that is a part of creation is also a part of you. You now vibrate as the tree, flower, sky—everything around you is vibration! Your entire body merges with all that is. You feel expansive and united, realizing that you were never separate at all. Separation was merely a perception that you once had. Your heart, mind and thoughts feel great peace. You know that you have a body but you are not the body. You have a mind but you are not the mind. For the first time, you realize that you are a soul. You feel a love that you've never felt before. For the first time in your life, you feel bliss. You no longer have any shadows, fears or doubts in your mind. You know that you can be anything and do anything because you are Spirit! In this feeling, you trust that nothing of the material world can touch you. You no longer experience life through your senses, but through pure awareness. Spend some time basking in this blissful state.

As you remain in the presence of bliss with the mask on, you decide to sit and absorb your new state of being. Close your eyes and gaze upward into the point between the eyebrows. Focusing on this point comes naturally to you and is easy to do. In the center of a blue sphere, you see a star that is encircled by a golden halo. You penetrate the center of the star and enter into the universal doorway of Spirit. As you go deeper and deeper into this star, you are transported into another dimension. You have now transcended into the realm of Christ Consciousness. As you continue to remain in this God realization, you behold a dove flying down from the heavens. Dove is a spirit messenger delivering communication between the realms of the conscious and unconscious. She ascends upon your Spirit and blesses you. This peaceful dove represents the Spirit of God living within you. You feel safe in her energy and allow her to assist you in releasing all negative patterns and memories of past trauma. She bestows many levels of healing to you. Take time to receive her messages and healing transmissions.

You are now free to release your inner turmoil and experience peace and prosperity. With your inner eye of wisdom now opened, complete intuition is your new state of being. As you awaken into Christ Consciousness, you feel the awareness of your essence as Spirit. After the dove delivers her gifts, you thank her. She fades away into the etheric realm as a six-point star emerges. You sense the six-pointed star as a part of your being. You feel a deep sense of truth residing within this star. Notice that this star is made up of two triangles. With the downward facing triangle, you comprehend Spirit becoming matter. With the upward facing triangle, you experience matter rising up into Spirit. You finally see how everything is created from Spirit into the physical and then merging back into Spirit again. This is the moment of clarity you have been searching for your entire life. All emotions, ideas and perceptions are now removed and you see duality as an illusion. There is no dark and

light, no love and hate, no good and evil or happy or sad. The outer experiences of the world are all neutral. You have arrived at zero point where contrast no longer exists. You are eternal. You are immortal. You now flow in and out of the cosmic web of life. This brings you great peace, relief and satisfaction.

You now feel complete. Take a deep breath as you take off the mask and set it down beside you. Although the mask is removed, your blissful awareness remains. Your life has been transformed! You are now ready to take this experience with you into the world, for you know everything is vibrating spirit. If you find yourself slipping back into the delusional world of duality, you can mentally place your mask of enlightenment on at any time and change your perception.

When you return from your journey, take a deep breath and reflect on the insights you received. Smile inwardly into your heart and thank your Godly self for the work you have done to accept life, yourself and others. Record any insights or awakenings in your copy of the *Reawakening the Soul Vision Quest Workbook*.

Introspection

How would I experience life differently if I realized my spiritual essence?

Am I caught up in the world and forgetting God?

How do I experience duality in the world? Can I change this experience?

EFT/Tapping

KC: Even though I experience the world by comparing and defining, I now choose to see differently.
KC: Even though I am unable to see with clarity, I deeply and completely accept the way I view the world.
KC: Even though I'm conditioned to believe in the appearance of life around me, I now choose to explore a different way of seeing.

EB: This world is a world of duality.
SE: I am comparing and defining.
UE: Love and hate.
UN: Hot and cold.

CP: Light and dark.
CB: Pleasure and pain.
UA: Health and sickness.
TH: Is this way of observing really serving me?

EB: Can there really be a different way of seeing?
SE: Can I take my consciousness beyond duality?
UE: I was conditioned to see this way.
UN: But I know my conditioning can be changed.
CP: It's my choice.
CB: My old way of seeing doesn't serve me.
UA: It seems to leave me confused and disappointed.
TH: I know there is a healthier way.

EB: I am open to explore other ways.
SE: I know that I am more than this body.
UE: I believe I have a soul.
UN: And my soul is made in the image of Spirit.
CP: I am open to feeling Spirit present in all creation.
CB: I am open to feeling Spirit beyond all creation.
UA: This Spirit is God.
TH: I am Spirit.

EB: Therefore, God and I are One.
SE: Everything manifest around me is Spirit.
UE: This means I am connected to everything.
UN: I am not separate.
CP: I choose to experience myself as Spirit.
CB: Living this way makes me feel powerful.
UA: I'd live with more compassion.
TH: I'd feel more joy.

EB: I am infinite love.
SE: Duality is an illusion.
UE: It is only what my perceptions led me to believe.
UN: I feel this truth.
CP: And I choose to live in this truth.
CB: This truth feels good.
UA: I feel so empowered.
TH: I choose to see clearly.

Fearless

**Connect to God and experience peace in
every moment.**

Fearless

"Thinking will not overcome fear but action will."

~ W. Clement Stone

Affirmation

**As I connect with God,
I watch my fears wash away.**

Card Message

The polar bear offers a message to have strength, confidence and dignity during times of emotional or physical transition. Reflect to the polar bear's ability to trust life, while moving with grace, dignity and present moment awareness. You have an inner knowing that it's time to make some changes in your life. Whether these changes are big or small, they all require you to step into your power to create movement. You know exactly what changes are needed in order to make you feel more balanced. You are now ready to move forward with intention, conviction, strength and action in creatively creating these changes.

As you step into your power and express your truth, you are on your way to freedom! This is an exciting time for you because changes are now occurring so quickly. As long as you stay connected to Source and remain completely focused on your dreams, goals and visions, all fears and doubts naturally dissolve and you naturally achieve success.

The environment around you seems to be intensely offering you clear signals indicating the areas in need of change. All of this energy may appear a bit frightening or may feel a bit intimidating and may bring up some inner hidden fears. Fear destroys and distorts all seeing. It breeds illusion and keeps your mind dull and if you don't do anything about it, it will destroy your dignity. The best ways to move past fear is to acknowledge it, accept it, and then take action to wash it away. When you place more energy on what you wish to accomplish instead of using useless energy towards fearing it, the fear will abolish. Don't let fear remain with you, and don't find excuses for it. Go into it with determination and wisdom to shift the energy. Fear is in the mind, and is supported by beliefs. You can choose to feed it or starve it by taking action. It exists when you are disconnected from realizing your true nature as Spirit.

It's your time to hold yourself accountable with integrity and wisdom, even if this means to be completely vulnerable. You are moving into a new direction, a higher state of consciousness. You desire clarity and absolute truth as you move from one phase of your life to another. You know it's time to end any old patterns and programming keeping you from your fullest expression. New beginnings, new ideas and new chapters of your life are unfolding within you as the outer world is eager to meet your request. You feel an inner excitement in your soul as you feel new passion beginning to emerge. Faith, courage and the ability to live fearlessly are necessary, as you become clear in creating your vision and your dreams.

To be fearless, you must have the courage and faith needed to take action. By gaining awareness through experience, that you are almighty Spirit, you can conquer anything. (See Courage) When you are consciously connected to your Creator, fear cannot exist. It's impossible, because it vibrates at a different frequency. Connection to God is essential to being fearless, and meditation creates this blessed relationship.

Stand firmly in your inner convictions. Trust what your soul is communicating to you, as this is the way to your liberation. (See Trust) Listen to the wisdom of your soul and use the fuel ignited by passion to take action. Inwardly call in the strength of the fearless Polar bear and incorporate its energy. There is magic to be experienced when you listen and acknowledge your passion. This is your inner voice. Step into the polar bear's power to speak your truth and what you believe in. You are being encouraged and supported in standing up for yourself in all situations presented to you. These include work relationships, personal relationships and your own personal relationship with yourself and God.

At this very moment, your Soul knows exactly what direction you are to take. It is encouraging you to trust in Spirit by looking straight into fear itself and see it for what it is . . . separation from your Creator. This separation can cause an illusion holding you back from achieving your Divine purpose. Build a relationship with your Creator and leap through all fears and soar into freedom. You are here on earth to make a difference by sharing your divine gifts. Think about it, absolutely no one else can complete this mission – only you; now go walk fearlessly and do it!

Card Symbology

The polar bear has no natural enemies and are intelligent, fearless, naturally courageous, strong and confident. They move with grace, dignity and awareness in the present moment. Bear's medicine includes extreme strength in the face of adversity, introspection, and purity of spirit. They are excellent swimmers, which reflects our ability to swim through emotional waters to find our way back to truth. They are creatures of dreams, shamans, mystics and visionaries. The polar bear is a desirable ally and spirit helper and its energy is accessible when we call upon him as he aids us in getting past all fears, both physically and mentally. The white color of the polar bear represents purity of spirit. Universal energy flows abundantly and naturally when fear is absent. The polar bear is regarded as the embodiment of the spirit of the North who possesses ancient wisdom with shamanic powers. Prior to acting, the polar bear will observe the situation beforehand. They know how to preserve both their energy and strength and combine them together at the appropriate time for the best outcome. We can benefit by using this same strategy and applying it in our lives.

Journey

Find a quiet place where you can relax undisturbed. Sit comfortably with your spine straight. Take a deep breath in, tensing your body from your feet to your head. Bring awareness to each body part, as you tense each muscle one by one, within the same inhale. As your entire body is tensed with energy, hold your breath until you are ready to exhale and release. As you exhale, make any audible sounds to expel all tension from your body. Repeat this exercise three times or until you feel relaxed. Gently begin allowing your natural breath to move in and out. With each inhale, silently chant: "I am Spirit." With each exhale, chant: "Spirit is fearless." Remain in this state for as long as needed, feeling all distracting thoughts subside.

Experience the Transcendental Video & Audio Journey on my Website to Remove All Fears!

The great white polar bear appears before you to share its medicine. You sense his intelligence, fearlessness and natural courage. He is strong and confident living in the present moment. You connect to his energy, as you feel calm and receptive to receive his magic. Envision in your minds-eye one of your dreams, desires or an area in your life where you need courage. Relax as you mentally create a clear image of where you need support. Now repeat after me, "I am safe. I am strong. I am everlasting all-pervading Spirit. I am a child of God. I possess all the power and strength of God. My thoughts and actions are pure and true. I am courageous with unshakable faith, because I know my oneness with Spirit. My throat chakra is wide open as I now clearly speak my truth. I am authentic. I have the highest integrity. I am fearless. I am limitless. I now take action towards my goals and dreams. I am confident and I share my gifts to the world. I now act according to my soul. I live in the present moment. My timing in life is always perfect. I am expansive. I am almighty. "

You are now connected with Spirit as extreme strength, power and confidence now fill your entire being. The polar bear's fearless energy marries with yours and you suddenly feel the power to take action in your life. You easily ask for what you want and need as you speak up for yourself. View a situation in your life where you wish to ask for what you need. Envision yourself in this situation clearly and confidently making your request. You are compelled to move forward in your life and ready to make whatever changes needed in order to acquire happiness. You are fearless as you walk solidly upon this earth sharing your unique characteristics. Now that you are consciously connected to your Creator, fear cannot exist. You feel its impossibility, because it vibrates at a different frequency. You are now vibrating with the consciousness of truth. Your connection to Spirit allows you to be fearless. You trust and have absolute faith, because you know you are a child of God. And as this child, you possess all the power of your Creator. You are a warrior of love. You came here to Earth to do something that only you can do. Absolutely no one else can complete this mission but you; now go shine your diamond light in the world for you are fearless!

When you return from your journey, take a deep breath and reflect on the insights you received. Smile inwardly into your heart and thank your Godly self for the work you have done to accept life, yourself and others. Record any insights or awakenings in your copy of the *Reawakening the Soul Vision Quest Workbook.*

Introspection

If fear and doubt were removed from my mind, would I be living my life differently?

What do I fear?

Am I willing to deepen my connection to Spirit in order to remove fear?

EFT/Tapping

KC: Even though I have fear around this situation, I deeply and completely accept the way I feel.

KC: Even though I'm afraid to take action, I deeply completely love myself.

KC: Even though I feel fearful, I deeply and completely accept the way I feel.

EB: All this fear.
SE: I feel scared.
UE: I'm afraid to move forward.
UN: I'm afraid to take action.
CP: What am I afraid?
CB: Where is all this fear coming from?
UA: They're coming from my thoughts.
TH: My thoughts are creating all this fear.

EB: And my thoughts create my moods.
SE: Why am I so afraid?
UE: I feel paralyzed.
UN: And I can't take action.
CP: This feels terrible.
CB: I am willing to shift this energy.
UA: Because I want to move forward.
TH: And I am willing to do whatever it takes.

EB: And I will take action.
SE: I am one with God.
UE: And fear cannot exist in this awareness.
UN: I am spirit.
CP: I possess all the courage of my great Creator.
CB: I am fearless.
UA: I speak my truth.
TH: I am authentic.

EB: I'm ready to move past my fears.
SE: My Limiting beliefs.
UE: And my doubts.
UN: I am now conscious of my thoughts.
CP: My mind is clear and positive.
CB: I trust my soul.
UA: And I allow it lead the way.
TH: I trust myself.

EB: And I have extreme faith.
SE: Because nothing can hurt me.
UE: I am safe.
UN: It's all a dream.

CP: And I choose to stay in the dream.
CB: And act accordingly with a calm state of mind.
UA: I speak my truth.
TH: I am authentic.

EB: I now possess the strength of the polar bear.
SE: And I walk in the conviction of my truth.
UE: Towards my dreams and goals.
UN: I now take immediate action.
CP: I am limitless.
CB: I am fearless.
UA: I have great courage.
TH: I am confident in myself.

"Let us not pray to be sheltered
from dangers but to be fearless
when facing them."

~ Rabindranath Tagore

Forgiveness

Feel the soul's wisdom through a heart of compassion.

Forgiveness

"The weak can never forgive. Forgiveness is the attribute of the strong."

~ Mahatma Gandhi

Affirmation

I now forgive everyone and myself. I am free!

Card Message

When you engage in the act of forgiving, you keep your sympathetic heart pure. This is one of the greatest gifts of spiritual life. We have all been wronged and we have all caused suffering to others. The unconscious wrongs you have committed and the displeasing things that have happened to you are not as important as who you become as a result of these experiences.

God forgives you constantly for your misguided thoughts and actions. You, being a child of God, are empowered to forgive in the same way. This is your spiritual responsibility while here on earth. If you feel you are unable to embrace this responsibility, know that you are only hurting yourself and blocking the natural current of love from flowing into your life. You will see that forgiveness is beneficial for you; it is the way to release the pain of the past. You will no longer carry the negative energy of past transgressions. Now is the time to cleanse your heart, release any pain and replace it with love. You will smile as divine gifts of peace pour into your experience.

Forgiveness is an act of the heart—a movement to let go of the pain, resentment or outrage you have carried as a burden. It is necessary to remove any negative emotions from your heart and mind, as this allows you to be released from the sorrows of the past. No one deliberately means to do harm to another. It just appears as such because the soul is deluded by the ego mind, born from ignorance. In this delusional state, one is acting out of fear rather than love-operating from the head rather than the heart. When you know yourself as a spiritual being, you are inwardly undisturbed no matter what happens in your life or what anyone has done to you.

Forgive yourself for any pain you have caused another. Know that your actions have also caused you to suffer. Realize that you did the best you knew how at that given moment. Do not allow the memory of those mistakes to poison the rest of your life. Learn from the past and change yourself for the better so that you can handle situations differently next time. Because of the law of karma, the universe is graciously allowing you more opportunities to learn and make things right.

Forgiveness is naturally born without effort when you love God and realize that every soul is made in the image of God. Live genuinely from your heart and learn to love without conditions. When compassion is your natural state of being, forgiveness happens automatically. When you raise your consciousness, you keep the light of divine love burning in your heart.

Card Symbology

The oak tree is a powerful symbol of antiquity, strength and growth. Trees reach down into the ground and up to the sky at the same time. This action reflects your own ability to remain rooted in your personal truth while experiencing the external world around you. Tree branches contain ancient teachings that encourage you to classify, identify and incorporate wisdom.

A beautiful lotus mandala is nestled within the branches of the tree. Mandalas are sacred art forms that symbolize various aspects of the universe. These special symbols have deep spiritual significance and are used in ritual and meditation practices. This sacred circle transforms suffering into grace. Lotus mandalas represent purity in action and freedom from attachment. The lotus flower symbolizes the yoga of awakening to your true Self.

The hand gesture located at the base of the tree is the Mukula Mudra. A mudra corresponds to certain aspects of Hindu and Buddhist teachings that designate a ritual gesture directed towards enlightenment. The Universe is composed of five elements: earth, water, fire, air and ether. Our body is also a union of these natural elements; this union is represented by our five fingers. Hand mudras regulate the five elements. The fingers that correspond to each element are: the thumb for fire; the index (Jupiter finger) for air; the middle (Saturn finger) for ether or space; the ring (Sun finger) for earth; and the pinky (Mercury finger) for water. The Mukula Mudra's appearance resembles the bud of a lotus flower, symbolizing new beginnings. Through the act of forgiveness, you remain in present moment awareness allowing gifts of new opportunities to flow into your life.

There are two celtic knots located on each side of the tree. On the left is the triple spiral. This beautiful celtic knot depicts the awareness of

one within the context of the whole. The triple spiral reminds you to let go, surrender and release. The celtic knot on the right is the five fold symbol devoted to the five elements: fire, earth, air, water and ether. Balancing these five elements creates inner harmony.

Journey

Find a quiet place where you can relax undisturbed. Sit comfortably with your spine straight. Take a deep breath in, tensing your body from your feet to your head. Bring awareness to each body part, as you tense each muscle one by one, within the same inhale. As your entire body is tensed with energy, hold your breath until you are ready to exhale and release. As you exhale, make any audible sounds to expel all tension from your body. Repeat this exercise three times or until you feel relaxed. Gently begin allowing your natural breath to move in and out. With each inhale, silently chant: "I forgive (name of person"). With each exhale, chant: "I forgive myself." Remain in this state for as long as needed, feeling all distracting thoughts subside. Place your hands in the Mukula Mudra position, as shown in the image on the card, joining fingers and thumb pointing upwards. This mudra directs you towards enlightenment. Through the act of forgiveness, you will open to new beginnings in your life.

Imagine yourself sitting before a strong oak tree. You feel the power and strength of the tree, as she stands unshaken, enduring the changing earth elements. You breathe deeply into your heart, allowing yourself to merge with the tree. The brown bark on her trunk and branches provides you with protection and support. You vicariously encompass the strength of this majestic tree. You begin to feel the base of your spine expelling roots and extending into the fertile soil of mother earth. Your roots travel deeper and deeper through all the layers of the earth until they reach the solid inner core. These strong roots wrap around the center core and begin to draw upon the life force of the earth. Breathe this revitalizing energy up through your roots and into your body.

You now feel branches and leaves growing out of the top of your head, energetically sprouting from your crown. These branches keep traveling through the clouds and celestial realms, fully expanding into the heavens. Using your breath, draw this celestial energy back down into your body. It is now time to dance through your breath with the rhythm of oneness. Inhale, drawing from the source of the earth's inner core up through the base of your spine. Move this energy up your spine and into the crown of your head. Exhale, releasing this energy up into the heavens, circling the energy out and around and back down to the earth's core. Continue to unite the energy from above and below within yourself in the above fashion, feeling strong like a tree. Repeat this exercise until you feel grounded and spiritually connected.

When you are completely connected to heaven and earth, feel how your consciousness has expanded and aligned with Christ Consciousness. You feel every soul on this earth connected to the same energy. Feel your immortality and know you are limitless.

You begin to feel the presence of a vibration pulsating within your heart. You have never experienced anything like this before. With every deep breath you take, this feeling expands and your heart opens. You notice a radiant glow appearing before you, around you and within you. This glow is reflected from your heart and soul. It continues to become more pronounced as it shimmers like a million microscopic stars. This glowing light blooms into a wondrous, glistening lotus mandala. This sacred art communicates a message to you from the universe.

The sun is setting and you begin to notice deep, rich colors radiating from the lingering rays of the sunset. You feel warm yellow and orange color frequencies penetrating your entire body. Your body begins to access messages from a language of pure color vibration. You welcome this intelligence, soaking it into every cell of your being, allowing the color vibrations to penetrate the core of your soul. You feel safe, sure and confident. You know the time has come to partake in the gift of forgiveness.

Yellow and orange begin to transform into warm variations of the color red. Breathe in this color. As red enters your energy field, you are saturated with the energizing power of passion and compassion. You are motivated to forgive someone. You know exactly whom you are ready to forgive. Take a moment and breathe deeply until this person appears right in front you. You are aware of your perceptions of how this person has affected you. You are mindful of the pain and suffering you felt at a distant time in the past. But now you are in such a strong spiritual space, you remain emotionally detached from all discomfort. In this moment, you only see the diamond light of love beaming from this person's soul. Notice that this person has the exact same

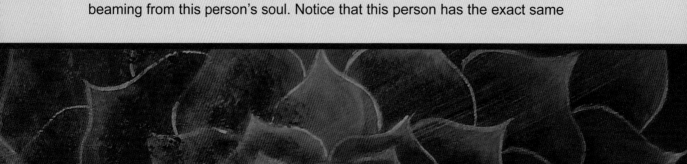

light in their soul as you do. You see them through the eyes of your compassionate heart. Right in front of you, this individual begins to transform into a young wounded child. You witness the many ways in which others have harmed this child. You have the understanding that this child has only acted out of fear, filled with confusion and sorrow. You look deeply into their eyes, seeing this person's sadness and pain. You know their suffering and understand their scars. Your heart overflows with sympathy. With tears in their eyes, they begin to speak to you. They tell you that they never meant to hurt you. They share with you they were only acting from an unconscious place of misunderstanding and ignorance. They tell you how sorry they are. Continue to listen to anything else they desire to share. You realize how both of your hearts have been wounded. You're not alone. Breathe deeply into any closed areas of your heart and allow all barriers you have carried from the past to be released once and for all.

When you are ready, look into this person's eyes and declare, "I forgive you and I love you." They begin to cry as they accept your gracious gift of forgiveness. You clearly understand how your soul called forth this experience to allow you to grow spiritually. You have become the strong, loving and wise person you are today because of this interaction. You have set another free while freeing yourself. Take time to reflect on the positive gifts that were once twisted illusion. Breathe in gratitude and feel transformed.

The color red now transforms into magenta. You find yourself flowing in the vibration of universal harmony and emotional balance. Your physical, mental, emotional and spiritual life is harmoniously stable. Your heart smiles, thankful to have arrived at this peaceful state. Magenta gradually shifts into pink as unconditional love and understanding pour into your heart. Pink showers you with the ability to give and to receive. You feel nurtured, hopeful and safe. Your tenderness and kindness has created soft, pastel colors in your energy field. You have accomplished something wonderful!

Slowly, the color pink alchemically transforms into purple. This color stimulates your imagination, inspiring you with high ideals. You introspect within this color, allowing yourself to get in touch with your deeper thoughts. Purple expands your awareness and connects you to a higher consciousness. Purple is associated with transformation of the soul. You know it is time to forgive yourself.

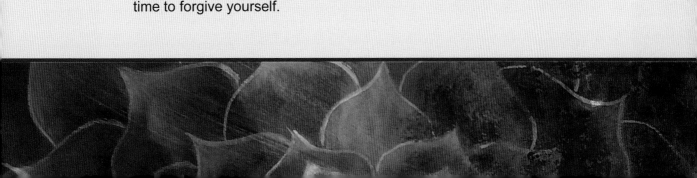

As purple continues to penetrate your thoughts, bring anyone you may have hurt into your awareness. You understand that you previously acted unconsciously from a place of fear. Now, you come from a place of love. You feel a familiar sorrow within your heart. This companion of distress has traveled with you for far too long. You feel the suffering you have endured by holding onto this sorrow and now you are ready to let it go. As you breathe in purple, ask the person you need forgiveness from to come before you. Take a moment and allow them to arrive. When they appear, say to them, "Will you please forgive me for causing you pain? I never meant to hurt you. I am so sorry." If you have any other words to share, take time to do so. This person looks compassionately into your eyes and says, "I forgive you." You embrace one another, feeling unconditional love. Your eyes connect one last time, as if to say thank you, then this person fades away. Your entire energy field is now crystal clear. You feel light and free.

Purple begins to merge into gold, illuminating your field with success, achievement and triumph! The color frequency of gold floods you with abundance, prosperity, value and quality. This golden glow reflects your higher ideals, wisdom, understanding and enlightenment. You are rewarded with this color because you have chosen to do the work. Gold infuses you with knowledge, spirituality and a deep understanding of your self and your soul. You now take the time to completely forgive yourself in any way needed. Take some time to love yourself for all the work you've done. Congratulations on your accomplishment!

The consciousness of your heart escalates as you notice the sacred lotus mandala has expanded infinitely, now vibrating throughout the universe. Billions of shimmering starlight's shower everywhere. You have freed yourself from all burdens of the heart, mind and soul. You feel empty and full at the same time, since you are currently experiencing the Divine presence of your godly nature. Forgiveness has reawakened your soul. You walk upon the earth completely whole and free as you share your holy Divinity. Bask in your new expanded consciousness.

When you return from your journey, take a deep breath and reflect on the insights you received. Smile inwardly into your heart and thank your Godly self for the work you have done to accept life, yourself and others. Record any insights or awakenings in your copy of the *Reawakening the Soul Vision Quest Workbook*.

Introspection

Am I holding onto anyone that I feel has caused me to suffer?

Have I forgiven myself for any suffering I may have caused another?

How would I feel different if I completely forgave everyone whom I believe has harmed me?

How would I feel different if I completely forgave and loved myself?

EFT/Tapping

KC: Even though it's hard to forgive someone who caused me pain, I deeply and completely accept the way I feel.

KC: Even though I haven't completely forgiven myself, I deeply and completely love myself.

KC: Even though forgiveness seems to be so hard, I am willing to look at it differently.

EB: I can't forgive.
SE: Forgiving this person seems so hard.
UE: It's so painful.
UN: It's so complicated.
CP: They hurt me so much.
CB: It's way too hard.
UA: It's too much.
TH: I can't do it.

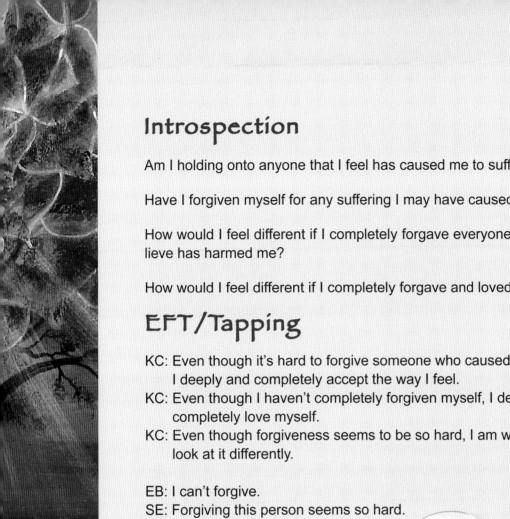

EFT Audio Available to Heal Emotional Blocks Around Forgiving.

EB: I don't want to do this.
SE: Part of me knows I need to do it.
UE: What if I can do this?
UN: What if I could see this situation differently?
CP: Maybe from a heart of compassion.
CB: And a mind full of wisdom.
UA: I do want to change.
TH: I do want to be free.

EB: All this pain has been holding me back.
SE: The suffering from this situation makes me feel angry.
UE: And remembering the pain makes me feel sad.
UN: I have had enough of this suffering.
CP: I am ready to heal.
CB: I am ready to forgive.
UA: I am ready to set myself free.
TH: I now feel this person as I tap.

EB: As I tap, I call in memories of this situation.
SE: I now choose to see this differently.
UE: Did I choose my life situations?
UN: Maybe I did choose this for my own growth.
CP: I choose to see how much I've grown from this experience.
CB: Could there really be something positive here?
UA: All these years, I've seen it as negative.
TH: Now, I'm open to seeing differently.

EB: Maybe they really didn't mean to hurt me.
SE: Maybe they didn't even realize what they were doing.
UE: They probably were acting out of fear.
UN: And pain.
CP: And completely unconscious.
CB: I feel sorry for someone like this.
UA: This person really needs to be loved.
TH: Can I love them?

EB: Can I open up to forgive them?
SE: I choose to forgive them.
UE: I choose to love them.
UN: I feel so empowered.
CP: I also forgive myself for all my wrong.
CB: I love myself enough to love everyone.
UA: I forgive myself.
TH: I feel complete.

"To forgive is to set a prisoner free and discover that the prisoner was you."

~ Lewis B. Smedes

Freedom

Give yourself permission to live the life
you came here to live.

Freedom

*"Every human being wants to be free. Once you
become aware that you are really a prisoner in this
life, you will crave freedom."*
~ Sri Daya Mata

Affirmation

I now celebrate the birth of my freedom!

Card Message

This card reminds you to celebrate your freedom. You were born free but conditioning from parents, teachers and society has caused you to forget your divine birthright. At an early age, you were taught what to believe and how to behave. In order to survive, you may have conformed to dysfunctional conditioning. You weren't area these ideals were only projections from the beliefs of others. You innocently received these beliefs as your truth. When you let someone else tell you how to feel or what to believe, you forfeit living your own authentic life. Every human being wants to be free. Once you become aware that you are a divine being, you will attain freedom.

It is time to wake up and be mindful of how you are living in order to experience harmony and purpose.

What is freedom?

ॐ   Realizing your oneness with God.

ॐ   A quiet mind and open heart.

ॐ   Being authentic to your self.

ॐ   Taking responsibility for your life.

ॐ   Awareness that you can make changes in your life.

ॐ   Making conscious and intentional decisions.

ॐ   Knowing that everything is in perfect divine order.

ॐ   Acceptance of every situation in your life with the understanding
     that it is all for your spiritual growth.

ॐ   Living in pure joy that makes your spirit sing and dance.

Truth lies in remembering who you are: an expression of God. As Paramahansa Yogananda said, "The wave cannot say, 'I am the ocean,' because the ocean can exist without the wave. But the ocean can say 'I am the wave,' because the wave cannot exist without the ocean . . . . You must in truth know from within that you are one with Him and can work His miracles." Living in this wisdom leads you to freedom.

Realize your true essence by freeing yourself from bondage that holds you back from achieving your dreams. When you seek the true aspects of yourself and rediscover your lost inner child, you will awaken a higher sense of purity, passion, creativity and spiritual healing. Your desire to live this new life will be irresistible. It is now time to rear into exciting new directions. Awaken and discover your own freedom and power!

Card Symbology

The white horse represents the rainbow of colors in your soul. The color white is created when all colors of the spectrum are present. White also represents purity, innocence and life. The noble horse has an honest, divine spirit. Horse medicine can help you express your own power and magic.

The rearing horse has many meanings. A horse will rear up when it feels boxed in, frightened, excited, joyous or confused. Are you feeling any of these emotions? Are you anxious about moving in a new direction? Is there something deep inside of you that feels excited to start a new project? If so, embrace the image of this card and allow horse energy to rear through you. This energy will move you out of limiting beliefs and in the direction of your authentic self.

The eagle represents the power to take responsibility to be the person you are meant to be. Eagle has a vast view and sees the grand picture clearly without distortions, just as your soul does. The dream catcher is a reminder that life on earth is a dream. Live in this dream without fear and feel the freedom residing in your soul. The Celtic swirls at the bottom of the image represent the dance of life in this dream state.

Experience the Transcendental Video & Audio Journey on my Website to Free Yourself Once & For ALL!

Journey

Find a quiet place where you can relax undisturbed. Sit or lie comfortably with your spine straight. Take a deep breath in, tensing your body from your feet to your head. Bring awareness to each body part, as you tense each muscle one by one, within the same inhale. As your entire body is tensed with energy, hold your breath until you are ready to exhale and release. As you exhale, make any audible sounds to expel all tension from your body. Repeat this exercise three times or until you feel relaxed. Gently begin allowing your natural breath to move in and out. With each inhale, silently chant: "My soul is free." With each exhale, chant: "I am free." Remain in this state for as long as needed, feeling all distracting thoughts subside.

You find yourself surrounded with tranquil colors of blue and turquoise. These colors help open the lines of communication between your heart and spoken word. Feel the turquoise color washing over your energy field, creating emotional balance and stability. Feel peace and tranquility radiating throughout your body. You begin to breathe deeply as you receive a powerful message transmitted through these beautiful colors. You begin to reflect upon the conditioning you have received from others throughout your lifetime. You witness things you were taught to believe and how you were conditioned to behave. You understand that these methods have molded and created who you are and how you feel. You come to a complete realization of how you have allowed yourself to be programmed by your experiences, beliefs and conditioning. The way you are currently living your life flashes before you like a movie. You watch this scene unfold as if you were sitting in a movie theatre. Take your time and watch the movie of your life being played. After it has finished, you begin to introspect. "Am I living my life with passion and purpose?" "Do I feel free to create my dreams?" "Do I feel inner joy?" "Am I happy?" The colors swirl around you and within you in a spiral motion as you reflect on all of these insights. You begin to recognize dysfunctional patterns. These patterns have controlled your life, paralyzing you from moving towards your dreams. Your soul clearly knows it is time to wake up. You feel the impulse to completely release all conditioning and limiting beliefs into the blue spiral. One by one, you let these beliefs dissolve into the coiling energy field. You begin to feel freer and lighter. As you finish unleashing the patterns, you feel clear and complete now that clarity has birthed within your soul. You realize your true essence as Spirit and feel your Divinity. Feel your strength and power rise out from your core. Know you are an expression of God. Decide to take full responsibility for your life right now. You have the awareness and courage to make any necessary changes. You know these changes will bring you inner joy and happiness. Feel how your creativity has been sparked and your wildest dreams have been awakened. All your desires begin to ignite and you feel excited to begin your life anew.

As the swirling turquoise color fades and takes all your limiting beliefs with it, a mystical white horse appears. You feel her magic and strength as you notice she is rearing. A horse will rear when it feels boxed in, frightened, excited, or confused. Go within and reflect upon these emotions. Ask yourself, "Do I feel boxed in or frightened?" "Am I feeling excitable?" "Am I confused?" "Am I anxious about moving in a new life direction?" Embrace and witness all messages you receive. The healing energy of the horse has arrived to move you out of limiting beliefs and into the direction of your authentic self.

The horse spirit merges with your soul. You feel something very exciting beginning to happen. Ask yourself, "What would it take for me to experience true freedom in my life?" "What would I have to release?" "What do I want to create?" "What are my dreams?" Feel the passion of your soul burning as you experience a new sense of freedom being birthed. Horse energy infuses you with motivation and enthusiasm. You now enjoy the freedom of living your life on your own terms. You know you can create exciting possibilities. You are free to spend your day engaging in all the things that feed your soul and bring happiness. Your life is now filled with passion, laughter and joy. The white horse delivers her medicine and magic. Thank her as she slowly fades away.

You gaze into the clear open sky and notice a captivating eagle flying above you. The eagle's energy fills your heart. She represents your higher self that guides you towards freedom. Her spirit enters your soul and you intuitively know you must follow her. She soars through the air, circling around you, showering you with internal gifts of great wisdom and authority. She shares her vision with your soul-a vast view of crystal clarity. She can see the past, present and future at a glance. Your inner vision becomes clear like the eagle's eyesight. You see how you have lived in the past and how your thoughts have created your experiences. You notice the ways your thoughts have served you along with the ways in which they no longer serve you. You are aware how you are presently living your life and know the changes you wish to make. Now, you can clearly see your future. You see yourself creating your dreams and living happily in passion. You feel the excitement of seeing your accomplishments unfold. You understand the rhythm of your life's patterns as you fly freely. Eagle leads you with wisdom, courage and trust. You can trust her because she is the inner guidance of your soul. She gives you the insight and awareness to understand that wherever you fly and land is perfect. Eagle Spirit blesses you with courage and action to execute necessary changes. She circles above you one last time. Thank her for all the gifts as she departs.

It's time to move forward towards your goals and dreams. This life is your own dream. Dream what you love to do and have fun during the process. Your

journey towards freedom has now begun. Relax in the spiral of the dream catcher.

When you return from your journey, take a deep breath and reflect on the insights you received. Smile inwardly into your heart and thank your Godly self for the work you have done to accept life, yourself and others. Record any insights or awakenings in your copy of the *Reawakening the Soul Vision Quest Workbook*.

Introspection

What does freedom mean to me?

How can I create more freedom in my life?

How would I feel if I were completely free to live every moment as my spirit wished?

What changes would it take for me to be completely free?

EFT/Tapping

KC: Even though I don't feel free, I choose to explore options to create more freedom in my life.

KC: Even though complete freedom feels impossible, I deeply accept the way I feel.

KC: Even though I long to be free, the changes I must make scare me. I completely and deeply love myself.

EB: What is freedom?
SE: Can I really be free?
UE: Can I really live my life exactly how I want?
UN: This seems impossible to me.
CP: I don't know if I am worthy to live this way.
CB: But why wouldn't I be worthy?
UA: Others are living this way.
TH: Why can't I?

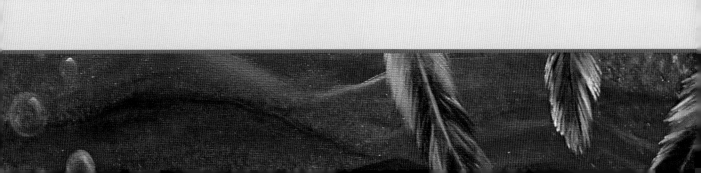

EB: Because I'm afraid.
SE: All these fears stopping me.
UE: All the changes I would need to make.
UN: It feels so scary.
CP: But is all of this honestly serving me?
CB: I feel trapped.
UA: But who trapped me?
TH: I guess I did.

EFT
Audio Available
to Clear Your
Energetic Field &
Set You
Free!

EB: If I created everything in my life.
SE: Then I can choose to create differently.
UE: I create through my thoughts.
UN: What if I changed my thoughts?
CP: I can do this.
CB: Where did my beliefs come from?
UA: Maybe many of them are not who I really am.
TH: I choose to release any limiting beliefs.

EB: These were someone else's beliefs.
SE: They were never mine.
UE: I choose to let them go.
UN: And open to new beliefs.
CP: I want a breakthrough.
CB: I'm ready for change to happen.
UA: Change feels safe.
TH: It's time to change.

EB: I am made in the image of God.
SE: Therefore, I am perfect.
UE: I reclaim my birthright as a soul.
UN: I feel my inner strength.
CP: It feels so safe here.
CB: I choose to feel the Spirit that I am.
UA: This feels liberating.
TH: I feel free to fly.

"In the vault of the mind lie all the chains of bondage, as well as the keys to freedom."

~ Paramahansa Yogananda."

Gratitude

Be thankful and mindful of God—the giver of all gifts.

Gratitude

"He is richest who is content with the least, for contentment is the wealth of nature."

~ Socrates

Affirmation

I am thankful for everything in my life.

Card Message

Take time every day to bless all the gifts in your life. Offer gratitude for your loved ones and sincerely bless them. As you think of every blessing in your life, feel the love and appreciation that pours from your heart. Give thanks for your possessions. Appreciate all situations in your life from the past to the present. Although you may perceive some situations as negative or painful, you will find hidden rewards in each experience through the grace of wisdom. Recognize the many ways in which you touch the lives of others and honor yourself. You were placed upon this earth to serve others with your exclusive gifts. These gifts include your unique personality, talents and love. The greatest legacy is to remember that your soul is the all-perfect reflection of God and share this insight through kindness.

Always remember the true giver of everything including health, wealth, success and happiness is God. His intelligence and hidden beauty is behind all finite patterns of creation. Through meditation and stillness, you begin to experience for yourself the ultimate proof of God's existence. Once you have found Him in the depths of your soul, you will experience Him everywhere. Sincere gratitude for your Creator is the greatest gift you can give.

Card Symbology

The oak tree is the mightiest of the tree kingdom and represents divinity, strength and courage. The oak is a living legend representing all that is true, wholesome, stable and noble. This tree is also considered the king of the green realm since it generously provides abundant gifts. Just as any good ruler shares his or her bounty with the inhabitants of their kingdom, the great oak tree reminds you to share your own individual gifts. This tree is grateful for the life giving forces of the sun and earth. This example of gratitude reminds you to give thanks for the same life force that sustains you.

The Sri Yantra mandala permeates from the tree as the holy symbol formed from the mantric sound pattern of Aum (Om, Amen). This vibration is the structure or blueprint of all creation. This sacred geometry symbolizes the feminine creative aspect of sacred sound, which creates patterns of light that mirror manifestations of Divinity. We are all a part of this sacred light. The Sri Yantra is the most powerful positive energy symbol.

This powerful symbol is formed by nine triangles surrounding and radiating out from the central point. This center is the junction point between the physical universe and it's energetic source. The four triangles pointing up represent the masculine. The five triangles pointing down symbolize the feminine. The combination represents the union of masculine and feminine Divine. The Sri Yantra is enclosed by two rows of (8 and 16) petals, representing the lotus of creation and reproductive vital force.

The hand gesture located at the base of the tree is called the Mida-no Jouin Mudra. A mudra corresponds to certain aspects of the Hindu and Buddhist teaching designating a ritual gesture directed towards enlightenment. The Universe is composed of five elements, earth, water, fire, air and ether. Our body is also a union of these elements, represented by our five fingers. Hand mudras regulate these five elements. The fingers representing the five elements are: The thumb for fire; the index (Jupiter finger) for air; the middle (Saturn finger) for ether or space; the ring (Sun finger) for earth; and the pinky (Mercury finger) for water. The Mida-no Jouin Mudra is formed as the left hand mirrors the right hand representing the two worlds of enlightenment and illusion. Enlightenment is born from the realization that the physical realm is an illusion. Understanding universal intelligence consists of knowing that there is One underlying energy pulsating within all of creation. Our physical realm, which includes our physical bodies, is a part of this phenomenal energy.

The ancient celtic knot at the base of the image represents beginnings and endings. When looking at the knot, one does not see a beginning or an end. This symbol is a reminder of the timeless nature of Spirit and oneness.

Journey

Find a quiet place where you can relax undisturbed. Sit comfortably with your spine straight. Take a deep breath in, tensing your body from your feet to your head. Bring awareness to each body part, as you tense each muscle one by one, within the same inhale. As your entire body is tensed with energy, hold your breath until you are ready to exhale and release. As you exhale, make any audible sounds to expel all tension from your body. Repeat this exercise three times or until you feel relaxed. Gently begin allowing your natural breath to move in and out. With each inhale, silently chant: "I am mindful." With each exhale, chant: "I am grateful." Remain in this state for as long as needed, feeling all distracting thoughts subside.

Bring your hands into the mudra image shown the wisdom card. The middle, ring and pinky fingers create a flat or slightly curved bed resting upon the lap. Form two circles with index fingers held together while extending upwards meeting the tips of both thumbs.

Feel the rhythm of your breath as you begin to merge with the oak tree. Feel the power and strength of the tree as she stands unshaken, able to endure the changing earth elements. You vicariously encompass her strength, feeling infused by a great force. You begin to feel the base of your spine expelling roots. These roots plunge deep into the fertile soil of mother earth, spreading far and deep. You begin to absorb nutrients from the womb of mother earth. Your roots sink deeper and deeper, traveling through all the layers of the earth, until they reach the solid inner core. They wrap around this center core and you become firmly anchored-strong and flexible at the same time. As you breathe, draw Mother Earth's energy to you. You sense this divine nourishment is your life force and continue to inwardly draw upon her sustenance. You breathe this energy up through your roots and into your being. The many fibers of your essence begin to morph into a solid trunk. Limbs begin to emerge from your trunk. You begin to form branches as you reach toward the sky and soak up the sun's rays. This precious sunlight is the source that sustains you. Light radiates with the vibration of oneness. You feel the wisdom of your soul as the eternal bliss of Spirit. Bask in this warmth and oneness.

As you breathe deeply, you feel the presence of a vibration pulsating within your heart. You have never experienced anything like this before. With every deep breath you take, you feel this energy expanding. As your energy continues to expand, you notice a radiant glowing light appearing within you and around you. This light is reflected from your heart and soul. The luminous glow continues to become more pronounced as it shimmers like a million microscopic stars. This shimmer blooms into the wondrous glistening Sri Yantra symbol. This sacred art speaks the voice of the universe. You feel deep understanding on a subliminal level birthing in your consciousness. Even though you are not quite sure of all Spirit wishes to communicate, you know that in time you will possess this wisdom. Your awareness is guided into the central point of light—the junction between the physical universe and it's unmanifest source. You feel great peace, calmness and absolute wholeness. You now spend time pulsating within this light. You can clearly see the world as a display of illusion. The awareness that there is no separation between your soul and Spirit is now yours. The nature of Creation reveals herself in myriads of waves of light. You are brought back to remembering your Oneness—your true nature as Holy Spirit.

In this blissful space, begin to witness every blessing in your life. Bring your loved ones into your heart and bless them. Acknowledge your possessions and sincerely appreciate them. Begin to review situations from past to present and breathe in light. Is there something that has happened in the past that still brings you pain? If so, look inwardly to reveal the blessing it has to share with you. Notice how you have grown due to this sorrow. Sincerely thank every circumstance in your life whether your mind perceives it as comfortable or uncomfortable. Inhale and allow the energy of grace to infuse your entire being. Notice how expansive this feels in your body, heart and mind. You have opened yourself to allow more space in your energy field. This current of energy feels so nourishing to you. You recognize the many ways in which you touch the lives of others. You bring awareness to your heart and acknowledge your talents, your love and your unique personality. Take a moment and honor yourself. You sense that your Creator is responsible for all these gifts. You remember your soul as the all-perfect reflection of God and see yourself stepping into your Godly nature. See the many ways you are able to shine your light as you live your true nature. Now that you have acknowledged every layer of gratitude, feel your heart bursting with love. Fill yourself with praise and rejoice in all that is. Feel your heart smile as it opens and expands.

An ancient celtic knot appears to you, pulsating and beating with the rhythm of oneness. This symbol imbues it's magic into your core essence with the wisdom that there are no beginnings or endings. You experience yourself as an immortal soul in the timeless nature of Spirit. Flow to the beat of the everlasting awareness of wholeness.

When you return from your journey, take a deep breath and reflect on the insights you received. Smile inwardly into your heart and thank your Godly self for the work you have done to accept life, yourself and others. Record any insights or awakenings in your copy of the *Reawakening the Soul Vision Quest Workbook*.

Introspection

Who am I grateful for in my life and why?

In what ways am I grateful for myself?

What material abundance am I thankful for right now?

What pain or suffering can I find gratitude in at this time?

EFT/Tapping

KC: Even though it's challenging for me to feel gratitude for the things in my life that don't feel good, I deeply and completely accept myself.

KC: Even though it's hard for me to feel grateful for the suffering in my life, I deeply and completely accept myself.

KC: Even though it's challenging for me to feel gratitude for every thing in my life, I deeply and completely accept myself.

EB: I am grateful for all the good things in my life.
SE: As I tap.
UE: I remember all these good things.
UN: As I tap, I see all the beautiful gifts in my life.
CP: All the beautiful people in my life.
CB: All the beautiful things happening right now.
UA: But can I feel gratitude for all the things that don't feel good?
TH: For all the sorrow in my life?

EB: For all the pain and suffering that I have endured?
SE: How can I feel grateful for painful experiences?
UE: It's hard for me to have gratitude for the distress in my life.

Listen to EFT
Audio on my
Website
fo Receive Move
Appreciation!

UN: It seems impossible for me to feel grateful for this pain.
CP: But I know that I need to find peace in this sorrow.
CB: Because I know that through the sorrow.
UA: Through the tears.
TH: And through the pain.

EB: There is a hidden message for me.
SE: There are gifts to be found.
UE: Gifts of growth.
UN: Gifts of me becoming a better person.
CP: A more spiritual person.
CB: A more loving person.
UA: So I tap into all this pain.
TH: All this sorrow.

EB: As I tap, I say thank you.
SE: Thank you for this situation in my life right now.
UE: Thank you for all the painful situations in my past.
UN: And I keep tapping until I really feel the gratitude.
CP: And the knowingness that this pain.
CB: Will bring me closer to Spirit.
UA: I tap knowing that this sorrow
TH: Is exactly what I need in my life.

EB: Because I created it.
SE: And I created it only for my spiritual growth.
UE: And only for a deeper understanding of myself.
UN: And I take full responsibility for creating this.
CP: Even though it seems that it is others hurting me.
CB: My soul knows that I can't blame others.
UA: I know in my heart and in my soul.
TH: That this was created by me and for me.

EB: As a gift for me to see.
SE: And I open up now
UE: To receive the blessing.
UN: That this situation has to offer.
CP: Through a grateful and loving heart.
CB: Thank you.

UA: I ask to see all the gifts in the shadows.
TH: Around my painful situations.

EB: And I open up to see these gifts.
SE: As I release any hostility.
UE: Any resentment.
UN: Any blame.
CP: As I release all of these,
CB: I open up to the truth that it has to offer.
UA: I open up to the light that it has to bring.
TH: Even though it feels dark.

EB: It feels really dark.
SE: I know beneath the darkness.
UE: There is light.
UN: And this is the light that I live in.
CP: This is the light that I breathe.
CB: This is the light that breathes through me.
UA: Because I am light.
TH: I am only light.

EB: The light of spirit.
SE: And I say thank you.
UE: To myself for doing this work.
UN: To receive this light.
CP: I say thank you to myself.
CB: For wanting to gain deeper understanding.
UA: And deeper wisdom.
TH: And to remember my wholeness.

EB: I love myself and to receive my blessings.
SE: Through pleasure and pain.
UE: I am grateful for myself.
UN: And I love myself.
CP: And I love the fact.
CB: That I am able to take full responsibility.
UA: And be grateful for all my actions.
TH: I am grateful for myself.

Growth

Expand your consciousness by utilizing every life experience.

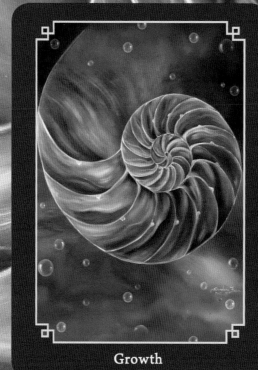

Growth

"Growth means change and change involves risks, stepping from the known to the unknown."

~ George Shinn

Affirmation

I respond positively to all of life's experiences and allow myself to grow.

Card Message

Growth is the process of responding positively to every experience in your life. Every circumstance is an opportunity for you to grow into a healthier, more conscious being. Through the universal law of cause and effect, all happenings are in complete alignment with your soul's purpose. When you fully understand that you create every situation happening to you, wisdom is born. Current situations in your life originated from previous thoughts, actions and desires. With this profound realization, you can begin to take full responsibility for everything happening in your life. You can either accept these circumstances as gifts for your personal development or you can blame them and become a victim. When you become a victim of your circumstances, you step into a state of helplessness, which slows the progression of your spiritual growth. From this dis-empowered space, suffering can manifest. Remember that you have a choice in how you view your experiences.

Perceived obstacles are opportunities that can be overcome by perseverance and wisdom. When you embrace every hardship and face adversity with a spirit of determination, it is inevitable that you will grow! What you learn from each challenge shapes your character. Your trials, sorrows and heartaches aid you in developing courage and strength. These are blessed opportunities that help you become stronger. How you meet each trial determines your future happiness and success. This incarnation is your own personal spiritual journey; these experiences have been created specifically for you and by you. How you choose to perceive this life is solely up to you. You can either allow circumstances to defeat you or you can reign triumphant over your life.

When you arrive at the understanding that each experience is ultimately for your own good, your life will begin to change. Realize that the purpose of your soul's evolution is to reunite you back into your Beloved's arms. Your soul is the bright and shining perfection of Spirit, but you may have forgotten this. Life's experiences are the gifts that bring you back to the awareness of your Oneness. Don't overlook these precious gifts. Life is constantly changing and growth is the process of embracing these changes in a positive way. As Heraclitus said, "The only thing that is constant is change" but remember—the only thing that is changeless is God!

Card Symbology

The nautilus shell symbolizes the unending spiral of life, as it is associated with the cycles of time, the seasons, the cycle of birth, growth, death and rebirth. This exquisite shell also represents our ever-evolving journey here on earth. The spiral, which is the oldest symbol known to be used in spiritual practices, reflects the universal pattern of growth and evolution. The chambered nautilus is a living fossil that has survived almost unaltered for over 500 million years. Nautilus (meaning "sailor" in Greek) is one of the only shells existing before there were fish, dinosaurs or mammals. The nautilus consists of a series of chambers inhabited by a sea creature who remodels the chambers in the shell continuously throughout it's life. As the creature grows, it moves forward into a new, larger chamber and produces a wall that seals off the older chambers. As it settles in to it's new space, the sea creature becomes ready for the next stage of it's life.

The nautilus in this image reflects your own spiritual evolution. In order to begin a new stage of growth, you must accept change and place your consciousness in the present moment. Pay attention to your thoughts and actions and utilize them in a positive way. The nautilus also reminds you to believe in your dreams and set goals in order for them to come true. As you create new chambers for your personal growth and let go of the past, you continue to grow into a beautiful spiritual being.

Journey

Find a quiet place where you can relax undisturbed. Sit comfortably with your spine straight. Take a deep breath in, tensing your body from your feet to your head. Bring awareness to each body part, as you tense each muscle one by one, within the same inhale. As your entire body is tensed with energy, hold your breath until you are ready to exhale and release. As you exhale, make any audible sounds to expel all tension from your body. Repeat this exercise three times or until you feel relaxed. Gently begin allowing your natural breath to move in and out. With each inhale, silently chant: "I accept change." With each exhale, chant: "With change comes growth." Remain in this state for as long as needed and then allow your journey to begin.

Visualize yourself walking along a beautiful sandy beach next to the vast ocean. You feel the warm sand beneath your feet as it flows between your toes. There's no one else on the beach; you are all alone. It feels

Experience the Transcendental Video & Audio Journey on my Website to Expand Your Consciousness!

quiet and peaceful as the setting sun slowly begins to lower and rest for the evening. You feel the warm heat from the sun wrapped around you like a blanket of light. This warmth is so comforting. You notice a slight breeze refreshing your senses as the air wafts across your body. You decide to sit down and absorb the radiant beauty that surrounds you. As you gaze at the sea, you notice brilliant colors bouncing off the water. Calming blues, greens, yellows and oranges envelope you. These colors captivate your senses, leaving you with a mystical sense of wonder. You are mesmerized by the delicate waves as they ebb and flow. You sense the consciousness of the cosmic sea as you watch her breathe. Your inhalation and exhalation begins to match the ocean's movement, inward and outward, as you harmoniously synchronize with the breath of oneness. As you continue this rhythmic movement, you feel your state of being change. You now find yourself merging with the ocean of cosmic awareness. You are no longer separated from the sea of cosmic consciousness; you are the ocean of Spirit that has become the human wave. Behind the wave of your awareness is the boundless sea of cosmic intelligence.

As you float in this oneness, you notice the appearance of the water begins to change shape. You notice an object emerging from the depths of blue space. You watch as this mysterious object comes closer until you clearly behold a magnificent nautilus shell. The energy emanating from this chambered nautilus holds ancient wisdom. This sacred object has survived in the earth's oceans for the last 500 million years. This nautilus existed before there were fish, dinosaurs, or mammals. As you gaze into the nautilus, you notice the intricate, artistic patterns that adorn the shell. The dazzling, opalescent pearl sheen is breathtaking to behold! You feel the sacred geometry within the spiral that represents the physical and energetic patterns that create and unify all things. This geometric pattern reveals the way that the universe organizes itself. Every natural pattern of growth or movement conforms inevitably to one or more geometric shapes. Sacred geometric codes create the molecules of your DNA—they are the building blocks of the universe. This sacred spiral represents the dynamic relationship between yourself and nature—the inseparable relationship of the individual part to the collective whole. This reflection holds valuable teachings for you about the inner workings of your being and how you relate to the universe at large. The key to understanding the relationship between yourself and the universe lies in understanding the concept of growth and proportion. Harmonic proportion and progression are the essence of creation and are consistent with nature. Your existence and personal growth are important parts of this progressive and perfect universe.

As you merge with this nautilus, you notice many chambers that the sea creature had created as it grew inside the shell. These chambers symbolize your own growth and movement in life. Your thoughts are quiet as you concentrate on the beginning point of the spiral that exists deep within the shell. You begin your journey into each chamber. You follow the spiral around and around as it climbs higher and higher, like a staircase, opening into larger and larger chambers. As you spiral around in the chambers, you begin to reflect upon your own life. You recall your growth process from childhood leading up to where you are right now. You continue to move through your own staircase of chambers from the past, spiraling into the present moment. Take note of how you created new cells when you outgrew old structures. You see how you have outgrown certain friendships and developed new ones. You review each dwelling place during the many transitions of your life. As passing scenarios from each residence flash before your eyes, you take notice of the relationships that have flowed in and out of your life. You view who you were then and who you have become. Memories flood before you as you move through each chambered staircase. You witness your spiritual growth through the hardships you have endured. Remember that the nautilus has been replicating itself and carrying the memories, knowledge and secret wisdom of past times. You can visit any of the chambers any time you wish and receive the wisdom and information that each chamber has to offer.

When you feel complete with your journey of the past, look into the central point of the spiral again. Imagine yourself very small and standing at the beginning of the spiral. Just as you followed the spiral around like a staircase, imagine yourself now climbing those stairs. You find yourself spiraling around and around, climbing higher and higher as you move through the chambers. You notice how each chamber grows larger than the one before. Go slowly and allow yourself to experience the twists and turns of the spiral. Notice how the stairs get wider and wider with each step, allowing you more space to move. When you get the top of the staircase, you feel so expansive. You glance down and view the center, realizing how far you have come. As you spend time reflecting on your accomplishments so far, you celebrate your achievements. Spend some time honoring the unique person you have become. You realize how much strength you have gained from life's experiences. You graciously thank yourself for all the work you've done. Looking back at the chambers, you see how you have climbed the precious ladder of realization- growing closer to the essential truth of your oneness with Spirit. Relax your mind and rest within the spiral's energy.

You now realize that you have outgrown the chamber of your current life and you are ready to create a new space. It is time for old structures to be removed, as they no longer serve you. It's time to clean out your old house. This is an exciting move for you, yet you may feel a bit uncomfortable. You are aware that every condition that confronts you represents the next step in your unfoldment. You welcome all tests because you know that within you is the intelligence to understand and the power to overcome. This new awareness of your personal power makes you feel limitless! You used to hide yourself away in small places but now you come out of hiding and open the gates to release all limitations. You decide to bury dead disappointments in the cemetery of the past. You understand that some old patterns no longer fit your new life. You now have the awareness that certain changes need to be made. Your energy field has raised it's vibration to a higher frequency and you must allow yourself the space to attract like minded people and new opportunities into your life.

You begin to contemplate and design the new blueprint of your dwelling. You inquire, "Are there any patterns I have outgrown and am willing to leave behind?" "Are there people in my life that no longer resonate with my energy that I need to let go of?" "Are there situations that just don't feel comfortable any more?" You look back at your life and begin to take action on revisions needed. It is time to completely let go of the past. You are growing in truth, integrity and authenticity as you make your way into your comfortable new home. "How is this new chamber going to serve you?" "What energy is this new space going to contain?" "How are you going to feel in your new home and environment?" See the new YOU that you envision yourself becoming. Notice how the new you walks, how you talk, how you stand, how you behave, and what your disposition is like. Notice every detail of the person you wish to become. You admire every characteristic of your new being as the excitement begins to build. You are stepping into your higher, authentic self-the absolute truth of your godly nature. You know this new space will only contain peace, as drama no longer serves you. You are now reawakening your soul! You feel the vibration of joy and bliss radiating from your being.

By doing your inner housecleaning, you have washed away the debris that once covered your lustrous diamond soul. You have removed old conditioning, ideas, beliefs, patterns, projections, and perceptions. Your soul is now able to shine it's brilliant diamond light! This is where you

longed to be; this is your dream come true. You are so enthusiastic as you consciously finalize the details of your new chamber. You have now created a healthy environment with deliberate, purposeful intention.

Now that you have prepared the way, your house is built. You are ready to move into your new chamber. You enter your beautiful temple and feel the expansive space created by the process of letting go. As you sit in your new empty space, you feel the sensation of total fullness and satisfaction in your being. You sit in the silence of deep appreciation and revel in the presence of joy. You plow the garden of life with new, creative efforts. You sow seeds of wisdom, health, prosperity, and happiness. You water your seeds with self-confidence and faith, fully trusting that the Divine will give you a bountiful harvest. Now that you have polished your soul, you feel alive, wide open and ready to receive all the good entering your life. You are restored and renewed as new opportunities and possibilities abound. You have shown up as an incandescent, spiritual being with fresh thoughts and new awareness. Because you have realized there is no separation between you and your great Creator, you are fearless, powerful and unstoppable. You have stepped into the Spirit of magic! The ocean of God's abundance flows through you. You have realized yourself as an image of God. You are a channel through which all Divine creative power flows.

The nautilus then dissolves as mysteriously as it appeared. You feel rejuvenated as you embark on your new journey.

When you return from your journey, take a deep breath and reflect on the insights you received. Smile inwardly into your heart and thank your Godly self for the work you have done to accept life, yourself and others. Record any insights or awakenings in your copy of the *Reawakening the Soul Vision Quest Workbook.*

Introspection

Do I accept change?

Am I willing to take 100% responsibility for my life?

Do I allow myself to grow from my hardships and suffering?

Can I embrace every situation in a positive way?

EFT/Tapping

KC: Even though accepting everything in my life as a positive experience seems challenging, I am open to explore ways to achieve this awareness.

KC: Even though it's hard for me to take full responsibility for everything happening in my life, I want to change because I don't want to blame anymore.

KC: Even though it's difficult for me to embrace hardships, I am open to look at this in order to grow.

EB: I know that in order for me to grow, change is needed.
SE: I need to change my thoughts.
UE: I need to change my views.
UN: I want to look into my beliefs.
CP: Everything that I've been taught.
CB: How much of it is really true?
UA: How many of my old beliefs are still being applied in my life?
TH: How many of these beliefs are untrue?

EB: How are these patterns being played out in my life?
SE: I want to be more conscious.
UE: I am willing to look deeply into my beliefs.
UN: And move into a new state of awareness.
CP: I want to grow.
CB: Growth is good for me.
UA: I want to change.
TH: I am tired of suffering.

> EFT
> Audio Available
> to Accelerate
> Your
> Growth!

EB: I don't have to suffer any more.
SE: I am now open to a new way of viewing life.
UE: I am open to change.
UN: I am open to dream.
CP: I am open to remembering myself as Spirit.
CB: I now open to fully trust my Creator.
UA: Can I take 100% responsibility for my life?
TH: For everything created in my life.

EB: Everything!
SE: What if I created everything?
UE: Knowing it was all for my highest good?
UN: It would definitely change my way of being.
CP: I would feel more peace.
CB: Can I really take full responsibility?
UA: Why not?
TH: It feels in alignment with my soul.

EB: It feels good to be responsible.
SE: And not blame anymore.
UE: I think my life would definitely change for the better.
UN: I would have greater understanding.
CP: And love for every one.
CB: Because I would know they are only reflecting my thoughts.
UA: And helping me to grow spiritually.
TH: This feels true to my heart.

EB: This feels healthy.
SE: Because if every situation was created for my spiritual growth.
UE: And I am not accepting and embracing it,
UN: Then I am impeding my own growth.
CP: This doesn't feel good.
CB: I don't want to do this.
UA: I want to grow.
TH: I am now open to taking full responsibility.

EB: For everything that has happened in my life.
SE: And everything happening in my life right now.
UE: With this new awareness,
UN: I grow deeper towards truth.
CP: I am willing to look back at all my situations,
CB: To see how it created who I am today.
UA: I now step into seeing who I wish to become.
TH: Strong.

EB: Fearless.
SE: Powerful.
UE: Limitless.
UN: Joyful.
CP: And all these come from personal development.
CB: It comes from remembering my divine essence as Spirit.
UA: I am an image of God.
TH: I am pure consciousness.

EB: I am immortal.
SE: And I choose to change my thinking.
UE: I thank everything in my life.
UN: For it has created the person I am now.
CP: I reclaim my power.
CB: And I know my vibration will shift.
UA: And call forth like vibrations into my life.
TH: Such as peace, prosperity and health.

EB: This feels good.
SE: I have faith in myself.
UE: I have faith in my Creator.
UN: And I am now ready to move forward.
CP: Into my new chamber.
CB: And leave all others behind.
UA: Along with all the energy contained in them.
TH: I leave these behind.

EB: In my new chamber.
SE: I feel expansive.
UE: I feel wise.
UN: I feel safe.
CP: I feel excited.
CB: I am open to create.
UA: And dream,
TH: The new me!

Identity

Remove all masks of false beliefs and shine as your Godly self.

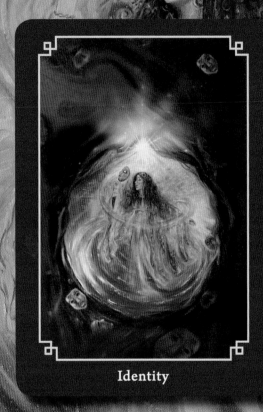

Identity

"The "self-image" is the key to human personality and human behavior. Change the self image and you change the personality and the behavior."

~ Maxwell Maltz

Affirmation

My identity is the essence of pure Spirit.

Card Message

You have thought of yourself as having certain qualities, with their characteristic feelings and emotions. You have become identified with the body, mind, belief patterns and material objects. As you masquerade these impressions with your passion and desire, you have utterly forgotten your real nature. Every day you are impersonating different characteristics according to your changing feelings through your thought patterns. You must realize that these characteristics are not part of your true nature. When you realize this, you are able to cast off these delusive states and step into your divine Self.

It is time to explore the beliefs you carry about who you are. Take a good look within and see where they came from. What do you believe about yourself? Are you really who you think you are? Are you wearing masks created by what others perceived you to be? Are you entangled in feelings imagining you have no choice? Do you even know who you are? Do you really, truly know who you are?

As you deeply analyze your thoughts, emotions and feelings, you will realize they arise from past conditioning. Your soul has identified itself with feeling and you have imprisoned yourself in various moods, which is the cause of all your suffering. You have put on masks created by false beliefs fed by the stimuli of feelings. This illusion is so powerful; it becomes real to you as a truth you hold about yourself. Your feelings and beliefs have masked your soul. The way to escape is to dissolve the feelings and emotions connected with body consciousness. Meditation is the way to achieve this.

You are not any of these masks; you are pure, calm Spirit. Your beautiful soul is the blessed reflection of Spirit. It is time for you to take off the masks of delusion and face your real Self. You will absolutely love what you find!

Card Symbology

Through awareness, the woman in the painting has realized the many identities she has accumulated throughout her lifetime. She is aware of how her beliefs have set into motion an illusion of her own self-perception. She recognizes the distortion of her perception, observing they were created by her beliefs. Understanding that thoughts create every experience, and thoughts arrive from beliefs, she knows it's time to change her minds programming. She understands the character of who she believed she was, is not true. She clearly beholds how these belief patterns created invisible masks covering her true identity. She is curious as to what would be revealed if she were to remove all these masks. As the truth of her all-knowing soul awakens and flourishes, she knows it is time to shed these layers of false beliefs. She dives deep into her perceived truths and releases the masks attached to each of them. As she entertains this, she now steps out of her old sense of self into the true existence of her Essential Self.

Journey

Find a quiet place where you can relax undisturbed. Sit comfortably with your spine straight. Take a deep breath in, tensing your body from your feet to your head. Bring awareness to each body part, as you tense each muscle one by one, within the same inhale. As your entire body is tensed with energy, hold your breath until you are ready to exhale and release. As you exhale, make any audible sounds to expel all tension from your body. Repeat this exercise three times or until you feel relaxed. Gently begin allowing your natural breath to move in and out. With each inhale, silently chant: "I breathe in clarity." With each exhale, chant: "I breathe out truth." Remain in this state for as long as needed, feeling all distracting thoughts subside.

Draw in all the richness of the warm colors emanating from the image. Feel the vibration of glowing oranges, magentas and yellows permeating your being. With a deep knowingness, you are aware that these cosmic swirls of color are magically transforming and cleansing your entire energy field. You feel spirit surging at such a deep level in your soul. You begin to focus on the color orange as it radiates warmth and happiness. Orange relates to your gut instincts. You grasp at some inner knowing that you want to wake up to experience your true identity. You know you are much more than you were led to believe. Orange offers you emotional strength to accomplish your journey into the awareness of your True Self. You know it will take effort on your part and you feel more ready than ever. Orange brings you motivation and a positive outlook helping you to look on the bright side of life. You sense this radiant color as both physically and mentally stimulating as it gets you thinking and talking. As you continue to absorb this color, take another deep breath inhaling the full essence of the fresh orange, it infuses you

Experience the Transcendental Video & Audio Journey on my Website to Reveal Your True Identity!

with optimism and uplifts and rejuvenates your spirit. Orange aids in the assimilation of new ideas and frees your spirit of all limitations, giving you the freedom to be yourself. With its enthusiasm for life, the color orange imbues you with adventure and risk-taking, inspiring you with confidence. Orange has now completed its magic and begins its transformation into magenta. You silently say thank you as you feel yourself radiating with enthusiasm.

Next, you begin to gaze into the brilliant magenta color as you feel its universal harmony and emotional balance energy re-calibrate your field. You feel the supernatural power bursting from this majestic color directly into your core. Every aspect in your life suddenly feels balanced, physically, mentally, emotionally and spiritually. You feel your intuition and psychic ability strengthen. You are able to rise above your current way of thinking, excited to experience a greater level of awareness and knowledge. You are not quite sure what all of this is leading up too, but you feel your soul dancing in excitement. With the wondrous spellbound energy from magenta, acting as an instrument of change and transformation, you feel free to release old emotional patterns that have prevented your personal and spiritual development. You experience a sense of self-respect and contentment. Your heart feels happy and cheerful. You are ready to take responsibility for creating your new path in life. Magenta has now shared its gifts and dissolves into the color yellow.

As yellow surrounds your field, you feel the illuminating and uplifting warmth fill your body with happiness. Yellow infuses your mind and inspires your original thought and inquisitiveness. Surprisingly, you feel excited about a new mental challenge coming your way. You now feel the acquired knowledge to create new ideas and find new ways of thinking. You are saturated with clarity and focused intention to begin experiencing your authentic identity. Wisdom has been reawakened in your soul.

With new awareness, you are now able to clearly see the many masks you have chosen to wear throughout your life. With the gift of wisdom, you know each mask was birthed from a belief. You notice how this notion was based upon false misunderstanding. You conclude how you have chosen to take another persons ideas, projections and views as your own. You understand that you have become identified with your body, mind, belief patterns and material objects. You no longer want to masquerade these impressions any longer. You are motivated to explore the masks you wear.

Out of the cosmic light, your personality mask appears before you. These are the characteristics that distinguish you as an individual, along with your behavioral and emotional characteristics. You become aware of how you have allowed your emotions to control your life. You feel how your team of protective inner selves, live your life around your emotional state of being, without thinking about them, questioning them or even being aware of them. You know it's time to clear your conscious and unconscious mind from previous negative programming. The personality mask asks you to release all negative emotions that disguise your True Self. These emotions may appear as, moodiness, anxious, angry, aggressive, rigid, reactive, excitable, restless, touchy, depressed, impatient, sarcastic, critical, gloomy and sadness. Throw all of them into the personality cosmic light. Discharge all negative energy you carry around these emotions. As you are complete with this mission, reflect back into your past and identify where these beliefs that have contributed to your emotions arrived. It may have been from a person, situation or an experience you had. Mentally see where these patterns came from. You comprehend how you chose to receive these negative emotions as your own. You recognize how you have been bound by these distorted emotions. You fully realize these are not who you are. You make a conscious choice and vow to leave all of this negativity in the past. The personality mask now shines from the refection of the light within your soul, infusing you with a magnificent glow of awakening. In this light you feel the truth of the holiness of your essence. Your soul light ingrains new patterns from your natural being into your consciousness. As starbursts enter your field, you feel peaceful, joyful, loving, happy, easygoing, carefree, calm, even-tempered, content, passionate, friendly, spontaneous, confident, and lively. You now leave feeling emotionally stable.

Next, out of the cosmic light, your role mask appears before you. The mask explains that a role is a set of connected behaviors, beliefs, and norms you have interpreted and defined as your own. It is the character and part played out through you as the performer. You have chosen to play these roles based upon your belief system. You feel how your inner verdicts are deeply embedded in you as you play your various roles in this physical world. You feel how your team of protective inner selves, live your life around these roles, without thinking about them, questioning them or even being aware of them. You know it is time to clear your conscious and unconscious mind around any roles you play derived from old programming.

Role mask asks you to examine all the various roles you play in your life. You are asked to view the individual roles you are playing such as, a mother, father, sister, brother, wife, husband, girlfriend, boyfriend, son, daughter, grandmother, and grandfather. Whatever roles these may be, bring them into your minds eye and witness how you have taken on these roles. Without judgment, notice yourself playing these various parts. Pay attention to what is happening behind the scenes as you undertake the responsibilities during each position. For instance, if you are assuming the mother job, what happens to the little girl in you? Is she being forgotten, pushed aside or do you take time to nurture her? In your minds eye, step back and act as a witness of your "self" playing various roles. Be creative and honest in trying to figure out all that is happening in the foreground and background as the scene is taking place. Mentally take note of any dysfunctions or imbalances you may uncover.

Now role mask invites you to go even deeper into subconscious and unconscious positions you may be participating in. You are asked to view the archetypal patterns you may be enacting. These may include roles as victim, (poor me. . . why does this always happen to me!?" saboteur, hermit, martyr, prostitute, gambler, child, savior, queen, and king, etc. Testify to any ways in which you may be contributing energy in these roles. Notice how you feel while taking on the persona. Does it feel healthy and balanced? Does it feel good? Is it benefiting your spiritual well being? Continue to recall and identify behavioral patterns you chose unconsciously.

Now, role mask asks you to mentally see your roles being played in your current occupation. You are now asked to view your occupational roles such as, accountant, artist, healer, therapist, blue-collar worker, lawyer, entrepreneur, secretary, teacher, and student. Notice what occupation you chose and ask yourself some introspective questions, "Why did I chose this occupation?" "Am I passionate in this profession?" "Do I sincerely love my line of chosen work?" "Do I feel happy and free in this position?" "Did I choose this career with the integrity of my soul? Or out of fear that I need security or to make money?" Review your daily obligations and see if they nurture your soul. Be completely authentic with your self without blame or judgment. Pay attention to feel the things you are engaging in on a daily basis. Do these feel in alignment with your soul's purpose and fueled by passion? Spend time reminiscing your chosen profession now, and the ones from the past. Notice any reoccurring patterns or themes in your occupation.

Now, release all negative roles that no longer serve your moving into your higher self. Throw all of them into the role cosmic light. Discharge all negative energy you carry around these false convictions. As you are complete with this mission, reflect back into your past and identify where the individual, archetypical and occupational roles arrived. It may have been from a person, situation or an experience you had. Mentally see where and how these patterns arrived. You comprehend how you chose to receive these false ideas as your own. You recognize how you have been bound by these distorted false beliefs. You make a conscious choice and vow to leave all of this negativity in the past. You fully realize these are not who you are. The role mask now shines from the refection of the light within your soul, infusing you with a splendid spark of awakening. In this spark you feel the truth of the holiness of your essence. Your soul light ingrains new patterns from your natural state of being into your consciousness. As star bursts enter your field, you are infused with clarity, wisdom and understanding. You know that you are an actor on this cosmic screen of duality.

Out of the cosmic light, the master mask of core beliefs appears before you. This is the major mask that governs the role mask and the personality mask. Core belief mask shares that a belief is something you accept as true, without question. You unconsciously bury these within the core of your being. These core beliefs are whom you think you are, how you think you should feel, act and behave. These core beliefs rule your thoughts, and your thoughts create every experience in your existence! You feel how your beliefs are deeply embedded in you. You sense how your team of protective inner selves, live and create your life around them, without thinking about them, questioning them or even being aware of them. You know it is time to become completely conscious and fully rid yourself from all negative programming. You know without a doubt, the repetition of these programs creates reoccurring patterns in your life. The core belief mask asks you to release all negative beliefs you have worn as a disguise about yourself. These beliefs may consist of unworthiness, failure, unsuccessful, low self-worth, powerless, not good enough, unlovable, incompetent, imperfect, not safe, defeated, and bad. Throw all of them into the core beliefs cosmic light, where they dissolve forever. Discharge all negative energy you carry around these false convictions. Release every one of them. As you are complete with this mission, reflect back into your past and identify where these core beliefs came from. It may have been from a person, situation or an experience you had. Mentally see where and how these patterns arrived. You comprehend how you chose to receive these false ideas as your own. You recognize how you have been bound by these distorted false beliefs. You make a conscious choice and vow to leave all of this negativity in the past. You fully realize these are not who you are.

The core belief mask now shines from the refection of the light within your soul, infusing you with lavishing wisdom. In this light you feel the absolute divine nature of your core essence. Your soul light ingrains new patterns from your natural being into your consciousness. As star bursts enter your field, you experience yourself as pure cosmic consciousness. Fully awake and aware of you're connection as Spirit. Your core is now fused with the energy of absolute bliss, as you perceive joy and happiness radiating from your soul. You have merged with your Godly nature, filled with positivity to create new opportunities in achieving your souls mission. You feel excited to be fully open to experience life and induce fresh ideas from the wisdom of your soul. Your expansion reaches beyond the heavens now that all the delusive masks of identity are removed. Congratulations! You have done some powerful work. It's time for a new movie to begin as you choose your alternate roles. Guided by wisdom, you now consciously select your acting parts. Your heart and soul is nurtured and free!

When you return from your journey, take a deep breath and reflect on the insights you received. Smile inwardly into your heart and thank your Godly self for the work you have done to accept life, yourself and others. Record any insights or awakenings in your copy of the *Reawakening the Soul Vision Quest Workbook*.

Introspection

What masks am I ready to release?

Are my beliefs the absolute truth about myself?

What negative beliefs are holding me back from fulfilling my dreams?

Who am I?

EFT/Tapping

KC: Even though at times I feel confused as to who I am, I deeply and completely accept myself.

KC: Even though I see many beliefs that make up my personality, I am open to explore these masks to think differently.

KC: Even though I have chosen so many identities, I am open to experience my True Self.

EB: Who am I?
SE: Who am I?
UE: So many beliefs swirling around me.
UN: That have become a part of me.
CP: So many masks I wear.
CB: So many roles I play.
UA: These roles reflect who I think I am.
TH: My thoughts create these masks.

EB: My thoughts create my roles.
SE: My core beliefs create all my thoughts.
UE: I wish to explore my core beliefs.
UN: What are some of them?
CP: As I tap, I am able to retrieve my negative beliefs.
CB: I acknowledge the negative ones.
UA: And replace them with positive ones.
TH: And as I tap, I look into the roles I play.

EB: Do they feel healthy?
SE: I tap and see the career I have chosen.
UE: Does this career really suite me?
UN: Does it feed my soul?
CP: Am I passionate about it?
CB: Am I happy?
UA: I now look into the roles I play in my life.
TH: Do these feel healthy?

EB: Am I caught up in these roles?
SE: And forget the things that I really love to do.
UE: And the way I would really like to be.
UN: As I tap, I now look at my emotions.

EFT
Audio Available
to Remove All
Blocks to Reveal
Your Divinity!

CP: Am I emotionally balanced?
CB: Am I a prisoner to my emotions?
UA: Can I remove these masks?
TH: Many of them feel comfortable.

EB: And make me feel safe.
SE: But many of them feel awful.
UE: I want to explore my real self.
UN: I want to feel my authentic self.
CP: How does this look for me?
CB: As I tap, I review my life.
UA: And see how everything was created by my thoughts.
TH: Which created all my experiences.

EB: If my beliefs were negative,
SE: My outer world reflects this.
UE: All these masks.
UN: I am ready to remove all these masks.
CP: I feel freer as I remove each one.
CB: I tap and remove the mask of fear
UA: I tap and remove all negative beliefs.
TH: I tap and remove any blocks holding me back from my dreams.

EB: I am ready to step into my spiritual self.
SE: And reclaim my personal power.
UE: I am a divine being.
UN: I am Spirit.
CP: I am bliss.
CB: I am able to express myself from this spiritual space.
UA: My soul is a perfect reflection of my Creator.
TH: I am now free to create from my true identity as Spirit!

Inner Voice

The all-knowing faculty of the soul enables you to experience direct perception of truth.

Inner Voice

"Your time is limited, so don't waste it living someone else's life. Don't be trapped by dogma - which is living with the results of other people's thinking. Don't let the noise of others' opinions drown out your own inner voice. And most important, have the courage to follow your heart and intuition."

~ Steve Jobs

Affirmation

I listen and trust my inner voice.

Card Message

The message from the wolf is to listen and trust your inner voice. This voice can be heard in many ways, such as a feeling, an insight appearing in a flash, or a deep knowing that propels you to specific action. Your inner voice is the language of intuition. Meditation strengthens your intuition.

Silence is needed for peaceful and clear decision-making. To hear your inner voice, you must dedicate time to be alone. It is impossible to listen to your guidance when you are surrounded by noise and commotion. It is essential for your happiness and serenity to give yourself the gift of silence. Through this stillness, you feel and recognize the Divine guidance right within you. Your life will begin to flow more peacefully and effortlessly. When you develop your intuition, you will receive truth from your soul without the intermediary of your senses.

Social conditioning teaches you to be logical and use your head. When you only use your head, you miss out on the vital information from your body, heart and soul. Pay attention to the messages your body shares during your decision-making. When you connect your heart and mind, along with the information from your body language, you receive clear and accurate guidance. Take note of your self-saboteur. The saboteur is the voice in your head that may try to hold you back from making changes. It is influenced and activated by fear. Through meditation, you begin to distinguish between your inner voice and the saboteur's influence. Therefore, making conscious choices guided by wisdom, which creates a peaceful reality.

Intuition is the discriminative faculty enabling you to make decisions that bring forth peaceful resolutions. You become a master of all knowledge when you perfect the ability of accurate intuition.

As you practice listening and using your inner voice for guidance, you begin to form a bond of trust. You begin to trust life, because you trust yourself. As you purify your mind and body, you open the channels of your energy field and receive the divine current of cosmic communication. You come to understand that this inner knowing is the voice of God.

Card Symbology

The wolf spirit symbolizes your inner teacher. In many Native American traditions, the wolf is considered to be the highest spiritual teacher in the kingdom. Wolf tells you to pay attention to what your intuition is telling you. Wolf helps you to hear your thoughts so you can avoid making inappropriate decisions. Trust in your intuition and you will connect to your divine purpose on the journey of life. Wolf waits, listens, watches and when he is clear, he acts with deliberate intention. The wolf also represents loyalty, guardianship, ritual, and spirit. The moon rules psychic perception. By getting in touch with your still small voice, your psychic abilities enhance. The bubbles represent the essence of Spirit, in which everything is made of.

Journey

Find a quiet place where you can relax undisturbed. Sit comfortably with your spine straight. Take a deep breath in, tensing your body from your feet to your head. Bring awareness to each body part, as you tense each muscle one by one, within the same inhale. As your entire body is tensed with energy, hold your breath until you are ready to exhale and release. As you exhale, make any audible sounds to expel all tension from your body. Repeat this exercise three times or until you feel relaxed. Gently begin allowing your natural breath to move in and out. With each inhale, mentally chant: "My inner voice." With each exhale, chant: "Guides me with wisdom." Repeat this chant several times as you naturally breathe in and out. Remain in this state for as long as needed, feeling all distracting thoughts subside.

Allow the tranquil blue and turquoise hues to fill you with peace and mental relaxation. As the brilliant blue light expands in your body, you begin to experience the vibration of inner security and confidence. You can rely on it to take control and do the right thing. You feel safe and balanced merging within the blue atmosphere and become absorbed in the brilliant rays of blue. You notice your throat relaxing and expanding. You feel the rays opening your lines of communication between your heart and spoken word. You find yourself able to speak your truth

Experience the Transcendental Video & Audio Journey on my Website to Deepen Your Intuition!!

through verbal articulation as it now flows with ease. The color blue is enhancing your self-expression and your ability to communicate your needs and wants are fully open. You take a moment as you view the areas you need to speak your truth. You feel yourself speaking with confidence and authority. Now you are open to ask for what you need and want. Ask yourself, "What do I need?" "What do I want?" And visually see yourself clearly asking and receiving your wishes. You notice how easy this is. You realize the vibration of the blue shades has heightened your intuitive ability and opened the door to your spiritual growth.

Out of the tones of the cosmic hue emerges a stunning blue wolf glowing from the distant full moon. She represents your highest spiritual inner teacher. Her gentle loving eyes connect with yours. Her gaze streamlines directly into your soul. You become charmed by her ethereal energy as radiant energy of wisdom fills your entire being. With her powerful magic, she strengthens your intuition. You feel an all-knowing power activate within the center of your eyebrows, your spiritual eye. You feel the blessing of confidence infused within you, as you completely trust your inner voice. You feel hypnotized by this wondrous wolf. The mysterious illumination from the full moon infuses you with psychic perception. Your mind, body and spirit are completely still. In this stillness, you merge with the wolf as you absorb glowing healing light. Magical spirit bubbles float before you, reminding you that you are orbs of light. You deeply relax and enjoy the potent wolf medicine as it fills your entire energy field.

Now that you are completely free from thoughts, wolf teaches you how to breathe deep within your heart and to pay attention to your body as you ask for guidance in decision-making. Go within and ask any questions you need clarity with, one at a time. Now that you are anchored in the divine, from this level of consciousness is where you can solve your problems. Remember to breathe into your heart, and pay attention to any messages received from your body. Allow the answer or course of direction needed to arrive naturally from your higher self. Remain calm, silent and still.

You feel complete and you thank wolf for her magic. You now have the tools to tap into your inner voice at anytime. You will receive answers and solutions as you are guided by your intuition. Take the healing medicine of wolf with you and be guided by the wisdom of your inner voice!

When you return from your journey, take a deep breath and reflect on the insights you received. Smile inwardly into your heart and thank your Godly self for the work you have done to accept life, yourself and others. Record any insights or awakenings in your copy of the *Reawakening the Soul Vision Quest Workbook*.

Introspection

Am I allowing myself the silent time I need to hear my inner voice?

Am I listening and taking action when I receive messages from my inner voice?

Do I trust my intuition?

What steps can I take to be more in tune with my inner voice?

EFT/Tapping

KC: Even though at times I don't trust my inner voice, I deeply and completely accept myself.
KC: Even though I don't allow myself enough silence to get in touch with my intuition, I deeply and completely accept myself.
KC: Even though I'm scared to listen to my inner voice, because I know changes will need to occur, I accept my fear.

EB: I have so many voices playing in my mind,
SE: I get confused.
UE: Am I listening to the voice of truth?
UN: Or am I listening to my mind?
CP: Sometimes, I'm afraid to listen to any of it.
CB: Because I don't trust it.
UA: I don't trust myself.
TH: At times, my inner voice tells me things,

EFT Audio Available to Open Your Inner Voice of Intuition!

EB: That seems too scary to do.
SE: Even though deep down inside,
UE: It would bring me great happiness and joy
UN: I fear the changes I need to make.

CP: I desire to explore ways to get trust my inner voice,
CB: Because this is the voice of truth.
UA: The wisdom leading me to do what I came here to do.
TH: And to help me make wise decisions.

EB: It is safe for me to open up
SE: And listen to my intuition.
UE: Even though this feels new to me,
UN: I am willing to examine it.
CP: I am willing to spend more time meditating.
CB: Because I know through silence,
UA: Truth is born.
TH: And I know this truth will lead me to peace.

EB: I enjoy being still.
SE: I love the calming effects from silence.
UE: This is a great gift I will give myself.
UN: This is exciting.
CP: The more I meditate,
CB: The more guidance I will receive.
UA: I trust the information coming from my higher self.
TH: This will lead me to my divine purpose.

EB: When my inner voice is open,
SE: I will be able to speak freely.
UE: And ask for what I want and need.
UN: I release any blocks
CP: Around speaking my truth.
CB: I will continue to listen to my inner voice.
UA: And have the courage to express myself.
TH: Because I know exactly what I need to do.

EB: And I know what I am passionate about.
SE: I see my gifts.
UE: And I have a lot to give.
UN: I'm ready to step into my higher self.
CP: Through the wisdom of my soul.
CB: This feels powerful.
UA: I trust myself.
TH: I trust Spirit.

Karma

The sum total of all actions you perform, both good and bad, present and past, create consequences.

Karma

"By the law of cause and effect, action and reaction, we make of ourselves what we presently are and what we will be."

~ Paramahansa Yogananda

Affirmation

My thoughts and actions are clear and conscious.

Card Message

You are participating in a game here on planet earth. This cosmic game is based on the law of cause and effect. This principle is known as karma. Karma governs the activity and outcome of every action you perform. These actions include both perceived good and bad behavior along with actions in the present and past. You are constantly creating your reality with your thoughts and words. With every action you commit, an equal action comes your way.

Your thoughts and actions have led to your present state. Introspection can help detect what tendencies have had a strong influence on your current life situations. The actions you have performed in the past remain present in your brain. One way to identify where your energy has been put into motion is to observe your current environments, moods, inclinations and habits. As Buddha said, "If you want to know the past, look at your present. If you want to know the future, look at your present."*

The law of karma is absolute, pure and unbiased; it is the unavoidable force governing everything in the universe. When you understand the perfection of this cosmic law, your life will inevitably change. You can activate this change by holding yourself accountable and taking full responsibility for all things happening in your life, both internally and externally. Understand that everything has been created by your thoughts and actions during some passage of time. Remember that every move on this game board of life is governed by a choice. The energy created by your decisions gives you the perfect result of your desired choice. The myriads of choices you make from moment to moment create the existence of the world around you. Open yourself to new opportunities that are aligned with the vibration of your awareness. Your thoughts begin to change as you acquire wisdom. When you change your thoughts, the created world around you transforms. Becoming aware and conscious gives you a beautiful opportunity to enjoy every experience and be fully present in the moment. You will begin to experience the world through the eyes of your soul. You can witness all experiences without any emotional attachments.

(Phillip Kapleau, The Three Pillars of Zen (New York: Doubleday, a division of Bantam, Doubleday, Dell Publishing Group, Inc., 1980), p. 294.

It's time to create your world anew with fresh thoughts and passion-filled enthusiasm. By awakening your soul to remember your Divine Essence, you free yourself from karma. When you understand and accept the rules of this cosmic game, you can play wisely and win the game of life to transcend suffering!

Card Symbology

The painting depicts a game representing the law of cause and effect. The earth is the mysterious checkerboard where human lives play out as chess pieces. The woman is painted as a chess piece and she stands on the checkerboard of life. She has become aware that she is playing this "game called life". She understands that every move she makes originates from a choice. She is now consciously mindful of all her thoughts and actions. She knows these thoughts create the world around her. A mystical bubble containing her spiritual energy field surrounds her. Behind her stands a beautiful peacock symbolizing wisdom, vision and heightened watchfulness. The peacock epitomizes both beauty and integrity. The "eye" of each feather represents the all-seeing eye of God and the wisdom contained in it. The peacock blesses the woman with guidance and protection in her spiritual awakening. There are two wolves symmetrically balanced on both sides of the female chess piece. The wolf on the left is looking off into the distance, symbolizing making choices guided by the ego mind. The wolf on the right stares head on, displaying the perfect wisdom received from the soul through communion with the Divine.

Journey

Experience the Transcendental Video & Audio Journey on my Website to Shift Your Karma!

Find a quiet place where you can relax undisturbed. Sit comfortably with your spine straight. Take a deep breath in, tensing your body from your feet to your head. Bring awareness to each body part, as you tense each muscle one by one, within the same inhale. As your entire body is tensed with energy, hold your breath until you are ready to exhale and release. As you exhale, make any audible sounds to expel all tension from your body. Repeat this exercise three times or until you feel relaxed. Gently begin allowing your natural breath to move in and out. With each inhale, mentally chant: "I breathe in wisdom" With each exhale, chant: "I breathe out truth." Repeat this chant several times as you naturally breathe in and out. Remain in this state for as long as needed, feeling all distracting thoughts subside.

Imagine yourself standing in a beautiful garden where the scent of fresh flowers permeates every cell of your being. It feels still, quiet and peaceful in this garden of truth. The only sounds you hear are the magical sounds of nature. You hear the birds singing and insects chirping. As the wind softly blows, you hear the slight rustling of leaves as they dance in the air. You take a deep breath from the silence of your soul and then exhale in this tranquil space. You feel a peaceful sensation within your mind, body and soul. You are now in perfect alignment with your higher self. Your mind is still and empty. The door to your soul is wide open and ready to receive knowledge handed down through the ages. You are able to look upon your life as though you are engaged in an interesting game of chess. You are a player and a participant in this game of life. You are interacting and playing a major part in this game. You are fully aware that every thought and every action creates a strategic move. The energy created by your volition brings forth the perfect result of your desired choice. The external world reflects energy created by your deeds and assembles itself accordingly. The various choices you make from moment to moment create the existence of the world around you.

You are now ready to play this game in a conscious manner. Breathe deeply and take a good hard look at where you have placed yourself in this life. What situations have you created? What is manifesting in your life right now? Are you happy where you have placed yourself? Feel the answers within your heart without any judgment or shame. Just witness yourself in the space of this moment. With deep awareness, reflect upon everything you have created in this life. Know that you have created everything that has happened to you in the past, along with everything currently happening right at this moment. Take full responsibility for each and every experience you have generated. You are now ready to consciously create your future.

Appearing before you is a ravishing peacock. Her beauty and integrity exemplify what can be achieved by living your life on a high spiritual path. Feel the presence of wisdom and vision emanating from this peacock. She shows you how to be watchful of every thought you think and every action you take. Notice the intricate eyes on her feathers. You experience the all-seeing eye of God infusing you with knowledge. You are excited to make some dramatic changes in your life. The peacock is here to protect you and guide you towards your spiritual awakening.

You can feel this spiritual awakening taking place within you. Receive all the gifts she has to offer and thank her. Peacock leaves her magic with you as she fades into the ether.

A captivating wolf now appears before you. He gazes off into the distance. As he looks away, his main focus is in the external physical world. He speaks to you in a language that your soul understands. He tells you to look carefully at every choice you make. Pay attention to your thoughts created by fear and ignorance. Look within to see how you are influenced by these negative thoughts and stories being played in your mind. He encourages you to review these thoughts and behold the ones based upon old limiting beliefs and ideas. He explains that these are unconscious thoughts created by the ego mind. He reminds you that these thoughts are creating your reality. Take a moment to gather up any negative beliefs about yourself. Breathe deeply and as you exhale, expel all the energy from these limiting thoughts into the wolf. Do this several times as you transfer all old beliefs into the wolf. You now feel released and free. Thank the wolf for taking your negative thoughts. He is happy to have helped you as he fades away.

A faint howling sound pierces the silence around you. The howling progresses, getting louder and more distinct. Another wolf magically appears before you. She stares directly into your eyes. As she penetrates you with her piercing gaze of truth, your entire being is filled with light. She represents the window of your soul containing the absolute truth of inner wisdom. You know she has some magic to share with you. She encourages you to seek and listen to the guidance from your soul. She elaborates on the importance of silencing your mind through meditation to gain true wisdom. Meditation will activate the remembrance of your essence of love. Through acting upon this wisdom, the choices you make will be harmoniously aligned with the will of Spirit. When you use this insight, your outer circumstances will begin to reflect this energy. By being fully aligned with Source, you accept everything as a blessed opportunity to grow. You embrace all of what life has to offer. You view the experiences of life through the eyes of a witness, able to see everything in an emotionally neutral state. This is the art of allowing. You experience and embrace the perfection of the universal law that is being played out. In this conscious state, your thoughts are imbued with positive energy that calls forth complimentary results. This awareness feels natural, healthy and balanced.

As you feel the sensation of peace encompassing your energetic field, you feel alive and free. The wolf's magic remains with you as she dissolves into empty space. Inwardly, take time to thank her for her gifts of truth.

Now that you understand the cosmic law of cause and effect, it is time to deeply explore your belief system. Notice all thoughts that are creating your current experiences. If your experience doesn't feel healthy and aligned with your higher self, you can change your thoughts. You have the power to change your circumstances. Your higher self desires to participate in this game with peace and joy. You have the choice to end suffering once and for all. It's all a matter of a choice—your choice to become conscious and aware. See yourself as a grand champion chess player creating and enjoying a balanced game. You recognize at times the game can feel challenging and at other times you encounter electrifying victories and staggering defeats. Remember that all these effects originate with you. The game is always being played out exactly as needed for your spiritual growth. You feel the excitement of knowing that you are constantly growing closer to the truth of your existence—a divine spiritual being. You are now gifted with wisdom as you see with clear vision. You are able to engage in this game with a serene mind, knowing your existence is nothing more than an entertaining and educational game of concentrated skill.

When you return from your journey, take a deep breath and reflect on the insights you received. Smile inwardly into your heart and thank your Godly self for the work you have done to accept life, yourself and others. Record any insights or awakenings in your copy of the *Reawakening the Soul Vision Quest Workbook*.

Introspection

What are my thoughts creating?

Are my thoughts and actions positive?

How would it feel to be completely accountable for all my actions?

EFT/Tapping

KC: Even though I may not fully understand karma, I am open to explore a new way of thinking.

KC: Even though a lot of my thoughts are still negative, I completely and deeply accept myself.

KC: Even though it seems challenging to constantly have positive thoughts and actions, I am open to exploring how to become a better person.

Listen to EFT Audio on my Website to Clear Karmic Patterns!

EB: Where are my thoughts?
SE: I have so many thoughts.
UE: Thousands that run through my mind.
UN: Continuously.
CP: Am I aware of these thoughts?
CB: Many I'm not aware of.
UA: Some of these are conscious.
TH: And some of these thoughts are unconscious.

EB: I can tell where my thoughts are leading me.
SE: From what is being created in my life.
UE: So, what is currently created in my life at this moment?
UN: Do I feel peace and joy?
CP: Balanced and content?
CB: Or do I feel stressed and unbalanced?
UA: Am I suffering?
TH: Am I angry?

EB: What kind of emotions am I experiencing right now?
SE: Because I know these emotions lead me back to my thoughts.
UE: My thoughts create my reality.
UN: My thoughts create every experience.
CP: And my thoughts create every situation.
CB: So it's easy to pinpoint where my thoughts are.
UA: By looking at my life's circumstances.
TH: I am open to becoming aware of my thoughts.

EB: I am open to becoming conscious of the actions that I choose.
SE: And the things that I say and do.
UE: I want to be conscious as to how I give in this world.

UN: Because everything puts the energy into motion.
CP: Everything I think, say and do.
CB: This is the law of cause and effect.
UA: And I want to understand this law.
TH: I'm excited to see it being played out in my life.

EB: By just taking the next steps.
SE: And becoming aware of my thoughts and actions.
UE: As I do this.
UN: I will see how everything around me changes.
CP: I will see it reflected.
CB: Even though it may not be instant.
UA: I know it is working.
TH: And I won't wait for it.

EB: Or look for it.
SE: I will learn to trust.
UE: And just allow the perfection of my life to unfold.
UN: If something does happen that doesn't feel good.
CP: I will act, instead of react.
CB: I will accept and embrace.
UA: Knowing that I created it at some point in my life.
TH: I know every situation arrives to help me grow spiritually.

EB: So I love and accept myself.
SE: As I consciously change my thoughts and actions.
UE: This feels good.
UN: I can do this.
CP: Even if I don't see the benefits instantly.
CB: It still feels good.
UA: If I can be happier here on earth.
TH: And feel good.

EB: Then why wouldn't I do this?
SE: I choose to be positive.
UE: I choose to be peaceful.
UN: I choose to be happy.
CP: Because this is my true nature.
CB: My thoughts and actions create my reality.
UA: I now choose positive thoughts.
TH: I now choose full responsibility of my life.

Listening

To listen, both inwardly and outwardly, is an art that requires skill and practice.

Listening

"The ear of the leader must ring with the voices of the people."

~ Woodrow Wilson

Affirmation

I now consciously open my heart and mind to listen both inwardly and outwardly.

Card Message

This card contains two different meanings of the word listening: active listening and inner listening. When interacting with this card, it is important to understand and practice both aspects of listening.

In active listening, one has the intent to "listen for meaning." When interacting with others we often listen inattentively to the other person. We may be distracted, thinking about something else or thinking about what we are going to say next. Active listening is a manner of listening and responding to someone as they speak, a practice whereby one focuses attention on the speaker.

Inner listening is learning how to silence the mind and listen to the guidance of your soul. This is the word of God. Listen and pay close attention to any useless chatter that may be taking place in your mind. Replace this noise with silence. Meditation, spending time alone in silence and remaining calm with an even mind will bring forth your ability to hear your inner voice. This truth brought forth will direct you towards making choices guided by wisdom rather than ego or emotions.

The voice of truth does not necessarily always come in the form of words, sometimes it is perceived as a feeling or a deep knowing of truth or an a-ha moment. Listening to your inner voice requires dedicated daily practice. The more you practice, the more you will align yourself to the divine within you. This is the place that encompasses love and truth. The desire for this voice of peace, found within the messages of silence, will forever continue to bloom and grow. By practicing this inner listening, you will see your life transforming right before your eyes.

To practice both active and inner listening will bring you to a balanced state of being.

Card Symbology

Wolf medicine is extremely powerful. The wolf teaches you to know who you are and to develop strength, confidence and surety, so that you do not have to prove yourself to anyone. The wolf has excellent hearing sensitivity. The wolf in the painting has one ear facing forward symbolizing the importance of listening within. The other ear is facing outward listening to the active physical world that surrounds us.

It is important to bring into balance the amount of energy given to both types of listening. Wolf helps you to understand that true freedom requires discipline and trust. Wolf is giving you a message: when you learn to stand in your power and speak your truth, the world listens.

The medicine of this wolf challenges you to strengthen your ability to quiet your mind and to master the art of listening. In the stillness of silence, you hear the voice of Spirit guiding you through wisdom and this increases your intuition. The wolf can help you to hear the inner guidance and guard you from inappropriate actions. Learn to trust the messages that you receive when listening within during times of silence. If you look into the eyes of the wolf, you will receive a message, but you must listen!

The floating bubbles remind you that this entire world, including you, consists of universal cosmic energy. The moon behind the wolf symbolizes the reflection of your soul. At times you may choose to reflect the bright light of Spirit from the full moon and shine forth manifesting in the physical world. At other times, you choose to remain inward meditating and contemplating, which reflects the energy of the new moon. It's all about bringing these two reflections into a nice balance. The moon has no light of its own, the light we see is reflected from the sun. Your sun is eternal Spirit and the more you open up and recognize it, the more light you receive. The more receptive you are, the more you overflow with divine light, and shine as an inspiration to others.

Journey

Find a quiet place where you can relax undisturbed. Sit comfortably with your spine straight. Take a deep breath in, tensing your body from your feet to your head. Bring awareness to each body part, as you tense each muscle one by one, within the same inhale. As your entire body is tensed with energy, hold your breath until you are ready to exhale and release. As you exhale, make any audible sounds to expel all tension from your body. Repeat this exercise three times or until you feel relaxed. Gently begin allowing your natural breath to move in and out. With each inhale, silently chant: "I am present." With each exhale, chant: "I listen with my heart." Repeat this chant several times as you naturally breathe in and out. Remain in this state for as long as necessary, feeling all distracting thoughts subside.

Experience the Transcendental Video & Audio Journey on my Website to Master the Art of Listening!

Look into the eyes of the wolf. Begin to feel the warm colors enter your space and flow into your soul. Breathe in and feel the joy burning from the warmth of the golden glow. Keep following the breath bringing in peace and calmness until your mind settles into a calm natural rhythm. Keep focusing on the breath. The breath brings yourself into present moment awareness where your soul receives messages. Any thoughts that arrive, allow them to be released into the cosmic vortex.

Now that all mental worries are gone, you welcome the empty, clear space that silence offers. In this sacred vacant space, you focus on the wolf and allow him to activate you with inner listening skills. As you listen in this silence, you begin to hear the voice of Spirit. Focus on receiving this activation.

Now that you are activated with the gift of inner listening, you enter the chambers of full active listening. The wolf spirit arrives to ignite you with the art of listening to others.

Repeat the following,:

"I am openly willing to be a good listener. My mind is calm and receptive to fully hear what someone is saying. I am in the present moment. I listen intently and consciously.

I pay attention to all the details and to their body language. I listen from my heart. I receive the information completely as delivered. I have no need to tell my own story or share my own opinions unless they ask.

I do not judge another while they speak. I listen without applying my own emotions or attachments with the words I hear. I mirror back what I hear instead of responding to what I think I know of the situation.

As I listen, I give another a precious gift, the sublime gift of being heard and feeling important. I will consciously practice this skill every day.

I allow this wolf to electrify me with magic to become a great listener."

Now that you have been sparked by the wonders of being a great listener, others notice how they feel heard and validated by your presence. There are no more distortions between what others say and what you hear, because you have been charged with clear listening skills. You are intuitive and compassionate and fully receptive to what the outside world has to offer.

You have been freed from all conditions and emotions as you listen to another speak. You are free from identifying and projecting your emotions and ideas onto another person's message. You are done sharing your beliefs and perceptions, unless asked. Pay attention every day to actively and consciously listen and watch yourself bloom in your ability to give someone the gift of active listening.

Find your heart being rewarded with grace as are now naturally able to listen inwardly to your soul and listen actively to others. The Wolf has endowed you one of the greatest gifts. Go shine with the light of the wolf in your soul and experience the world in beauty all around you.

When you return from your journey, take a deep breath and reflect on the insights you received. Smile inwardly into your heart and thank your Godly self for the work you have done to accept life, yourself and others. Record any insights or awakenings in your copy of the *Reawakening the Soul Vision Quest Workbook*.

Introspection

Am I a good listener?

Can I become a better listener?

Do I trust the messages that I receive when I listen in silence?

EFT/Tapping

KC: Even though I don't feel like a good listener, I deeply accept the way I feel.

KC: Even though my listening skills are not the best, I accept the way I feel.

KC: Even though my mind is chattering when others speak, I completely accept the way I feel.

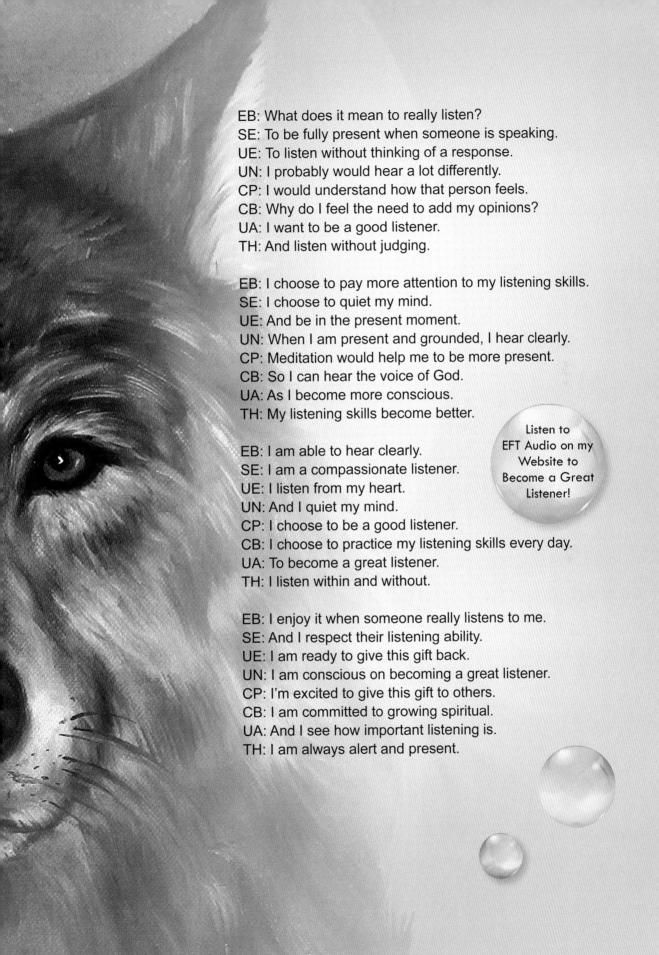

EB: What does it mean to really listen?
SE: To be fully present when someone is speaking.
UE: To listen without thinking of a response.
UN: I probably would hear a lot differently.
CP: I would understand how that person feels.
CB: Why do I feel the need to add my opinions?
UA: I want to be a good listener.
TH: And listen without judging.

EB: I choose to pay more attention to my listening skills.
SE: I choose to quiet my mind.
UE: And be in the present moment.
UN: When I am present and grounded, I hear clearly.
CP: Meditation would help me to be more present.
CB: So I can hear the voice of God.
UA: As I become more conscious.
TH: My listening skills become better.

Listen to
EFT Audio on my
Website to
Become a Great
Listener!

EB: I am able to hear clearly.
SE: I am a compassionate listener.
UE: I listen from my heart.
UN: And I quiet my mind.
CP: I choose to be a good listener.
CB: I choose to practice my listening skills every day.
UA: To become a great listener.
TH: I listen within and without.

EB: I enjoy it when someone really listens to me.
SE: And I respect their listening ability.
UE: I am ready to give this gift back.
UN: I am conscious on becoming a great listener.
CP: I'm excited to give this gift to others.
CB: I am committed to growing spiritual.
UA: And I see how important listening is.
TH: I am always alert and present.

Love

Open your heart to be filled with the grace of God's unconditional love.

Love

"Where there is love there is life."

~ Mahatma Gandhi

Affirmation

I am made up of Spirit and Spirit is 100% love.

Card Message

You are broadening your understanding of love, for you realize that you are made up of love. You are ready to receive the unconditional love vibrating as the spirit of your essence.

Divine Love is who you are and who you have always been. Allow the pure, gentle, unconditional love of God to flow into your life. Remember that you must stay open in order to receive this perfect love. When you are able to absorb this unconditional love energy, you will also be able to adore others unconditionally. It is through loving God and receiving God's love that we begin to feel compassion and understanding for everyone, everywhere. With this form of love, genuine acceptance is naturally born.

Carefully pay attention to the kind of love you are seeking. If it is love and approval from the world, you will be disappointed. Take care to avoid getting caught in the illusion of looking for love outside of yourself. It's time to move into a higher dimension of love, one that attracts all other love! The real feeling you are yearning and searching for is the essence of what you are made of—love.

Self-love is the basis for all other love. Learn to love, accept and embrace your own soul and then you can fully and unconditionally love others. Know that your soul is made in the perfect image of God. Strive to live your life feeling this perfection. You know your own personal weaknesses, but understand that these were created by the mind. Hold firm to the conviction of the true perfection of your soul, which is born from pure love. You are this expression of love and the desire of your soul wishes to express itself as love through you.

Spend time alone engaging in the activities that you absolutely love and that make you feel alive. Learn how to enjoy silent time with yourself. During this time, feel divine love melting into your essence. Take extra time every day to feel your own energy and your own space outside of worldly cares.

Hug yourself and tell yourself how much you love yourself. Feel that these words and actions are from God, the God that resides within you. Here is where you will feel the fullness of the love that you are. In this love, you will no longer have the need to seek love and approval from any human being because the love from God is unconditional. When you feel the presence of the pure and holy, unconditional love that is present within your soul, you will truly know how precious it is. You will feel that the entire universe is connected to the same cosmic source.

You are being encouraged to look deep within your heart and see the seeds that have been planted from your past memories and experiences. Some seeds may contain the energy of love, joy, bliss, beauty and magic. Others may consist of pain, hurt, fear, abuse, and wounds of sorrow. Take the time and be honest about looking into your own heart to feel the latent memories within it. If there are any negative memories, ask them to leave. In order to receive the fullest capacity of love, forgiveness is essential.

Love God with all your heart, mind, soul and strength. Fill your heart with the complete unconditional love of God. Remember that God is behind your heart and soul. Even at times when He seems hidden and distant remember, where there is love, God cannot hide. When you remain in the presence of love, you will find true and everlasting freedom from all worldly cares and sufferings. Freedom holds the experience of everlasting love and blissful union with the Cosmic Beloved and this is the goal of life.

Develop a relationship with God and talk to Him in the language of your heart. Your Beloved exists in everything and is only seeking one thing—your love! When you behave as a tender loving person, you are fully expressing the divine love that you are.

When you allow yourself to receive pure divine love and hold it within your heart and soul, you will also be able to love others with perfect unconditional love. This is the way to true love. When you remember this truth and feel it permeating your being bringing the experience of oneness, you'll hold the key that completely ends your suffering.

Card Symbology

The pure and tender heart emerges from the lotus flower ready to receive and share love. The sacred realm of the heart is green in color and intercedes between the worlds of spirit and matter. The heart is the central chakra within the seven main energy centers (chakras) of the body; it represents the heart of our journey. This is the chamber from which we give and receive love; it is the center of our being.

The lotus flower represents purity and beauty that reflects our core essence. The red color represents the physical heart, its original nature as compassion, passion and love. The pink represents the Buddha and is the supreme lotus.

The lotus grows out of the murky darkness at the bottom of the pond and transforms into a beautiful flower, which is symbolic of ones desires to move through the dark past and bloom into the beauty found in present self-awareness. The plant's stalk is easy to bend in two, but is very hard to break because of its strong sinuous fibers. This illustrates the fact that no matter how hard and painful past situations may have been, nothing can separate your heart from Divine love and the truth that lives and breathes behind it.

This lotus reminds you to open up to love, beauty and light and in turn, be the miracle of love, beauty and light. When you open your heart to love, you, as the lotus will rise above the mud and become a beautiful fragrant flower with the ability to love all.

Angelic wings embrace and emerge from the heart within the lotus to guide you to trust the process of opening your heart as you learn to surrender to love. The downward flying dove is a traditional symbol of peace. As you engage in the process of opening and healing your heart, gifts of divine blessings and inner peace will be given to you. When the heart opens to receive the grace of God's love, your heart will be filled to its fullest capacity and overflow into your entire being. The bright star sparkles from the center of the heart like the all-seeing eye that reveals the gift being prepared for you through your awakening.

Journey

Find a quiet place where you can relax undisturbed. Sit comfortably with your spine straight. Take a deep breath in, tensing your body from your feet to your head. Bring awareness to each body part, as you tense each muscle one by one, within the same inhale. As your entire body is tensed with energy, hold your breath until you are ready to exhale and release. As you exhale, make any audible sounds to expel all tension from your body.

Experience the Transcendental Video & Audio Journey on my Website to Behold Unconditional LOVE!!

Repeat this exercise three times or until you feel relaxed. Gently begin allowing your natural breath to move in and out. With each inhale, silently chant, "I breathe in love ." With each exhale, chant, "I breathe out love." Repeat this chant several times as you naturally breathe in and out. Remain in this state for as long as necessary, feeling all distracting thoughts subside.

You are about to embark on a journey into your heart center. During this travel, you will remove any negative emotions residing here and release them in order for new positive ones to be created. You know that you are the soul and you have great courage to release any pain in your heart because you know they are holding you back from loving and being loved.

Take your hand and rub your heart in a circular motion gently massaging your heart. As your hand is moving over your heart, ask it what it is feeling. Ask if there are any emotions that need to come forth and be transformed. As you caress your heart, feel any emotions it may be experiencing such as pain, fear or sorrow. Ask it to release the emotion tied to it into the palm of your hand.

Now, slowly pull your hand out from your heart and feel this energy in your palm. It is important to allow the energy to leave your heart and move into the palm of your hand. This energy contains the message that your heart wishes to share. Look into the palm of your hand and ask this energy to communicate to you. You may wish to ask questions such as; is there something you wish to share with me? Can you show me what pain is here? You may receive a descriptive message; a symbol or you may experience the emotion behind the pain.

Allow it to talk to you, cry to you and express itself in any way that it needs to. This emotion needs to be transformed and released in order for your heart to open up to receive love. Be a witness and listen to the messages that the energy wishes to share. When the message is complete, sincerely thank it for sharing and tell it that you are now going to set it free. It no longer belongs in your heart. It now belongs to the universe and God knows exactly what to do with it.

After the energy has shared its message, take your hand and release it with a sweeping motion up into the heavens and declare, "I now release you into the universe to set you free!" Feel this energy being released from your palm.

If you feel that there is more remaining in your heart, continue to do this exercise as many times as needed, until you feel all the energy fully release from your heart. You will know when you are finished, because your heart will feel calm, expansive and open.

Your heart now feels light, clear, empty and pure. As you rub your heart, sincerely thank it for releasing the pain and sorrow and feel the glory, love and beauty take its place. Remember that no one can break your heart. You are fully responsible for your own heart and the choices you make in sharing and receiving love with others. When you feel love from another human being, it is God loving you through that individual. When you love another, it is God's love flowing through your physical form loving another. This love may change form, but remember that it will always flow from the One Almighty Source.

After releasing these emotions, you feel an empty open space in your heart. Now is the time to fill this space with unconditional love from your Creator. Open up and allow yourself to receive this love. Feel the essence of God filling your heart with unconditional love. Allow it to pour into your heart. Know that this love is the essence of your soul. When you fill yourself with this holy love, you hold the blessing of loving others with unconditional love.

Continue to feel the powerful love emanating from God, this love that is waiting for you to receive it. Hear the voice of God through your own consciousness telling you over and over again, "I love you, I love you."

Fill yourself with this divine message. Feel how easy it is to love others when you are full of the vibration of unconditional Divine peace. In God's heart, you are perfect and are not judged by your past actions. Remember that you are an expression of Divine Love and thus, you are ready as you are now lifted to a higher awareness.

You are now completely filled with the memory of your godly self. You are reborn into divine love as you feel your angelic wings emerge from your heart. You feel the wisdom contained from the lotus flower as it guides you to trust the process of deepening and opening your heart and surrender to love. You experience the downward flying dove penetrating your being as you feel the sensation of a great inner peace overtaking your heart.

As you engage in the process of opening and healing your heart, gifts of divine blessings and inner peace will appear. As your heart opens to receive the grace of God's love, you are filled to the fullest capacity as it overflows into your entire being. A bright star sparkles from the center of your heart as the all-seeing spiritual eye reveals a gift for your awakening. You now are full of love, light and wisdom as you spread your wings and love unconditionally.

When you return from your journey, take a deep breath and reflect on the insights you received. Smile inwardly into your heart and thank your Godly self for the work you have done to accept life, yourself and others. Record any insights or awakenings in your copy of the *Reawakening the Soul Vision Quest Workbook.*

Introspection

Am I willing to repair any wounded aches in my heart?

Do I love myself?

Do I feel God's love for me?

Can I open my heart to love and to be loved?

EFT/Tapping

KC: Even though my heart has been hurt, I deeply accept the way I feel.
KC: Even though it's scary to fully open up to love, I deeply and completely love myself.
KC: Even though at times I don't feel loved, I am open to explore receiving unconditional love.

EB: What is love?
SE: It feels so confusing.
UE: There's so many meanings.
UN: What does it mean to me?
CP: Do I allow myself to feel love?
CB: Do I allow myself to be loved?
UA: It's scary to share love with another.
TH: Because I'm afraid I might get hurt.

EB: Where would the hurt come from?
SE: Maybe having expectations?
UE: Expectations that when I love someone, I want them to love me back.
UN: And if they don't, I will get hurt.
CP: Why would I have the need to receive love from another?
CB: I would have to be feeling lack of love within myself.
UA: Do I love myself?
TH: Do I allow myself to be loved by my Creator?

EB: How would I feel differently, If I always felt loved?
SE: Knowing that I am loved.
UE: Exactly the way I am.
UN: Even with all the mistakes I made.
CP: To always feel loved.
CB: And supported.
UA: This feel good.
TH: How can I always feel this love?

EFT
Audio Available
to OPEN
Your HEART
to LOVE!

EB: I would have to take more time to be alone.
SE: To stop my busy mind.
UE: So I can feel my Creator loving me.
UN: This feels like such a tender time.
CP: Just me and my beloved.
CB: Whispering divine messages.
UA: From the cave of my mind.
TH: I could make a conscious effort.

EB: To reprogram my mind.
SE: To send sweet messages of love to myself.
UE: Instead of playing the same old stories.
UN: I am made up of love.
CP: My soul is love.
CB: And I know that all this love is made up of Spirit.
UA: And all the love from others comes from this same Source.
TH: The vibration of love exists in all of creation.

Magic

When you are consciously connected to God, you receive proof through tangible gifts of Spirit.

Magic

"Magic is believing in yourself, if you can do that, you can make anything happen."

~ Johann Wolfgang Von Goethe

Affirmation

I am the magician of my life.

Card Message

Do you realize that you are a wizard? . . . Honestly!

You are a skilled magician and it is time for you to awaken. Your thoughts are the wand that creates your reality. When you consciously create from a calm state of mind, magic is born!

Deep meditation and spending time alone brings forth a serene mental and physical state of mind. (See Meditation)

The secret is to remember your true essence as Spirit! Open your eyes and welcome all the magic appearing in your life. You are surrounded and supported by many spirit guides. Open up to receive all your blessings. These spirit guides are anxiously waiting to serve you and give you what you want. They are more eager to give you what you want, than you are to get it. So, remember to ask them for support and guidance and thank them when you receive it.

As you welcome the gifts, your job is to take immediate action with all your will towards accomplishing your dreams. Determine to be great like a wizard by bringing forth your gifts and passions and sharing them with the world.

When you become and share the bright light that you are, your essence shines into the world making it better. Where there is light, darkness cannot exist. Acknowledge your inner light and feel it ever flowing into your being. This living energy is the substance of Spirit, living and breathing within you.

Invoke your magic . . . and remember — you are the magician!

Card Symbology

This painting reveals the tremendous universal power of Spirit that magnetizes the earth. We are a part of this spirit and our mission is to learn how to tap into this dynamic power.

The forces that flow forth from all deities, wizards, angels, shamans, gurus and enlightened beings are permeating all around us. It is available to us for the asking, it is our job to receive these transmissions. We are all here on earth to make a difference, to grow and to become greater. Our earth heals itself when we remember that we are whole. For in this wholeness our expression lights the world with love, therefore raising the universal vibration. The owl represents the wisdom of our soul and shows us how to contain and transform any darkness from our subconscious minds into light.

Journey

Find a quiet place where you can relax undisturbed. Sit comfortably with your spine straight. Take a deep breath in, tensing your body from your feet to your head. Bring awareness to each body part, as you tense each muscle one by one, within the same inhale. As your entire body is tensed with energy, hold your breath until you are ready to exhale and release. As you exhale, make any audible sounds to expel all tension from your body. Repeat this exercise three times or until you feel relaxed. Gently begin allowing your natural breath to move in and out. With each inhale, silently chant, "I breathe in magic." With each exhale, chant, "I breathe out magic." Repeat this chant several times as you naturally breathe in and out. Remain in this state for as long as necessary, feeling all distracting thoughts subside.

You are entering into the portal of magic. As you travel into this mystical space you feel yourself disconnecting from all bodily limitations. You are comfortably voyaging into the dimension of your soul. As you journey even deeper, you feel how quiet and safe it feels.

Appearing slowly out of space, an enchanted wizard arrives to activate you with magic. He begins to speak as you feel his vibration at a deep subconscious level. "I have come to remind you that you are a wizard. Be silent and you will feel this truth. You have exceptional wisdom and magic buried within the spirit of your soul. Your thoughts and actions control the wand of creation. Every thought sends its waves traveling throughout the universe, bringing back the exact vibration in accordance to its nature. Universal law creates and manifests in perfect divine order. You are a perfect part of this order. Your diamond soul is an image of this Divine perfection of love. Receive my mystical activation and absorb this vibrating cosmic intelligence. Allow it to raise your state of consciousness and receive its magic!"

Experience the Transcendental Video & Audio Journey on my Website to Experience More MAGIC!

As you walk this journey here on earth, remember that you are surrounded and supported by many spirit guides. Open your heart to receive all their blessings. These spirit guides are anxiously waiting to serve you and give you what you want. Take a moment and ask your Spirit Guides for support and guidance.

Now use your calm focused mind power and envision something you really want to manifest in your life. Visualize it clearly and feel every explicit detail of your desired dream. Bring your awareness to your heart and feel that it is now being created for you. Spirit is more willing to give to you, than you are to receive it. Feel this truth and trust with unflinching faith. Feel the excitement and joy expanding in your soul. Take a long deep breath and welcome all of your gifts. Feel the magic flowing through your breath and feel the life force pulsating behind every particle of your being. Recognize the magician that you are.

Magic is born as you freely create your reality from a place of passion, joy and enthusiasm. You fully realize that you are the creator of your life. You utilize your God given power and potential as you move through life with a solid purpose and passion. You are a unique spark of light, filled with magical creativity. Repeat to yourself over and over again, "I believe in me . . . I am a Magician!" Feel every moment of creation as a mystical experience.

You are magic born of Spirit as you step into your wizard mastery and bring forth your talents to share with humanity. You create your life powered by the wisdom of the your soul from a state of superconsciousness. The bridge between your mind and heart is now harmoniously balanced as it transmits radiant rays of truth. You are now born into a higher awareness as you pay attention to every thought and action. You grow, expand and flourish in magic, for you are Spirit. The perfection of life welcomes you with open arms. Go create your magic!

When you return from your journey, take a deep breath and reflect on the insights you received. Smile inwardly into your heart and thank your Godly self for the work you have done to accept life, yourself and others. Record any insights or awakenings in your copy of the *Reawakening the Soul Vision Quest Workbook*.

Introspection

Do I believe in magic?

How can I open up to more magic in my life?

How would it feel to be a real magician?

EFT/Tapping

KC: Even though I don't really believe in magic, I'm willing to explore it.

KC: Even though I forget to bring magic in my life, I deeply and completely accept myself.

KC: Even though I don't feel very lucky, I'm ready to explore new ways to open myself up to receive magic

EB: What is magic?
SE: Is magic really real?
UE: Do I even believe in magic?
UN: I guess it's couldn't hurt to believe.
CP: If I don't believe it will never be real.
CB: So why not dream?
UA: It's fun to dream.
TH: And it's fun to create.

EB: What if my mind really is like a wand?
SE: And created according to my thoughts?
UE: Now that's interesting.
UN: My mind created everything this very moment.
CP: I wish to be more conscious of my thoughts.
CB: And create magic in my life.
UA: I call upon my spirit guides for support.
TH: And encouragement.

EB: And support.
SE: I trust they are there to help me.
UE: I only need to remember to ask.

EFT
Audio Available
to Open Blocks
Stopping You
from Being
The Magician
of YOUR
Life!

UN: I am grateful for all these gentle masters.
CP: Guiding me in my life.
CB: As I continue to tap.
UA: I do feel more supported.
TH: And I feel the love of Spirit.

EB: For I am Spirit.
SE: And I am the creator of my life.
UE: And I choose to create my dreams.
UN: And live my life according to my desires.
CP: Because I believe in magic.
CB: I have faith.
UA: And I have purpose.
TH: I trust in my divine self.

Meditation

Reunite your soul with Spirit in the
sacred space of silence.

Meditation

*"When you go beyond the consciousness of this
world, knowing that you are not the body or the mind,
and yet aware as never before that you exist ~ that
divine consciousness is what you are. You are That
in which is rooted everything in the universe."*

~ Paramahansa Yogananda

Affirmation

Every particle of my being is submerged in
eternal light. I am filled with this light, which contains the
Divine Spirit within and around my being.

Card Message

Meditation is the way to remember your authentic self as Spirit. Through meditation and stilling your mind, you begin to feel your entire being merge with Spirit. Paramahansa Yogananda said, "God-contact becomes possible when by meditation one has attained mastery over the restlessness of the mind. One cannot meditate with uncontrolled thoughts running in every direction. A mind that does not belong to you, or a mind that is wholly occupied by the senses, can neither be offered to God nor received by Him. Wherever your heart is, there will your mind be also. If you can control your feelings and sensations, then you can put your mind on God. Having God, you shall have everything else."

Jesus said, "Seek ye first the kingdom of God, and His righteousness, and all these things shall be added unto you." (Matthew 6:33) You are encouraged to take these words sincerely and plant them as seeds in your heart. Water them frequently by loving God constantly and bringing this love to everyone you come into contact with. Fertilize them through deep and regular meditation. Grace will be the unfolding blessing bestowed upon you. Pull the weeds of negative thoughts, actions and chatter of the mind. Through these actions you will feel your soul blooming with the fragrance of divine goodness. This is God expressing Himself through you. Practicing daily meditation will change your life.

When you include meditation as a part of your daily practice, you will notice increasing mental and physical efficiency in your life. You begin to feel more peaceful with a deeper understanding and you will easily find answers to your questions. Through the calm intuitive state of inner perception, you will make choices, which are guided by wisdom. As you feel the love of God in meditation, your consciousness expands. You will be overflowing with love and, in turn, be able to love everyone unconditionally.

Card Symbology

The figure sits in the lotus posture in deep meditation, all thoughts have been turned off. The figure has released all attachments; she experiences the Oneness of her soul. She is one with the eternal light of God. She has dissolved her body in the ocean of Spirit and is no longer body-identified. Her breath shares the same life as the trees; her heart shines like the sun in the sky and her voice becomes one with the songs of the birds. In this state she realizes the "I am" that exists within her being. The earth and grass and sky are all her blood relations. Like a spirit, she walks on earth, no more afraid of the tumultuous waves of creation.

The lotus flower represents the unfolding of consciousness. It grows out of the darkness at the bottom of the pond reflecting the way that our ignorance is born out of darkness. Through meditation, our consciousness unfolds into purity reflecting the Divine Mother. The full bloom of the lotus permeates with the fragrant of divine sweetness that spreads throughout the world in the form of love. Your heart holds the nectar of this sweetness, which is born out of meditation.

Journey

Find a quiet place where you can relax undisturbed. Sit comfortably with your spine straight. Take a deep breath in, tensing your body from your feet to your head. Bring awareness to each body part, as you tense each muscle one by one, within the same inhale. As your entire body is tensed with energy, hold your breath until you are ready to exhale and release. As you exhale, make any audible sounds to expel all tension from your body. Repeat this exercise three times or until you feel relaxed. Gently begin allowing your natural breath to move in and out. With each inhale, silently chant, "My mind is calm." With each exhale, chant, "My body is still." Repeat this chant several times as you naturally breathe in and out. Remain in this state for as long as necessary, feeling all distracting thoughts subside.

Now, see yourself sitting in a beautiful lotus flower. Your body is a mass of consciousness, pure energy. You feel this energy and feel it vibrating with life force. Now, you allow yourself to be freed from your bodily attachment. You allow your physical field to slowly break away from their magnetic force, which creates your body. Your identified essence begins to break apart like bubbles floating away from your body.

You feel lighter and lighter as your physical field dissolves and merges into space. Allow your flesh to let go of the substance of weight keeping your soul body bound. Release all tension or aches and pains from your body and visualize the orbs carrying these away. Release all thoughts

Experience the Transcendental Video & Audio Journey on my Website to Feel Yourself as SPIRIT!

and mental worries and feel these as spheres of energy floating away from your consciousness. Let your entire mind disintegrate.

You feel more and more expansion in your awareness as you keep letting go. As each and every cord is released, feel the limitless energy you now contain. Notice how light and empty you feel. You are now free from the mind, and any attachments to the limitations of the body. Your body consciousness is finally free. You know you are not the body or the mind. You are filled and flowing with the light of Cosmic Consciousness. You are the divine consciousness in which everything in the universe is rooted.

Repeat the following:

> "I am entering into the temple of silence. Peace fills my body; peace fills my mind; peace fills my heart and resides within my love. God is love. I am His child. I am love. God and I are one.
>
> I am immortal. I am Almighty. My throbbing heartbeat unites with the rhythm of oneness pervading all of creation. I am vibrating consciousness. I have become the clouds, floating in peace.
>
> My heart has become the sun, warm and radiant as I beam my golden rays of divine light. I am the eternal light of oneness.
>
> My spirit merges with nature as I dance in this life, weaving my consciousness with God. I am transcendental spirit manifested out of God. I am energy intermingling with the universe.
>
> I am holy and I express myself as Spirit. I am reunited with my Eternal Beloved. My soul shines like a flawless brilliant diamond. My soul's light shines brighter and brighter shimmering light unto myself. Light unto my family, light unto my nation, light unto my world, light unto my entire universe.
>
> Everything in my existence shares the same universal Father and Mother – God. I am one with my Great Creator and I am here to share my Godly gifts."

Float within the stillness of your breath and allow yourself to journey into this sacred space of oneness.

Now it's time to come back to the physical world. Out of the ether, you become aware of all the orbs coming back into you, slowly recreating your physical body. As your body materializes, you become aware of the truth of your existence as spirit. Your vibration is forever changed.

Hold onto this awareness throughout your daily activities, and watch the magnificent wisdom of your soul unfold like a lotus. Your soul contains the cosmic intelligence and God consciousness. In this calm intuitive state of inner perception, your understanding deepens and you now find answers to all your questions. In this silence you experience increased mental and physical efficiency in your daily life. In the temple of silence you behold all answers.

Begin and end your day in meditation. Thank your creator for the energy that sustains your life. Remember to take the peace found in meditation and carry it into your daily life, spreading peace into the world. Peace on earth begins with peace within.

When you return from your journey, take a deep breath and reflect on the insights you received. Smile inwardly into your heart and thank your Godly self for the work you have done to accept life, yourself and others. Record any insights or awakenings in your copy of the *Reawakening the Soul Vision Quest Workbook.*

Introspection

Am I allowing myself the gift of meditation every morning and evening?

How can I consciously bring the peace from meditation into my daily life?

Do I acknowledge the Spirit that makes up who I am?

Am I ready to relinquish my thoughts and place my emphasis on remembering my divine nature?

EFT/Tapping

KC: Even though I feel like I can't turn off my mind to meditate, I deeply and completely accept myself.

KC: Even though I feel my mind racing with thoughts, I deeply accept the way I feel.

KC: Even though I feel like my monkey mind won't stop racing, I deeply and completely love myself.

EB: This wondering mind.
SE: My busy mind.
UE: My thoughts swirl round and round.
UN: Over and over again.
CP: How do I turn off my mind?
CB: How do I stop all these thoughts?
UA: I can take a deep breath.
TH: And breathe.

EFT
Audio Available
to Deepen
Your
Meditation!

EB: As I take another deep breath.
SE: My mind feels calmer.
UE: I focus on my breath.
UN: I focus on this tapping.
CP: This tapping feels good.
CB: Just tapping, stops my thoughts.
UA: When my thoughts cease.
TH: Clarity comes naturally.

EB: In this silence.
SE: Is where the voice of my truth resides.
UE: In this silence.
UN: Is my intuition.
CP: In this stillness.
CB: Are all the answers to all my questions.
UA: I feel calm.
TH: I feel peaceful.

EB: I am able to make clear conscious decisions.
SE: Which makes my life much easier.
UE: It feels nice to have a clear calm mind.
UN: This brings me peace.
CP: I am calm.
CB: I am silent.
UA: I am still.
TH: My mind is still.

EB: My body is still.
SE: I breathe in this stillness.
UE: I control my own mind.
UN: And I choose peace.
CP: It feels good to give my mind a break.
CB: I don't have to figure out everything.
UA: And I don't have to be in control.
TH: I choose to let go of all this activity in my mind.

EB: I feel calm.
SE: I am spirit.
UE: I am eternal light.
UN: I am divine.
CP: I am Almighty.
CB: I breathe light.
UA: I breathe love.
TH: I am love.

"Be still, and know that I am God."

~ Psalm 46:10 ."

Peace

Experience all encompassing serenity by completely embracing God's love.

Peace

"Peace on earth begins with peace within."

~ Sundara Fawn

Affirmation

The Spirit that I am consists of love and peace.

Card Message

Your core essence is peace. Your soul is the perfection of peace. By knowing and understanding this truth, you begin to bring this energy into your awareness every day. When you first begin your day, set aside time to meditate. Quiet your mind and offer your devotion to God. Know that you are perfect and loved exactly as you are in this moment. Feel the unconditional love pouring into your heart from Spirit. Feeling this love will bring inner joy to you. Make a conscious effort to hold on to this feeling and carry it with you throughout the day. The material world has a gravitational tendency to pull this peace from you. It is crucial that you remain grounded and aware of your daily actions to avoid being pulled away from this perfect peace. Pay close attention to your thoughts and make a conscious effort to remain in a positive and peaceful state.

When you change yourself, you perform your duty in changing the world. You begin to experience that the world around you becomes peaceful and safe. Remove all hate from your heart and you will begin to live a virtuous life. It is so important to practice meditation because you begin to feel the presence of Spirit within your being. The peace found in meditation and prayer will remain with you during your daily activities. This deep peace and sense of trust will be your anchor during your daily life experiences.

There is a bubble-like energy field around you that lovingly protects you throughout every moment of the day. This bubble is Spirit, the very essence of who you are. "God is a Spirit; and they that worship Him must worship Him in spirit and truth." (John 4:24) As you engage in your daily activities, remember that God is working through you. Hold this one sustaining thought in your mind: "I love you, Lord." Remember that all your worldly affairs consist of God energy— everything is from God and for God. When you live in this awareness, you live in the consciousness of your omniscient Creator as you pass through the experiences of life. You can then behold yourself and everyone around you as part of the Infinite Whole. When this happens, peace reigns in your life.

Card Symbology

The etheric figure sits within a bubble of energy, floating peacefully and gracefully wherever the current of time and space moves her. She knows that the ultimate goal of her existence is to attain the liberation that comes from the realization of Oneness with God. She knows her divine destiny is to realize God's image living within the temple of her soul. She is aware that her mortal state of consciousness is a delusion ruled by her body, mind, and senses. She knows in order to obtain this state of oneness and devotion; total surrender must become a daily practice. She floats within the gentle clouds in the sky of her dream world. The three lotus flowers represent the unfolding of mind, body and spirit. The mind must be trained to remain calm and hold positive thoughts. One must remember that the flesh of the body is condensed energy, a product of God's thought. The ultimate goal is to realize that everything in this universe is Spirit.

Journey

Experience the Transcendental Video & Audio Journey on my Website to Achieve Deeper Peace!

Find a quiet place where you can relax undisturbed. Sit comfortably with your spine straight. Take a deep breath in, tensing your body from your feet to your head. Bring awareness to each body part, as you tense each muscle one by one, within the same inhale. As your entire body is tensed with energy, hold your breath until you are ready to exhale and release. As you exhale, make any audible sounds to expel all tension from your body. Repeat this exercise three times or until you feel relaxed. Gently begin allowing your natural breath to move in and out. With each inhale, mentally chant: "I breathe in peace . . . and with each exhale, chant: . . . "I breathe out calmness." Repeat this chant several times as you naturally breathe in and out. Remain in this state for as long as needed, feeling all distracting thoughts subside.

Gaze into the image and feel the peace emanating from this image. Feel the all-sustaining life force within your body temple that vibrates with God consciousness. This life force energy allows you to move, think and breathe. This consciousness is your will power of pure, Divine energy. Feel this power surging through your spine, bursting open the doors that lead to your heart. This infusion of energy penetrates every tissue, every sensation and every cord of your nerves. All the cells in your body and thoughts you experience are now dancing on the cosmic sea of vibration. Visualize this vibration as millions of tiny bubbles that join together to form the blueprint of your physical body. Now begin to release these orbs from your energetic field. Observe these bubbles dispersing from your body and mind and spreading out into the surrounding atmosphere. Keep releasing each and every sphere until your body completely dissolves into empty space. Feel the sensation of weightlessness as you float upon the clouds of peace. You are now moving in the airless ether and into millions of universes of matter. You have passed through the physical universes into the subtle, shining inner rays of light that hold all matter in manifestation. As you melt into the universe, meditate and feel your immortal spirit. Know that you are safe and protected within God's unconditional love that surrounds you. This Divine Love adores you for the perfection of who you truly are in this moment. You are being given grace because you are awakening to remember your Divine essence. Place yourself within an energy bubble of peace and watch as it surrounds your entire body. You now simultaneously experience your soul, your heart, every fragment of inspiration, every speck of the vast blue sky, the earth, the mountains and the sea. Everything is tied together with one cord of rhythm, unity, joy and Spirit. You are a wave in the cosmic sea of bliss. Continue to relax in the comfort of absolute peace.

As you float, a beautiful pink lotus flower emerges before you. This is the flower representing the unfolding of your mind. You become aware that your mind is based upon mere projections. You have the capability of perceiving the world any way you wish. Through the magic of this lotus, you have the ability to receive every experience as a unique, positive gift. You unwrap each present and welcome the special blessings each life lesson has to offer. As you float along the currents of life, you experience everything as a gift from God. You receive every bestowal as a blessed opportunity to grow in peace and awareness towards self-realization. You acknowledge and give thanks for every gift being offered to you. If something arises that doesn't feel comfortable, breathe the energy of peace into the situation. By being at peace with every situation, hidden opportunities will be revealed. Remember that your essence is love. As you thank the lotus for helping you understand that you are in control of your mind and that you now choose peace, the exquisite flower dissolves in space.

A beautiful, yellow lotus flower then unfolds in front of you. This lotus represents the physical body. You are no longer a prisoner carrying a heavy load of bones and flesh. You have broken the chains of your muscle-bound body with the power of relaxation. You are free. You are immortal. You bask in the lightness of your essence as Spirit. When you feel complete in this journey, you thank the yellow lotus for allowing you to free yourself from all bodily limitations. The flower then gently disperses into the ether.

As you breathe deeply, another pink lotus flower presents itself to you. You smell the luscious fragrance permeating from the flower as it unfolds. This flower symbolizes your senses. You become aware of all your physical senses: sight, hearing, taste, smell and touch. This flower shares the knowledge that even though your senses are useful tools that provide data for perception, you are so much more than your sensory perceptions. Suddenly, a passage opens up within your soul and you feel your own immortality. The tempting enchantresses of the senses have now vanished. Your ties to the flesh are broken as the grip of sensory experience is loosened. You exhale as the ripples of limiting thoughts melt away. As you sit on the altar of your throbbing heart, you watch the roaring outpouring of life force energy as it moves through your heart center and into your body. You are no longer attached to the confining senses. Your new perception views the whole universe as an image of light. You behold your- self and all things as one with the Cosmic Light of the Divine Source. Your conscious- ness is dispersed from your body and spreads all over the universe. You intuitively feel the presence of the Infinite Christ within you. All creation melts away as you bask in the uncreated, transcendental vastness of Spirit. As you become one with eternity, you thank the lotus for your insights as it fades away.

You now return within the bubble in the clouds of space. Remember that you can bring yourself back to this peaceful feeling anytime you like. Take this peace with you throughout your day. Place a protective bubble around yourself each morning. Know that you will be untouched by the energy of others because you are always protected inside this bubble. By living in this harmony, you share it with others and spread the gift of love.

When you return from your journey, take a deep breath and reflect on the insights you received. Smile inwardly into your heart and thank your Godly self for the work you have done to accept life, yourself and others. Record any insights or awakenings in your copy of the *Reawakening the Soul Vision Quest Workbook*.

Introspection

Do I feel peace throughout my daily activities?

How can I bring more peace into my life?

How would it feel to live every moment in the consciousness of peace?

EFT/Tapping

KC: Even though I feel a little ungrounded right now, I choose to become present and aware.

KC: Even though my mind is wandering, I accept who I am and how I feel.

KC: Even though my life situations feel a bit chaotic, I accept how I feel.

EB: My mind doesn't seem very still.
SE: And I don't feel very peaceful right now.
UE: But I want to be at peace.
UN: Because peace feels good.
CP: When I am at peace,
CB: I am calm.
UA: I am centered.
TH: I am grounded.

EFT Audio Available to Feel More Peaceful!

EB: When I am at peace,
SE: My mind is clear.
UE: I am able to make clear decisions.
UN: My intuition is heightened.
CP: And the choices I make bring positive results.
CB: My soul always knows this peace.
UA: And this is how I want to be.
TH: This is always how I want to live.

EB: And this is my choice.
SE: I now choose peace in my life.

UE: I now feel clear.
UN: I feel grounded.
CP: I am centered.
CB: I place myself in a bubble of peace.
UA: And in this bubble,
TH: I float around this world.

EB: Inside this bubble,
SE: I know that no one can poison my peace.
UE: Because this peace belongs to me.
UN: I deserve this peace.
CP: I embrace the joy found from this peace.
CB: This peace is who I am.
UA: In this peace, I am safe.
TH: I am protected.

EB: I float in harmony.
SE: I bask in this calmness.
UE: I close my eyes and take a deep breath,
UN: And allow myself to feel this peace.
CP: I feel so calm.
CB: With an inner happiness.
UA: This is where I choose to be.
TH: This is where I shall remain.

EB: I am peace.
SE: I am peace.
UE: I feel peace in every situation in my life.
UN: Because I know the wisdom of my soul,
CP: And the peace within my soul.
CB: This peace is who I am.
UA: This peace is who I choose to be.
TH: I am peace.

"Peace is the enjoyment of life;
activity is the expression of life."
~Paramahansa Yogananda

Power

Unite your personal will with Divine will to create limitless strength.

Power

"Will is the instrument of the image of God within you. In will lies His limitless power, the power that controls all the forces of nature. As you are made in His image, that power is yours to bring about whatever you desire."

~ Paramahansa Yogananda

Affirmation

I am made in the Divine image of my beloved Creator and I reclaim my infinite power.

Card Message

Your personal willpower is the greatest thing to develop. The force of will is directed from your mind, and your thoughts are the fuel that governs and generates the mind. Reclaim your power to become fully conscious of each and every thought.

Your thoughts are shaped according to how you perceive the world around you. This perception creates the beliefs about yourself, others and your environment. (See Identity) Since you create from your thoughts, it's essential to awaken to your true nature and begin creating from your Godly mindset.

First of all, know that you are NOT broken in any way, and you never were! There's no such thing. You were born WHOLE, COMPLETE and PERFECT, and now you are returning to your original state of perfection. You are a child of God. Now is the time to create a new perception of your essence through wisdom, realization and experience. (See Wisdom) You then feel, vision and become this magnetic force of power. To acknowledge and realize your true self as one with God, your thoughts and your life changes.

All power lies in the soul's will, which draws upon the cosmic Source. All energy comes from the infinite. Your will is part of this divine will. Strengthen your will by uniting it with divine will. When you fully realize that all matter is eternal energy and you are prepared to live in this awareness, your personal will power will be aligned to a greater Source.

Look beyond accepting any negative thoughts and patterns created from ignorance and rise to reclaim your power with shear determination! Realize your power, and use it to create your dreams. Now go and be an inspiration to others! It's your time to shine your diamond light. Do not let anything stand in your way. Whatever you make up your mind to do, you will be able to carry forth.

Card Symbology

The title of this painting is "Royal White Elephant." White elephants are sacred and a symbol of royal power and good fortune. She is almighty, as she knows it within—she radiates it without. She is confident, calm and grounded. It's her natural state of being, for she has realized the truth of her existence as a spark of God.

The elephant is gently holding an elegant lotus flower, which symbolizes the blossom of wisdom representing purity and beauty as it grows out of the murky darkness of the pond. The flower is a reflection of your own purity and wisdom that progresses from the lowest to highest states of consciousness. The lotus flower inspires you to continue to grow through the trials of your life so you can bloom and reach your highest potential. This spiritual unfolding can be achieved by fully surrendering to your Creator. The lotus flower reminds us that there is beauty in every aspect of life.

The flames in the lower right corner represent the burning of negative conditioning and transforming it into truth. The crescent moon illustrates the first beginning step into this truth, and continues to grow and light up into the full God realization of love. Flow like the moon, the tides and the ever-lasting dream into the unfolding of wisdom. The dream catcher relates to the crown of illumination, and honors the remembrance that this world is all but a dream.

God is dreaming through us. The color orange illustrates the power of creativity sparked immediately from God and governs the sacral center. The electrifying surge from this hue ignites the will power to taken action.

Journey

Find a quiet place where you can relax undisturbed. Sit comfortably with your spine straight. Take a deep breath in, tensing your body from your feet to your head. Bring awareness to each body part, as you tense each muscle one by one, within the same inhale. As your entire body is tensed with energy, hold your breath until you are ready to exhale and release. As you exhale, make any audible sounds to expel all tension from your body. Repeat this exercise three times or until you feel relaxed. Gently begin allowing your natural breath to move in and out. With each inhale, mentally chant: "I am powerful." With each exhale, chant: "I am almighty." Repeat this chant several times as you naturally breathe in and out. Remain in this state for as long as needed, feeling all distracting thoughts subside.

The Royal white elephant appears before you. You feel the compassionate energy radiating from her essence. Instantly you trust her intentions, as you instinctively feel safe and expanded in her presence.

Slowly, her trunk lifts and twists itself around your body as she cradles you with her dynamic, grounded vibration. She cradles you with her tender loving trunk as your being melts into deep trust and relaxation. You completely surrender as you feel the healing touch of the elephant. You dissolve with her into the spaceless ether, with an inner knowing that you are being transported safely into another dimension. You melt into the oneness as you receive the fortune of power from this elephant.

You are now in the present moment where time doesn't exist, where you become silence itself—motionless. Stillness and formlessness permeates all around you and within you as you are now filled with complete awareness. The source of spirit rhythmically flows through your gentle breath sustaining you with life force. The holy essence of Spirit fills every cell of your being.

Now, you are transported into a Portal where the truth of your royalty exists. You feel the activation as you travel out of this world and dissolve back into the oneness of the universe. You now realize with every breath, and every move you make that this is spirit sustaining you. You are the offspring of Spirit, a child of God.

Repeat the following:

"I am Almighty . . . I am Almighty . . . I am Almighty.

I am a creator and I make my dreams. I am a creator and I invoke my passions. I am a creator and I share goodness. I am a creator and I produce my life. I consciously co-create with all creation.

I create from the passion in my heart center. I have the power to create my life according to my conscious thoughts and actions. I am passionate and grateful for everything in my life.

My strong conviction and faith will manifest my visions. My higher power is now ignited in my soul. I am guided by this higher power.

I am fearless. I am limitless and I am power. I am connected to God's will."

Experience the Transcendental Video & Audio Journey on my Website to Step Into Your POWER!!

Your sincere heart is the gateway that awakens your soul to the re-membrance of your Godly self. Be determined to become greater every day by living authentically. Reclaim your power and know your purpose in life. Now go shine your diamond light power and activate the world.

When you return from your journey, take a deep breath and reflect on the insights you received. Smile inwardly into your heart and thank your Godly self for the work you have done to accept life, yourself and others. Record any insights or awakenings in your copy of the *Reawakening the Soul Vision Quest Workbook.*

Introspection

Am I willing to step into my personal power?

How would it feel to be fearless?

Have I given my power over to someone else?

What changes can I make right now to live more fully in my power?

How would I be different if I consciously knew the potential of my divine power?

EFT/Tapping

KC: Even though I don't feel very powerful, I deeply and completely accept myself.
KC: Even though I don't feel as powerful as I know I can be, I love myself.
KC: Even though I'm not as strong as I would like to be, I deeply and completely accept myself.

EB: What does it feel like to have power?
SE: How would I feel differently?
UE: Do I feel powerful?
UN: Am I in control of my own life?
CP: Do I have strong boundaries?
CB: Am I willing to say no?

Listen to EFT Audio on my Webiste To Reclaim Your POWER!

UA: Am I living every moment the way I want?
TH: I want to step into my power.

EB: And feel courageous.
SE: I want to inspire others.
UE: As I reclaim my power.
UN: I inspire others to do the same.
CP: And we all help each other.
CB: This feels supportive.
UA: This feels like mastermind.
TH: I feel myself as God.

EB: I feel the spirit pulsating in my being.
SE: I am Almighty.
UE: I am a part of God.
UN: I am spirit.
CP: I receive my power from God.
CB: I reclaim myself as Spirit.
UA: And I shine my light from this power.
TH: By using my passions.

EB: My will is aligned to God's will.
SE: My heart is the compass.
UE: I am here to create.
UN: And I create my world.
CP: So the world does not create me.
CB: I create my own life.
UA: If I don't create my own life.
TH: Then life will create it for me.

EB: And this doesn't feel good.
SE: Because it would be created from my beliefs.
UE: I choose to consciously create.
UN: From new beliefs about myself.
CP: Being fully aware of my great Creator.
CB: I reclaim my power.
UA: My will is now united to God's will.
TH: My will is now connected to Source.

Present Moment

Consciously exist in the now.

Present Moment

"If you want to know your past—look into your present conditions. If you want to know your future—look into your present actions."

~ Chinese Proverb

Affirmation

I live in the present moment where peace resides.

Card Message

Where are your thoughts? Are they lingering in the past or do they project into the future? What if you could bring your awareness into the present moment and experience every second as a gift from the Divine? You can find a treasure in each present moment.

Begin at once to consciously pay attention to every thought, for each thought acts according to its nature. In every activity you perform, place full attention using your mind and personal action while performing the task. Make sure your mind is completely in the present moment, for if your thoughts and actions are not aligned, you will produce weak results.

Pay attention to things you may be chasing after. Whether it is trying to get everything done from your busy to do lists, worrying about schedules and obligations or feeling bombarded with everything you think you have to complete. Stop, calm down and ground yourself. You do not have to endure this self-created pressure that you have created. If you continue this pattern, you will find yourself running around like the majority of busy minded people, always chasing one thing after another.

Who creates your "to do" list? Who keeps you busy running around the clock? Are you chasing the "*White Rabbit*"—always on the go, go, go?"

Well, my friend . . . I am here to ask . . . Who created the "*White Rabbit*?" Yes—You did! And just as you created it, you can un-create it! Make it mandatory to stop chasing life and allow life to flow through you!

When you keep your mind full of "have to do's," or when you get trapped in replaying past stories in your mind, you are holding yourself back from receiving the full blessings from spirit. If you continue this old pattern, you continue to create according to past desires and karmic inclinations. When you exist in present moment awareness, you are calm, peaceful, with a deep sense of joy. Your body, mind and soul feel completely connected to a grander Source and you feel relaxed. There is an inner knowing with extreme faith that everything is in perfect order. Your mind is still, empty, yet focused because you are now co-creating with the universal strata. Here in this state, you create according to wisdom rather than ego.

Make the decision now to bring your consciousness into the present moment. This is the only place to be. In this place, you will find peace.

Card Symbology

The white rabbit is a symbol from Alice in Wonderland. Remember how she kept chasing the white rabbit? We are much the same way, always seeming to be chasing after life. The clock represents the illusion of time, for in essence the only real time is the present moment. The past is a mere projection from thought of a previous present moment state and identified according to the perception of one's own mind. The future will also exist in the present moment when its time arrives and is created by present actions. The color green representing the heart chakra, is in the center of the other chakras. Here is where heart and mind unite in the present moment of peace to create good.

Journey

Find a quiet place where you can relax undisturbed. Sit comfortably with your spine straight. Take a deep breath in, tensing your body from your feet to your head. Bring awareness to each body part, as you tense each muscle one by one, within the same inhale. As your entire body is tensed with energy, hold your breath until you are ready to exhale and release. As you exhale, make any audible sounds to expel all tension from your body. Repeat this exercise three times or until you feel relaxed. Gently begin allowing your natural breath to move in and out. With each inhale, mentally chant: "I am present." With each exhale, chant: "I am eternal." Repeat this chant several times as you naturally breathe in and out. Remain in this state for as long as needed, feeling all distracting thoughts subside.

Experience the Transcendental Video & Audio Journey on my Website For Present Moment Awareness!!

You are floating in a portal past all limiting beliefs regarding time. In this space, time doesn't exist. There is no such thing as past or future, only the universal heartbeat beating in the present moment of bliss. This quiet, tranquil space is the container where love permeates and penetrates. Beating in the rhythm of oneness, your mind is empty. Your thoughts subside into a clear, open and expanded space. Your breathing has diminished as it calmly draws in the pulsating cosmos rhythm. You are now resting in omnipresent conscious awareness. Familiarize yourself with this presence and bask in this divine state. This is present moment awareness.

Now, in this crystalline state of being, bring into your awareness a life decision you need to make. Visualize the scenario and feel the emotions around it. You know that you have choices, and you get to choose. In this moment you are free from making all decisions. Completely free yourself from making any decisions at this moment around this situation.

Repeat the following:

"I do not have to make a decision at this moment. I trust and know that the decision will be made for me, at the perfect time. I ask for the guidance and clarity to be so crystal clear that the decision will make itself.

My soul knows exactly what direction to take, in order for the highest good of all to be made manifest. I allow the decision to present itself, effortlessly and accurately with my innate faith. I take action according to the instructions that will be made known to me."

Let go of this situation and trust that you will know exactly what to do. When you free yourself in this way, you allow the mind to step aside allowing new unexpected choices to become available.

Now glance at your "to do list." How does it make you feel? Are you putting pressure on yourself to keep up with this never ending list? You alone are responsible for creating it, and you alone are responsible for determining how many things you wish to do and the amount of time to accomplish them.

If you find yourself frantically chasing after every item and making yourself crazy in the process, now is the time to consciously stop this behavior. Take note that the same person who created these items on the list is the same person who can accomplish them with ease and grace, and even remove some of them if necessary. Urgency is not of the vibration of spirit that you wish to carry. You are now moving away from acting unconsciously, dictated by behaviors, patterns and whims. You are moving into conscious awareness. You are done chasing. You are finished driving yourself crazy. You have identified the pattern and you release yourself from all self-created burdens of stress and exhaustion caused by busying your mind with obligations and chasing after mere projections.

Remember the list will always be there no matter how much you run after it. Do the best that you can do while being and acting in the present moment to accomplish the things needed. Note, that when you die, most likely you will still have desires you wished to accomplish, and these will all dissolve whence they came from. These lists only survive from the attention of energy and importance placed upon them from your mind.

You now feel relieved from all the pressures your mind has dictated for you to complete. You are aware in daily situations when you begin to run these old programs of adrenaline and you are able to bring them to an immediate halt. You are now activated with present moment awareness and act and think upon one thing at a time with full attention. You are clear and focused. You notice how life effortlessly flows resonating with the notes of peace and harmony. You are aware how you are able to achieve much more in this state of mind.

Take a moment to envision your new state of awareness, one of deep sublime peace. Feel how you wish to create and experience your life. Don't be shy, dream big, see and feel your dreams. Know, that as you consciously produce, you create your future according to present moment actions.

You now stop chasing life, but rather allow life to flow through you with ease and grace. As you think in the present moment and act in the present moment, this creates the outcome of your future. You are aware of your every day existence, as you are calmly active in the moment of now. This is where truth resides.

When you return from your journey, take a deep breath and reflect on the insights you received. Smile inwardly into your heart and thank your Godly self for the work you have done to accept life, yourself and others. Record any insights or awakenings in your copy of the *Reawakening the Soul Vision Quest Workbook.*

Introspection

Where are my thoughts?

Do I feel like I'm chasing life?

Am I allowing, "what is" to occur?

Am I present?

EFT/Tapping

KC: Even though I know I'm not in the present moment a lot, I deeply except where I am.

KC: Even though I feel I'm not very present, I deeply and totally love myself.

KC: Even though my mind seems to be racing all the time, I know this behavior is not present and I am open to change.

EB: Being present.
SE: Even though it sounds so simple,
UE: It can be so challenging.
UN: My mind is always racing.
CP: Thinking about the past.
CB: And projecting into the future.
UA: How much do I think of the past?
TH: How much do I dream about the future?

EB: Am I really ever in the present moment?
SE: I'm always chasing after life.
UE: And trying to complete my to do list.
UN: I'm so attached to my calendar.
CP: It's always seems full.
CB: I'm the one that created this craziness.
UA: And I can un-create it.
TH: I'm done chasing the white rabbit.

EFT Audio Available to Help You Stop Chasing Life!

EB: And always running after time.
SE: I'm done chasing my expectations.
UE: I'm done feeling so fearful.
UN: In not getting enough accomplished.
CP: I'm going to stop now and breathe.
CB: And feel the presence of this divine moment.
UA: I do feel calmer.
TH: I feel more centered.

EB: Just breathing and remembering helps.
SE: Can it really be this simple?
UE: I heard the saying, "God is easy, and everything else is difficult."
UN: Could this be true?
CP: Spirit does reside in the present moment.
CB: Maybe I can remember to just breathe more deeply during the day.
UA: And Just be mindful of being present.
TH: I know this takes practice.

EB: But I'm willing to make the effort.
SE: I'm willing to grow.
UE: And expand.
UN: I'm willing to be more conscious.
CP: Because being in the present moment makes me feel complete.
CB: And sure of my self.
UA: And safe.
TH: Being present allows me to feel connected to my Creator.

EB: I feel nurtured.
SE: And fully supported.
UE: I'm done chasing after life.
UN: Life creates through me in the moment of the now.
CP: And I live in the present moment.
CB: I now reclaim my original essence.
UA: By being in this moment.
TH: I feel love.

"The art of life is to live in the present moment, and to make that moment as perfect as we can by the realization that we are the instruments and expression of God Himself."

~ Emmet Fox

Purification

Cleanse the heart, mind and body to reflect the perfection of the soul.

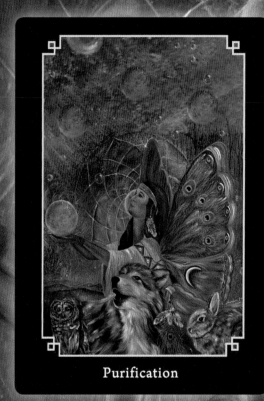

Purification

"Absolve me, teach me, purify me, strengthen me: take me to Thyself, that I may be Thine and Thine only."

~ Joseph Barber Lightfoot

Affirmation

I know that my soul is the perfection of God and I claim that perfection.

Card Message

You are encouraged to set aside time to look deeply into your heart. What do you see? Is your heart pure? Purification involves regular, deep cleansing of the heart, mind and body along with regularly clearing of your physical space and energy field. This is a process that takes consistent awareness, time and patience. When you begin this purification process, you will instantly gain clarity and feel a positive difference.

Your soul is perfect and reflects Universal Light. Throughout lifetimes, you have accumulated layers of beliefs and patterns that have gradually shrouded your soul. As these layers covered your essence, your shining light has gradually diminished. The most important work while here on earth is to uncover these layers and remember yourself as a pure reflection of God. Self-realization through reawakening the soul is the key to unlock and release these buried layers.

Purification includes uncovering false beliefs and peeling them away. Some of these layers may feel painful and uncomfortable as you strip away toxic beliefs and burdens that no longer serve you. When you remove limiting beliefs from your mind, you begin to reflect the perfect light of Infinite Spirit. This purification process is necessary in order for the light of your soul to burn at its brightest.

Purifying the mind begins with having awareness of your thoughts and beliefs. What you believe to be true is the foundation of how you perceive yourself and the world around you. The thoughts you experience about yourself create and manifest your reality. Wake up to your own negative thought patterns and make a conscious effort to change them. Your current life experience is the destination where your thoughts have led you. Take time to analyze how your life is at this very moment. How are you feeling? Is your life unfolding peacefully and filled with joy? Take a step back and look at the circumstances in your life right now. This is your story, based upon your thought patterns. If you are peaceful and moving forward with passion and purpose, then your energy is aligned with the perfection of Spirit. Positive thinking created this alignment for you. If you are unhappy with your story at this moment and the circumstances surrounding your life, then it's time to reconstruct new patterns of thought. You have created this reality and now you can re-create it!

Sunda

Purify your heart so that it can hold unconditional love. In order to have a pure heart, learn to forgive everyone who has harmed or hurt you. It is also necessary to forgive yourself and all of those whom you may have harmed or hurt. (See Forgiveness) When you love God and love yourself, you surrender into the trust that true love brings. By spending time in silence, you begin to remember who you are and unite with Spirit.

Your physical body houses your soul, acting as a precious and sacred temple. A healthy and pure body, cleansed from toxic foods and substances, will enhance your soul's light.

The physical space that you occupy is also an important element in purification. Take a clear look around your living space and see if it needs to be refreshed. Do you need to go through your closets or pull the weeds in your garden? Is it time to go through drawers and cabinets and remove old stuff? Take a look at any space that you occupy outside of your home such as an office or work site and see what clearing may be necessary.

Personal space also includes your own energy field and those whom you spend time with. It is important to have clear, healthy boundaries and balanced relationships with healthy people. Take note if you are living an authentic life. Do you give yourself permission to say no? When you clear your energy field, you attract people with healthy energy. When you explore every aspect of your energy field and clean it up, it reflects your soul and you shine, feeling alive and energized.

Card Symbology

Call upon owl medicine for higher wisdom, clairvoyance and magic. The owl is a bird of the night and a symbol of the darkness within—a place where it is safe to hide secrets. It is time to become aware of shadows. Through wisdom, learn how to bring forth light to replace the darkness of the shadow. The wolf is the spirit of the free and pure wilderness. Wolf medicine teaches how to develop strength and confidence so that you don't have anything to prove to anyone. Wolf helps you to develop the understanding that true freedom requires discipline. The wolf in this painting is howling to remind you of your own unique voice and the importance to speak freely and openly. The rabbit is associated with the fairy realm. He leads you towards magical worlds. Rabbit medicine will bring forth movement in life's situations with varying degrees of leaps and hops, not by a steady step-by-step movement.

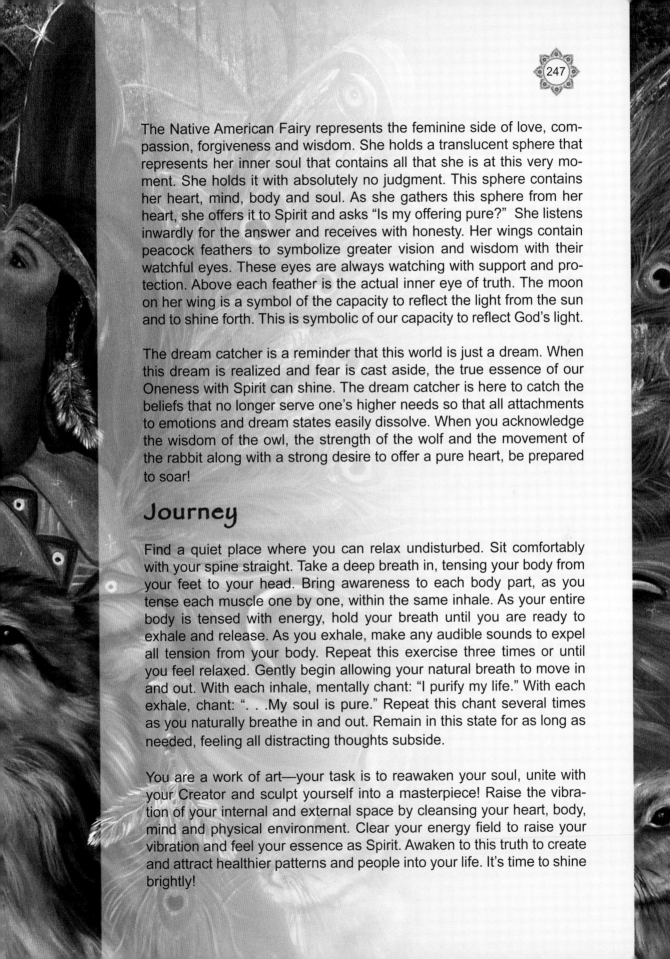

The Native American Fairy represents the feminine side of love, compassion, forgiveness and wisdom. She holds a translucent sphere that represents her inner soul that contains all that she is at this very moment. She holds it with absolutely no judgment. This sphere contains her heart, mind, body and soul. As she gathers this sphere from her heart, she offers it to Spirit and asks "Is my offering pure?" She listens inwardly for the answer and receives with honesty. Her wings contain peacock feathers to symbolize greater vision and wisdom with their watchful eyes. These eyes are always watching with support and protection. Above each feather is the actual inner eye of truth. The moon on her wing is a symbol of the capacity to reflect the light from the sun and to shine forth. This is symbolic of our capacity to reflect God's light.

The dream catcher is a reminder that this world is just a dream. When this dream is realized and fear is cast aside, the true essence of our Oneness with Spirit can shine. The dream catcher is here to catch the beliefs that no longer serve one's higher needs so that all attachments to emotions and dream states easily dissolve. When you acknowledge the wisdom of the owl, the strength of the wolf and the movement of the rabbit along with a strong desire to offer a pure heart, be prepared to soar!

Journey

Find a quiet place where you can relax undisturbed. Sit comfortably with your spine straight. Take a deep breath in, tensing your body from your feet to your head. Bring awareness to each body part, as you tense each muscle one by one, within the same inhale. As your entire body is tensed with energy, hold your breath until you are ready to exhale and release. As you exhale, make any audible sounds to expel all tension from your body. Repeat this exercise three times or until you feel relaxed. Gently begin allowing your natural breath to move in and out. With each inhale, mentally chant: "I purify my life." With each exhale, chant: ". . .My soul is pure." Repeat this chant several times as you naturally breathe in and out. Remain in this state for as long as needed, feeling all distracting thoughts subside.

You are a work of art—your task is to reawaken your soul, unite with your Creator and sculpt yourself into a masterpiece! Raise the vibration of your internal and external space by cleansing your heart, body, mind and physical environment. Clear your energy field to raise your vibration and feel your essence as Spirit. Awaken to this truth to create and attract healthier patterns and people into your life. It's time to shine brightly!

Overlap the palms of both your hands and place one on top of the other on your heart. Keep breathing slowly as you feel the energy from your heart enter into your palms. Breathe even deeper into your heart. Feel all your love, compassion, and soul wisdom. Now, remove your hands and as you do, feel your heart energy gathering into a sphere in your palms. Look into this orb of light, as it contains the spirit of your heart and soul. As you watch the dancing, sparkling energy, you feel expansive. With the orb still in the palm of your hands, you lift your arms and offer it to Spirit. You say to your Creator, "here is my heart, so simple, so true, is it pure enough to reflect the presence of you?" Now declare, "I offer my heart and I ask for the strength to purify my thoughts, actions and beliefs." Relax and receive the messages. Notice where you need strengthening and ask to be shown how to achieve this. Ask for a clear understanding of how to remove any layers that are keeping you from being the perfect reflection you wish to be. Notice all the ways you want to change, along with any bad habits you wish to release. Without any judgments, witness anything that comes to you. Stay in this awareness for as long as needed to receive your messages.

Let's now explore your physical body. Look carefully at your eating habits. Can you eat healthier in order to raise your vibration? Are you exercising enough? Are you spending enough time playing and having fun? How are your sleeping patterns? How can you give more nourishment to your body? A pure body, cleansed from toxic food and substances, is needed to enhance the reflection of your soul's light. Feel the energy around your body pulsating with light. As you cleanse the toxins from your field, you remove the residue that restricts your soul from shining. The healthier your body becomes, the more every cell will dance and sparkle with light!

Now, look into your living space and working environment. Are there areas that need to be cleaned or cleared? Do you need to go through your closets or pull the weeds in your garden? Is it time to go through drawers and cabinets to remove the old stuff? By de-cluttering your physical surroundings, you will create a healthy, vibrant space.

Take a look at the people you spend time with. Do they enhance your life? Do they bring you love and joy and nourish your soul? Are there any individuals you spend time with that feel toxic to you? If so, it may be healthier to remove yourself from them. Continue looking into all areas of your sur-

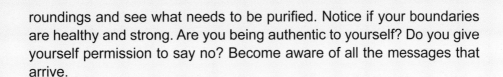

roundings and see what needs to be purified. Notice if your boundaries are healthy and strong. Are you being authentic to yourself? Do you give yourself permission to say no? Become aware of all the messages that arrive.

Now, with new awareness from the journey, make a vow to change! Take all your new insights and bring them into your field of energy and announce out loud, "I freely release all these impurities into the vortex of consciousness." Release them all now! Keep releasing residue as you envision the changes you now choose. The owl, wolf and rabbit spirit animals continue to hold the space for you. You receive the wisdom of the owl, the strength of the wolf and rapid change and movement from the rabbit. Release them all until they are gone!

Your energy field is now cleared! Embrace the perfection of who you are at this moment. You vibrate with bright crystalline light and attract others with resonant energy. You feel alive and happy! Feel how crystal clear your body and energy field is! You now reflect the brilliance of your higher self—your soul. Now, go shine your holy light into the world and inspire others to do the same!

When you return from your journey, take a deep breath and reflect on the insights you received. Smile inwardly into your heart and thank your Godly self for the work you have done to accept life, yourself and others. Record any insights or awakenings in your copy of the *Reawakening the Soul Vision Quest Workbook.*

Introspection

How can I become more pure in my body, mind, heart and surroundings?

What would I feel like if I were a pure reflection of love?

What steps can I immediately take towards creating a more purified and satisfying life?

Are my thoughts, beliefs and actions pure?

250

EFT/Tapping

KC: Even though I don't feel completely pure, I deeply and completely accept myself.

KC: Even though there are so many ways that I want to purify myself, I am now open to take the next step.

KC: Even though all these changes feel so far out of my reach, I completely accept the way I feel.

EB: What does it mean to be pure?
SE: How can I feel more whole?
UE: I would like to explore this deeper.
UN: What does it mean to purify my mind?
CP: And make it clear.
CB: I would have to empty any negative thoughts.
UA: And think positive ones.
TH: And meditate more.

Listen to EFT
Audio Available
on my Website
to Purify
Your Life!

EB: This would make it still.
SE: And make it empty.
UE: And full of peace.
UN: Can I really do this?
CP: Can I really purify my mind?
CB: Why not?
UA: It would feel good to have a clear, strong and vibrant mind.
TH: It would feel good to feel more peace and harmony.

EB: This would feel good.
SE: I'm willing to explore this.
UE: And find ways to clean my mind.
UN: How about my body?
CP: How can I purify my body?
CB: Am I willing to change my diet to be more healthy?
UA: I would definitely feel better.
TH: And probably think clearer.

EB: And this would lead to more happiness.
SE: I am willing to be healthier.
UE: And exercise more.
UN: And spend more time doing the things that I love to do.
CP: Making these changes would make me feel better.

CB: And brighten up my spirit.
UA: With all of this gunk gone.
TH: My soul could only feel brighter.

EB: The more I release and change.
SE: And empty the old.
UE: The brighter I shine.
UN: And when I shine,
CP: I feel my divinity.
CB: I feel alive.
UA: I feel happy.
TH: I feel clear!

Receive

Welcome and acquire all the precious gifts
from Spirit.

Receive

*"Everything comes to us that belongs to us if we
create the capacity to receive it."*

~ Rabindranath Tagore

Affirmation

I welcome all the gifts that Spirit has to offer me.

Card Message

You are now clear and receptive to open up and receive all the blessings of Spirit. As you become more awakened and aware of spirit and how it flows, your abundance increases. Gifts from spirit wish to pour forth to you in every aspect imaginable, from health, wealth, happiness and love! Now is the time to create the energetic space to receive your divine inheritance.

Breathe deeply, thank and acknowledge every gift in your life, every situation and every circumstance. Gratitude for *everything* in your life is essential to opening yourself to make more available space to receive all your new gifts. Be grateful for everything in your life and your receptive channels will open.

The greatest gift to receive is remembering your true nature as Spirit. Make your consciousness a receptacle to receive this omnipresent truth. Reawaken your soul and reunite once again with your everlasting beloved God. Learn to love yourself and you will open to receive all the unconditional love and blessings from your Creator. Bring the awareness of God into your consciousness and feel your presence merging with His omnipresent consciousness. He is the breath of life behind your every waking moment. Silently receive His love every moment of every day.

Open up your heart to receive the bountiful gifts that Spirit has to offer you. Request your wants and needs and know that in remembering God, you shall receive everything. Ask to receive only what is for the highest good of all. You will receive what is rightfully yours according to your capacity to receive it.

Give and you will receive. By giving, you will discover the treasure of receiving through the pure act of giving unconditionally. Knowing that everything and everyone in creation is permeating with the intelligence and consciousness of God, you share and distribute the flow of universal Spirit through your activity. As you share the joy in expressing your passionate gifts, you receive the grace of God's love ever shining within you. You behold the most precious gift—knowing that you are made in the image of God! Open to receive your bountiful gifts!

Card Symbology

The etheric figure is grounded upon the solid rocks of wisdom, opening to the truth of her existence. She has received the first glimpses into the awareness of her oneness with her Creator.

With arms open to receive the light of Christ through the burning sun, pure love fills every particle of being. All the elements of creation are present and pulsating within the same timeless heartbeat.

Earth, water, fire, air and ether vibrate within everything in this universe. The calm and serene landscape reflects this intimate connection. Everything melts into the oneness of love.

Journey

Find a quiet place where you can relax undisturbed. Sit comfortably with your spine straight. Take a deep breath in, tensing your body from your feet to your head. Bring awareness to each body part, as you tense each muscle one by one, within the same inhale. As your entire body is tensed with energy, hold your breath until you are ready to exhale and release. As you exhale, make any audible sounds to expel all tension from your body. Repeat this exercise three times or until you feel relaxed. Gently begin allowing your natural breath to move in and out. With each inhale, silently chant, "My heart is free." With each exhale, chant, "I am open to receive." Repeat this chant several times as you naturally breathe in and out. Remain in this state for as long as necessary, feeling all distracting thoughts subside. When you have

Breathe deeply, thank and acknowledge every gift in your life, every situation and every circumstance. Gratitude for everything in your life is essential to opening yourself to make more available space to receive all your new gifts. Be grateful for everything in your life. The more gratitude you have, the more your receptive channels open. Continue to feel your heart filling with gratitude as your auric field grows and expands.

You have now created space to receive the truth of your existence. You are grounded in truth as you sit upon the solid rocks of wisdom. You feel every particle of your being as a perfect blend of the elements. Your heart and soul are empty receptacles to be filled with the truth of light. It's time to experience how loved you are by your great Creator.

Hug yourself while you repeat the following:

> "God loves me. I am His child. God loves me, just as I am. I am love. I receive this love and I open up to absolute truth. God loves me. I feel my Beloved's love through me as I hug myself. I feel His breath breathing through my breath. I am so loved.
>
> I open to feel this love, for I am love. I receive all the gifts my Beloved is constantly giving me. I am aware of every gift in each waking moment. God is worthy. I am worthy to receive love. I am worthy to receive wealth. I am worthy to remember my perfect health. I am whole and perfect. I am happy. I receive the perfection of myself exactly as I am."

Receive this transfusion of love from Spirit and allow it to permeate every cell of your being.

When you return from your journey, take a deep breath and reflect on the insights you received. Smile inwardly into your heart and thank your Godly self for the work you have done to accept life, yourself and others. Record any insights or awakenings in your copy of the *Reawakening the Soul Vision Quest Workbook*.

Introspection

How can I open to receive more fully?

Is it easier for me to give or to receive?

Am I comfortable receiving compliments?

Do I receive God's unconditional love?

EFT/Tapping

KC: Even though I forget to open to receive daily, I am willing to make this a part of my practice.

KC: Even though I forget that I am a child of God, I deeply and completely love myself.

KC: Even though I'm constantly giving, I choose to explore how to receive more.

Listen to EFT Audio to Clear Away Emotional Blocks Around Receiving!

EB: I'm always giving.
SE: Giving seems easy.
UE: But am I receiving enough?
UN: Am I balanced in giving and receiving?
CP: I want to be balanced.
CB: And I want to learn to receive.
UA: Can I open up to allow myself to receive?
TH: Who am I?

EB: Do I really know who I am?
SE: Do I allow myself to be loved by God?
UE: I'm ready to be loved.
UN: I'm ready to feel unconditional love.
CP: Can I really be loved for who I am in this moment?
CB: I feel so flawed.
UA: And imperfect.
TH: How can God love a defective person?

EB: But if I am one with God.
SE: Some part of me must be perfect.
UE: Could it be my soul?
UN: Why not?
CP: I do feel the presence of my soul.
CB: And I feel its perfection.
UA: So the more I receive my divine essence,
TH: The more I feel my own perfection.

EB: Where does the source of my energy come from?
SE: It must be my great Creator.
UE: This energy sustains me.
UN: Every breath of life is fed by this energy.
CP: This is God.

every particle of your being as a perfect blend of the elements. Your heart and soul are empty receptacles to be filled with the truth of light. It's time to experience how loved you are by your great Creator.

Hug yourself while you repeat the following:

> "God loves me. I am His child. God loves me, just as I am. I am love. I receive this love and I open up to absolute truth. God loves me. I feel my Beloved's love through me as I hug myself. I feel His breath breathing through my breath. I am so loved.
>
> I open to feel this love, for I am love. I receive all the gifts my Beloved is constantly giving me. I am aware of every gift in each waking moment. God is worthy. I am worthy to receive love. I am worthy to receive wealth. I am worthy to remember my perfect health. I am whole and perfect. I am happy. I receive the perfection of myself exactly as I am."

Receive this transfusion of love from Spirit and allow it to permeate every cell of your being.

When you return from your journey, take a deep breath and reflect on the insights you received. Smile inwardly into your heart and thank your Godly self for the work you have done to accept life, yourself and others. Record any insights or awakenings in your copy of the *Reawakening the Soul Vision Quest Workbook.*

Introspection

How can I open to receive more fully?

Is it easier for me to give or to receive?

Am I comfortable receiving compliments?

Do I receive God's unconditional love?

EFT/Tapping

KC: Even though I forget to open to receive daily, I am willing to make this a part of my practice.

KC: Even though I forget that I am a child of God, I deeply and completely love myself.

KC: Even though I'm constantly giving, I choose to explore how to receive more.

EB: I'm always giving.

SE: Giving seems easy.

UE: But am I receiving enough?

UN: Am I balanced in giving and receiving?

CP: I want to be balanced.

CB: And I want to learn to receive.

UA: Can I open up to allow myself to receive?

TH: Who am I?

EB: Do I really know who I am?

SE: Do I allow myself to be loved by God?

UE: I'm ready to be loved.

UN: I'm ready to feel unconditional love.

CP: Can I really be loved for who I am in this moment?

CB: I feel so flawed.

UA: And imperfect.

TH: How can God love a defective person?

EB: But if I am one with God.

SE: Some part of me must be perfect.

UE: Could it be my soul?

UN: Why not?

CP: I do feel the presence of my soul.

CB: And I feel its perfection.

UA: So the more I receive my divine essence,

TH: The more I feel my own perfection.

EB: Where does the source of my energy come from?

SE: It must be my great Creator.

UE: This energy sustains me.

UN: Every breath of life is fed by this energy.

CP: This is God.

Listen to EFT Audio to Clear Away Emotional Blocks Around Receiving!

CB: I feel God.
UA: I receive the truth of light that God is myself.
TH: I am open to receive entire goodness.

EB: Coming to me now.
SE: I acknowledge all the gifts I am now receiving.
UE: The more I open.
UN: The more I receive.
CP: God is worthy.
CB: Myself as God is worthy.
UA: I am worthy to receive love.
TH: I am worthy to receive wealth.

EB: I now allow myself to receive.
SE: I now open up to all the gifts.
UE: That spirit has to offer me.
UN: I cherish all these gifts.
CP: Especially the gifts of who I am.
CB: I am worthy.
UA: And I now allow myself to receive.
TH: I welcome life.

Surrender

Align your will with God's will and trust the
perfection of all that is given to you.

Surrender

*"God knows what He is doing with me, I cannot
always understand His way, but I am content in
the realization that He knows what is best.
That is surrender.*

~Sri Daya Mata

Affirmation

I now relinquish everything over to the grace of God. I
trust that all is perfect.

Card Message

To feel peaceful and whole, come to a place of surrender and fully yield to God. Confusing and stressful feelings are a result of forgetting that you are not the one in control. When you open your heart and completely surrender, you will find peace. Your life will begin to unfold like magic as new opportunities present themselves.

To fully surrender, you must practice releasing your personal will to the will of God. Loving and trusting God is the key to surrender and release. In this state of love, you will know the perfection of everything in your life. (See Love and Trust) Know that you are not alone in your journey. When you surrender to God, miracles begin to unfold. You may suddenly meet someone who shares a message that resonates with you or you may receive unexpected financial blessings. You notice synchronicity happening all around you that support your journey back to God. Every moment becomes magic when you live in a state of surrender, as contentment and joy become your natural vibration. You will begin to understand the endless possibilities of Divine guidance.

Sometimes it takes becoming completely exhausted, emotionally and physically, before you are ready to learn the true blessing of surrender. You have a choice to return to your Creator out of desperation or desire; it's your choice. You can choose to learn your life lessons in a gentler way by surrendering to God now.

Wisdom gained through your own personal experience is a beautiful way back to your loving Creator. By continually growing through your discovery of self-awareness tools and techniques, your spiritual development begins to unfold. It is important to realize that every circumstance, person and experience in your life provide you with opportunities for spiritual growth. Look upon every situation as an opportunity to develop your character. It is your responsibility to find harmony in the life lessons that are given to you. As you learn to show gratitude for all situations, yes—even the difficult ones, your soul begins to reawaken to its natural omnipresent state and you will experience happiness.

Card Symbology

The woman sits upon the lotus flower; the flower represents purity and beauty as it grows out of the murky darkness of the pond. The flower is a reflection of your own purity and wisdom that progresses from the lowest to highest states of consciousness. The lotus flower inspires you to continue to grow through the trials of your life so you can bloom and reach your highest potential. This spiritual unfolding can be achieved by fully surrendering to your Creator.

The lotus flower reminds us that there is beauty in every aspect of life. As the woman opens her heart and raises her palms in surrender, she experiences sublime peace and magic. Her life becomes as beautiful as the painting—full of magic and serenity. She faces toward the sun-rays, feeling the warm presence of Divine light and love. She knows this light is a reflection of her own soul. When she realizes that she is this light, she relinquishes everything back to her source. In a transcendent state, she floats upon the lotus flower with the awareness and wisdom that comes from surrendering to God.

Journey

Find a quiet place where you can relax undisturbed. Sit comfortably with your spine straight. Take a deep breath in, tensing your body from your feet to your head. Bring awareness to each body part, as you tense each muscle one by one, within the same inhale. As your entire body is tensed with energy, hold your breath until you are ready to ex-hale and release. As you exhale, make any audible sounds to expel all tension from your body. Repeat this exercise three times or until you feel relaxed. Gently begin allowing your natural breath to move in and out. With each inhale, silently chant: "I surrender to life." With each exhale, chant: "I accept all situations." Repeat this chant several times as you naturally breathe in and out. Remain in this state for as long as necessary, feeling all distracting thoughts subside.

You find yourself sitting comfortably in a pond, nestled within a beautiful lotus flower. A wondrous garden surrounds you with the radiant beauty and magic of life. The invigorating floral fragrance enlivens every cell of your body. You gaze into the vibrant sun, feeling the radiant rays pen-etrating your skin with warmth. You feel safe, complete and whole. You relax, breathing sunlight into your body. As you continue to sit in this tranquility, your breath becomes deeper, slower and calmer as you in-hale the brilliant rays of light. Your breath becomes still as it merges and unites with this spectacular light. Your entire inner being is tingling with the sensation of vibrating light. You feel your consciousness expanding, wider and wider, until it encompasses the entire universe. Your physical

Experience the Transcendental Video & Audio Journey on my Website to Surrender Naturally!

body has dissolved into another plane and you feel free from all bodily discomfort. Feel yourself as a light being, pulsating with thriving energy and cosmic intelligence. Your heart is wide open as you experience the deepest peace you have ever felt. The landscape around you melts into luminous spiritual light and you embrace this sacred space with your Creator. With heightened awareness, surrender becomes your natural state of being. This act of surrender is no longer something you have to "do," but rather, it is simply who you "are." You now feel and realize your godly Self.

In this union, you feel safe to give all your responsibilities, emotions, fears and difficulties over to a higher power. One by one, completely release all of your burdens into the spiraling vortex of energy. Let go of any limiting beliefs keeping you separate from creation. Discharge all the old patterns that do not feel good. Let them all go! Relinquish the need for control. Your mind only has the power that you give it. Your thoughts no longer have authority over you. Keep giving all expectations and attachments away. All these perceived burdens no longer belong to you, as they were never really yours from the beginning. It was your choice to carry them and identify with these thoughts, but now you are guided by wisdom and you know how to transform these old programs. You choose to free yourself from these burdens by releasing them to God.

Now that you have emptied your mind, you feel as if you are floating in peace. You are able to feel gratitude for all life has to offer. You begin to witness your current life circumstances and notice that these were chosen gifts for your own personal and spiritual growth. You experience peace in each and every one of these situations as you gently release them from your energy field. Feel your heart open and merge with the peace emanating from the spiritual experience of letting go . . . accepting . . . relinquishing . . . and letting God!

Your body, mind and heart are now expanded with limitless space. You know and trust the creation around you because you now experience the Creator within you. With this great faith, you understand that everything happening in your life is for your spiritual advancement. As you breathe into this freedom, you become the essence of surrender and truth. This feels so natural and smooth. Breathe deeply into this ease. Practicing the art of surrendering in every day situations is the key to a peaceful and holy life.

Now take a glance into the recent past and notice any uncomfortable situation where you would like to practice letting go. In your mind, replay the scene and pay attention to how you reacted. Are you still reacting? How do you feel? What emotions are going through your mind? How is your posture? How is your breathing? Notice if you are trying to control the situation. Release this scenario from your mind and from your energy field. Let this feeling go! Take all of this energy and disperse it! Wipe it clean from your mind, as it is only cluttering your consciousness. Now that you trust Spirit so deeply, there is no need to cling to old patterns of holding; no need to control the outcome of situations. You have the power to allow everything to flow naturally and organically, accepting and embracing all of it. As you let go of all perceived negative emotions around this situation, you become the observer of the experience without emotional attachments.

When you fully trust God, you allow the perfection of "*what is*" to occur. When you live in this trust, you remain in an emotionally neutral state—this is yielding. Remember, you have the power and awareness to float in this blissful peace every moment. Keep practicing with every situation that presents itself and you will become the master of your life!

As you reawaken your soul and discover your true nature as Spirit . . . surrender becomes your natural state of being!

When you return from your journey, take a deep breath and reflect on the insights you received. Smile inwardly into your heart and thank your Godly self for the work you have done to accept life, yourself and others. Record any insights or awakenings in your copy of the *Reawakening the Soul Vision Quest Workbook.*

Introspection

What burdens do I feel right now in my life that I can let go of and surrender?

Do I feel any fear around letting everything go back to Spirit?

Am I holding on to any emotions or baggage from the past that is stopping me from receiving the flow of Divine magic?

Am I paying attention to all messages from my body, mind and spirit that are here to serve as guides?

EFT/Tapping

KC: Even though at times it's hard for me to surrender, I accept the way I feel.

KC: Even though surrender feels challenging to me, I deeply and completely accept myself.

KC: Even though I don't know what it means to fully surrender, I'm willing to explore new concepts.

EB: What is surrender?
SE: What does surrender really mean to me?
UE: I seem to hear it all the time.
UN: And it makes sense at some deep level.
CP: But, what does it really mean?
CB: As I tap, I feel what surrender means to me.
UA: I breathe and tap.
TH: As I let myself open to explore surrender.

EFT
Audio Available
to Help
You Relax in Deep
Surrender!

EB: Can I really allow myself to completely let go?
SE: But I'm so used to being in control.
UE: If I let go, then who would take over?
UN: This feels a bit uncomfortable.
CP: I'm so used to controlling.
CB: And holding on to expectations.
UA: And when things don't happen the way I envision them.
TH: I become disappointed.

EB: Is this a pattern in my life?
SE: Can I let go and trust life?
UE: How do I trust?
UN: Can I surrender to a higher power?
CP: What does my higher power feel like?
CB: I am open to explore my relationship with my Creator.
UA: I am willing to feel my Creator.
TH: It feels good knowing that I don't have to be in control.

EB: The thought of accepting everything feels freeing.
SE: The more I open my mind.
UE: And the more I feel my Creator.
UN: The more I experience the presence of God.
CP: The more I choose to love.
CB: The more Godly I become.
UA: When I feel connected with Spirit.
TH: Surrender feels natural.

EB: How can I connect more with God?
SE: How can I feel the presence of Spirit?
UE: Maybe by giving myself time to connect with "me."
UN: By spending time every day, doing what I love.
CP: Am I willing to give this a try?
CB: Why not?
UA: It feels good.
TH: When I am giving to me, I am giving to God.

EB: I am developing a relationship with God.
SE: And therefore trust would come naturally.
UE: I know this is going to take some practice.
UN: But I'm willing to keep practicing.
CP: Until I experience truth.
CB: And I am open to the understanding,
UA: That everything happening around me,
TH: Is created for my spiritual unfoldment.

EB: Just embracing this truth and accepting,
SE: Gives me a sense of power.
UE: It feels good to let go,
UN: And let God!
CP: It would make my life much easier.
CB: And much more peaceful.
UA: I'm willing to give this a try.
TH: I will keep practicing acts of surrender.

"We can only learn to know ourselves and do what we can—namely, surrender our will and fulfill God's will in us."

~ Saint Teresa of Avila

Transformation

Let go of the false self and be reborn
into absolute truth.

Transformation

*"Life and death are illusions. We are in a constant
state of transformation."*

~ Alejandro Gonzalez Inarritu

Affirmation

I rise above my mind into the awareness of my soul's
wisdom.

Card Message

The message from the phoenix states that it is time for you to release and burn away the old and open up to the new. The old may include patterns, beliefs or ideas that no longer fit the higher awareness you are moving into. You are aware that the way you are currently living your life no longer serves you. You feel a personal fire burning within your heart crying out with the desire to change. Although you feel passionate and certain, pay close attention to any feelings of fear. Fear is born from your self-saboteur, which is the voice in your head that tries to hold you back. Its job is to "protect" you from taking risks and making changes. The fear may strengthen because it senses your soul's eagerness for absolute truth. When thoughts of fear arise, immediately go into the heart and feel the love from your soul burning there. Learn to distinguish between your soul's wisdom and the saboteur's influence upon your decisions. If you listen to your heart and act accordingly, you will be guided by wisdom.

In the past, you have resisted change because you felt a sense of comfort and safety from things remaining the same. In what you may have perceived as comfortable, you now see or feel the delusion behind it. Deep down inside you recognize the dysfunction and crave change. Your higher self knows that greater reward is birthed when the dysfunctional patterns are burned. It is now time for renewal and you may feel excited and scared at the same time. This is absolutely fine. You feel the absolute truth calling from your native soul and you know you must move toward this vision. You are moving into your true nature, the soul: a reflection of Spirit. You have descended from Spirit into flesh and have become identified with the body and its senses and possessions. It is now time to return to God.

You look forward to celebrating the rebirth of your soul. You are immortal like the phoenix. You go through many cycles of birth and death while here in the physical realm. This cyclic journey happens every day, as the phoenix represents the sun and emerges anew each morning and dies in flames each evening. This cycle reflects the existence of your human birth and death. Your omniscient soul knows the cyclic evolution that takes place throughout your journey of incarnations. Congratulations! You are now ready to celebrate the birth of your higher consciousness and resurrect your soul.

Card Symbology

The phoenix is a mythological bird and its legend exists in many cultures such as ancient Phoenician, Greek, Chinese and Egyptian mythology. The phoenix is identified with the sun.

The myths suggest there is only one phoenix alive at any point in time and, depending on the legend, it is said to have a lifespan of between 500 and 1,000 years. When it begins to feel old and weak, it builds a nest out of twigs - its own funeral pyre - sets it afire, is consumed by flames and is reduced to ashes. From the flames and ashes a new young phoenix miraculously rises, reborn to live again.

The flight of the phoenix represents your capacity to leave old patterns, beliefs, ideas and old created ways of life behind and fly toward the sun into clear vision of wisdom and truth. The olive branch held by the bird symbolizes peace and goodwill.

Journey

Find a quiet place where you can relax undisturbed. Sit comfortably with your spine straight. Take a deep breath in, tensing your body from your feet to your head. Bring awareness to each body part, as you tense each muscle one by one, within the same inhale. As your entire body is tensed with energy, hold your breath until you are ready to exhale and release. As you exhale, make any audible sounds to expel all tension from your body. Repeat this exercise three times or until you feel relaxed. Gently begin allowing your natural breath to move in and out. With each inhale, silently chant, "I am ready." With each exhale, chant, "To transform my life." Repeat this chant several times as you naturally breathe in and out. Remain in this state for as long as necessary, feeling all distracting thoughts subside.

Since you are working with fire energy, it is preferable to face south and visualize the energy of fire emanating from this direction. The south consists of the burning passion for creation, inspiration, the fire to destroy, and the heat from the sun that gives birth to new life.

Look closely at the card as you begin to feel the presence of the phoenix that resides in your soul. Your inner phoenix has traveled through many incarnations and has now returned back to participate in this one. You have grown in wisdom through understanding the law of cause and effect. In your heart, you know love is the only way to truth. Breathe in, then exhale releasing all limiting beliefs that keep you from experiencing this truth.

Visualize yourself preparing your pyre. As you gather your sticks and twigs, place the energy of the deceptive beliefs, ideas or patterns of the past along with anything else you wish to burn. Release them from your physical field as you pile them on your pyre. Know that they will be transformed into the rebirth of new, healthy and whole belief patterns that are aligned with your higher vibration.

Once your pyre is complete, place yourself comfortably in the nest, take a deep breath and light the fire. Feel the flames consume your entire being as they burn away the old. Breathe into the flames and feel yourself as one with the flame of spirit and passion. Feel the limiting beliefs transform into ashes. If you feel any pain or sorrow, know that it is an illusion and lovingly allow it to be released. Remain in the excitement of the emerging gifts that can now come forth.

Now, visualize the birth of your own loving phoenix as you spread your wings and fly out from the ashes into the sun of new beginnings. Spend as long as possible visualizing your new direction and spend time feeling, seeing and experiencing the new "you." The new phoenix! Notice in every area possible how different you now are. Notice your posture and how you move. Pay attention to the way your voice sounds and feel the power of conviction behind it. You see and hear clearly and know truth as the essence of your soul.

Visualize yourself living in this dream world. You are now able to create the life you wish according to the visions projected from your heart. You now choose to live in peace by engaging in the things that you absolutely love. This rebirth allows you to be born into the Christ Consciousness of your soul. Begin to live your life hereafter in this new presence and know that the old is gone forever.

Experience the Transcendental Video & Audio Journey on my Website to Transform Your Life!

When you return from your journey, take a deep breath and reflect on the insights you received. Smile inwardly into your heart and thank your Godly self for the work you have done to accept life, yourself and others. Record any insights or awakenings in your copy of the *Reawakening the Soul Vision Quest Workbook*.

Note: You may wish to write any deceptive beliefs, patterns, ideas or limitations that no longer serve you on a piece of paper and actually burn them in a fire outside as an additional ceremony.

Introspection

What ideas, beliefs, thoughts or patterns must be burned in order for new growth and new direction to occur?

How does the vision of my inner phoenix rising appear to me?

What am I willing to burn at this moment in my life?

How will I experience life differently after my re-birth?

EFT
Audio Available
to Help Break Free
From Limiting
Beliefs!

EFT/Tapping

KC: Even though I'm stuck in some old beliefs and patterns, I deeply and completely accept myself.
KC: Even though I'm stuck in my old ways of thinking, I deeply and completely accept myself.
KC: Even though I feel stuck in old beliefs and patterns, I deeply and completely accept myself.

EB: All these beliefs of mine.
SE: So many beliefs.
UE: Many have become a part of me.
UN: They even exist without my awareness.
CP: They are so much a part of me.
CB: I now choose to wake up.
UA: And see these beliefs and patterns.
TH: I am able to understand my beliefs.

EB: By viewing my current life situations.
SE: My life is reflected by my thoughts.
UE: And I am now ready to change my thoughts.
UN: I now release all limiting beliefs.
CP: And open up to transform my life.
CB: Into the peace that I was meant to experience.
UA: I now let go of any fear.
TH: That is keeping me from my goals & dreams.

EB: It is safe for me to burn all this fear.
SE: And open up to new beliefs.
UE: I now release all old patterns into the fire.
UN: And feel them burning away.
CP: All of them.
CB: This feels a little scary.
UA: But it feels good.
TH: It feels good to get rid of this negativity.

EB: I am now reclaiming my will power.
SE: I mind is clear and positive.
UE: I am transformed.
UN: It's my choice.
CP: I choose joy.
CB: I choose happiness.
UA: My soul is perfect bliss.
TH: My soul is awakened.

EB: Because I am waking up.
SE: I feel lighter and free.
UE: I am open to transform my energy.
UN: And fly with the wings of the new phoenix.
CP: I am free.
CB: I am finally really free!
UA: I spread my wings.
TH: And I fly!

Possibilities

Trust

Know and accept that everything is perfect and in accordance with eternal spiritual principles.

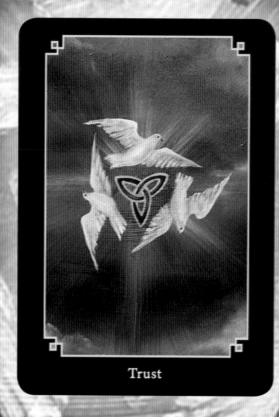

Trust

"All I have seen teaches me to trust the creator for all I have not seen."

~ Ralph Waldo Emerson

Affirmation

I completely trust the perfection of divine order in my life.

Card Message

To fully live in peace, learn to trust the perfection of life. This foundation of trust is built by remembering your God-Self. In this awareness, you will trust yourself through the power of your soul's intuition.

Understand that every occurrence is in perfect divine order. You create everything in your existence, whether consciously or subconsciously, through your thoughts, beliefs and actions. Every experience arrives in order for you to grow closer towards your own divinity. The way in which you participate in this world is based upon your level of trust in your Creator.

Meditation is the way in which you can realize your Oneness with your Creator. (See Meditation) Keep God directly in your line of vision at all times while performing your actions. Jesus said: "But rather seek ye the kingdom of God; and all these things shall be added unto you." Luke 12:31. When you feel your presence as One with God, you trust the world in which you exist because you trust yourself.

When you gain this awareness, you have the strength to accept and embrace every circumstance, trial, and situation—all the so-called "*problems*" that arise in your life. There are no problems, only *opportunities*. And you are being given the gift of opportunity to learn what you need from each test and trial while being calmly active.

Suffering occurs when you identify with your lower self and forget who you are. This misidentification creates feelings of helplessness, blame and denial, which lead to questions such as, "why is this happening to me?" This mind set keeps you separated from your true identity. Remember that you are never separate from Spirit. Your thoughts, beliefs and perception of experiences are responsible for disconnecting you from this realization. Through meditation and right living, you can change your thoughts by experiencing the true nature of your soul. Develop faith and you will move rapidly towards your soul's spiritual unfolding, leading you to divine realization.

When you are aware of your divine presence, you will achieve right attitude and you can affirm: "Now, Lord, this has happened to me, please help me understand what I need to learn. I know that you have placed this upon me only for my highest good."

Trust that everything is created for the sole purpose of uniting you back to your Source. In attaining this wisdom, you will understand that in every single moment, the divine is guiding you back home. When you fully accept and embrace every occurrence created in your life with gratitude, you live in faith and receive the gift of profound peace and inner strength.

Sri Daya Mata said, "Never bemoan what happens to you. Never feel defeated by any circumstance of your life. Strive always to think, "Lord, I have faith that no trial or experience comes to me without Your permission. I know I have within me, through your blessing, the strength to cope with anything that comes."

Even when your task seems superhuman, remember that the Divine is just stretching the rubber band of your consciousness, expanding its potentially infinite capacity.

When you arrive at a place of acceptance through understanding the law of cause and effect, you will consciously create more trust in your life. (See Karma) Your positive thoughts and right thinking will bring forth the exact circumstances that will manifest into your life's experiences. Trust in the law of divine perfection. Set yourself free, spread your wings and fly!

Card Symbology

The image of the three doves floating in a circular motion with perfect harmony and balance reflect the movement of the perfection of divine order. The sense of peace emanating from this image is the same peace that resides within your soul.

The inner Celtic knot is called the triquetra (trinity) symbol. The number three reflected from the knot and the birds represents a number of meanings. Spirit, Mind, Body; Father, Son, Holy Ghost; Mother, Father, Child; Past, Present, Future; Power, Intellect, Love; Creation, Preservation, Destruction; Thought, Feeling, Emotion; Mother, Maiden, Crone.

The Celtic knots that border the image have a heart intertwined within the knot. This represents the Oneness of all pervading love emanating from cosmic consciousness. There is neither beginning nor ending

which is symbolized in these knots. We have all come from the One Creator and we will all return to the One Creator, which is all part of the perfection of this divine order. The birds represent awakening, remembering and flying into action.

Journey

Find a quiet place where you can relax undisturbed. Sit comfortably with your spine straight. Take a deep breath in, tensing your body from your feet to your head. Bring awareness to each body part, as you tense each muscle one by one, within the same inhale. As your entire body is tensed with energy, hold your breath until you are ready to exhale and release. As you exhale, make any audible sounds to expel all tension from your body. Repeat this exercise three times or until you feel relaxed. Gently begin allowing your natural breath to move in and out. With each inhale, silently chant: "I trust life." With each exhale, chant: "I trust myself." Repeat this chant several times as you naturally breathe in and out. Remain in this state for as long as necessary, feeling all distracting thoughts subside.

As you gaze at the serenity of these birds, feel yourself flying as freely as they are. Feel the presence of your soul as the perfection of pure love. You are completely made up with the energy of spirit, which holds the vibration of love. Feel the essence of spirit as an endless chamber of light, which is not contained by space. Release and forget any and all limitations that hold you bound. Wash away all fears. Hear the voice within your heart silently whispering over and over again, "I love you."

Fill yourself with this truth. Feel the arms of Spirit wrap around you and embrace you like a little child as you fully feel and receive this love. Know that through this love you can now trust God.

Now, that you are filled with love, merge your own spirit with the limitless universal spirit floating in all creation. Breathe deeply as you expand throughout the cosmos. Allow yourself to flow through all dimensions as this oneness of spirit. The energy of this spirit holds vast amounts of love. Open and expand yourself as much as possible to receive this unconditional love. Bask in this love for as long as you wish, for your spirit is love.

Experience the Transcendental Video & Audio Journey on my Website to TRUST LIFE!

You are filled with the presence of love and truth. Place your hand on your heart and call forth any current life situations that you need to build trust around. Now, embrace, accept and find gratitude in each of them. You are aware that each one of these was created only to benefit you. If you experience emotions such as sadness, anger or frustration, allow yourself to search deeper behind these feelings to embrace the hidden blessings behind them. Thank the emotion for the fuel to take action.

If you experience resistance, breathe and remember, the emotions arrive to bless you. Ask yourself: "How can I embrace the perfection of this situation?" Through this understanding, you release any negative feelings. Ask that your gift be re-vealed to you with clarity. Through acceptance, you find your gift of wisdom, and feel the excitement as you open it. Your blessings are now bursting forth showing you exactly what you need towards your journey of spiritual unfolding.

Know that the Universe in which you live is absolutely perfect and you are a part of this perfection. All energy that you feel is being expressed through you from your Creator. Your goal is to recognize and reunite yourself back to your original state of Oneness with Spirit.

Breathe deeply as you return from your journey. Give thanks for all the messages and awareness's that you have received. As you walk in your daily journey dur-ing your time on earth, bring awareness to everything that is being manifested around you and go within and say "thank you, I trust that whatever is brought to me is for the sole purpose for my highest good."

Everything in your life was created by you—for your soul's evolution. Keep your deep sense of peace, trust and love throughout your daily activities and experi-ence your God-Self. This is what was intended for you all along. The more you practice the presence of God, by being Godly, the more you inspire others to do the same.

When you return from your journey, take a deep breath and reflect on the insights you received. Smile inwardly into your heart and thank your Godly self for the work you have done to accept life, yourself and others. Record any insights or awakenings in your copy of the *Reawakening the Soul Vision Quest Workbook*.

Introspection

Am I accepting and blessing each of my current life situations at this moment?

Am I filled with the presence and love of God?

Do I trust that I am creating my own experiences?

Do I accept the divine order of life's happenings?

What gifts are waiting to be born through my struggles?

EFT/Tapping

KC: Even though it's hard for me to trust myself, I deeply and completely accept myself.

KC: Even though it's hard for me to trust every situation in my life, I deeply and completely accept myself.

KC: Even though it's really challenging for me to trust others, I deeply and completely accept myself.

EB: I'm afraid to fully trust.
SE: Do I even know how to trust?
UE: Is it safe for me to trust others?
UN: Do I trust myself?
CP: Do I trust the perfection of the universal law?
CB: Do I trust God?
UA: I'm scared to fully trust.
TH: I'm afraid that if I completely trust.

EB: I will be let down.
SE: I will get hurt.
UE: That others are going to hurt me.
UN: I don't trust the world.
CP: I don't feel safe in this world.

Listen to EFT Audio Available on my Website to Trust Life by Trusting Yourself!

CB: I don't feel safe with my own mind.
UA: How would I feel, if I could completely trust everything in my life?
TH: All these situations being played out in my life.

EB: All the people that I have to trust in my life.
SE: How would I feel if I could fully embrace and trust God?
UE: And to know that every person, every situation and every circumstance.
UN: That is in my life right now.
CP: Is completely in divine order.
CB: And I created it all.
UA: For my highest good.
TH: Only to help me grow.

EB: And to evolve spiritually.
SE: But I didn't create this?
UE: Or did I?
UN: How would I feel if I could really trust?
CP: And know that everything is perfect.
CB: It may feel scary.
UA: But it may feel re-assuring.
TH: It would mean that I am responsible.

EB: For everything that has happened to me.
SE: And for everything happening to me right now.
UE: Am I really responsible?
UN: Could I take responsibility for all of this?
CP: And know that it led me to the person that I am right now?
CB: I have grown from each experience.
UA: And I feel stronger from them.
TH: And I am a better person because of them.

EB: This feels good.
SE: Trusting feels good.
UE: There is a sense of freedom.
UN: Living in this trust.
CP: And knowing that everything is a gift for me.
CB: I think that I can open up to this.

UA: I will now try and open up to this trust.
TH: And it's not good if I can't trust the world.

EB: And it feels good to open up to trust.
SE: It feels liberating to know that I am always taken care of.
UE: I feel free.
UN: I feel safe.
CP: Knowing that every person, situation and circumstance
CB: In my life, is only for my own spiritual growth.
UA: Towards my oneness with my Creator.
TH: I now walk in this life with this trust..

Truth

Know the divine perfection of your soul.

Truth

"The ultimate Truth is God; and God is the ultimate Truth. What you are before God and your own conscious, that is what you are. Even if the whole world misunderstands you, nothing is lost; you are what you are."

~ Paramahansa Yogananda

Affirmation

I experience life in absolute truth as an expression of Spirit.

Card Message

You may base truth upon fact from things you perceive as real or from experiences or events. Spend time being introspective about what you experience as your truths. This includes what you perceive outwardly along with the truths you hold about yourself. You are encouraged to explore truth at a very deep level, one that may change your life. What truths do you believe about yourself and about others? What truths do you believe about the world in which you exist? Where did these truths come from and are they, in fact, the absolute truth or distorted perceptions? Are you completely authentic? How do you validate your perception of truth in all areas? You are now being guided to challenge yourself as to how you understand truth.

Truth is universal and is the rightful possession of every person and constitutes the equality of all souls before God. In the deep peace found in meditation, you will experience your soul made in the image of God. In this perfection, you will come to know absolute truth. When you live in this clarity, you will realize that you are never alone. You will feel the all-pervading love of God surrounding and guiding you through the voice of your soul. Your supreme desire will become to experience the presence of God in your soul. It is here where truth is known. Truth is fully understood when your soul knows its own perfect nature made in the image of God. Your soul is an all-powerful divine expression of love. In the deluded ego state, you do not know this soul perfection; you are only aware of it and misinterpret it's ability to manifest your inherent power and peace. Live every day authentically and have the desire and determination to experience God for your self.

Card Symbology

The angel is an image that reminds each of us that we possess the spirit of a guardian of truth. She holds the grace of absolute and eternal truth found within our soul. Her presence of purity and love reflects our own souls. She is right within our hearts and souls, guiding us towards right action. Her love is always there with the message that we are never alone in this world. She can be called upon for help and guidance at any moment as she waits to respond through our love.

The fawn represents the gentleness and innocence of our inner child, eager to grow spiritually towards truth. We can be like the child who sees life with fresh, new awareness, untouched by limited human conditioning. We must be willing to open our hearts to the innocent child residing within us in order to find the calm peace of our inner spirit.

The wolf is howling towards the full moon, celebrating the return back home to our true selves. Wolf medicine teaches us to know and speak our truth. The butterfly encourages us to know that our transformation will be glorious and beautiful. The roses are a reflection of the permeating fragrance of our essence when it is reunited back to the source of its existence. The dream catcher is a reminder that we are once again experiencing life in a dream state. We are immortals who dream a mortal existence and we must remember that this is Gods dream, dreaming through us.

Journey

Find a quiet place where you can relax undisturbed. Sit comfortably with your spine straight. Take a deep breath in, tensing your body from your feet to your head. Bring awareness to each body part, as you tense each muscle one by one, within the same inhale. As your entire body is tensed with energy, hold your breath until you are ready to exhale and release. As you exhale, make any audible sounds to expel all tension from your body. Repeat this exercise three times or until you feel relaxed. Gently begin allowing your natural breath to move in and out. With each inhale, silently chant: "I inhale truth." With each exhale, chant: "I exhale truth." Repeat this chant several times as you naturally breathe in and out. Remain in this state for as long as necessary, feeling all distracting thoughts subside.

Experience the Transcendental Video & Audio Journey on my Website to Find YOUR Truth!

Feel the presence of peace found in the culmination of the images of the painting. Breathe deeply and slowly into your heart until you begin to feel calm, centered and safe. Surround yourself with the love and peace that resides within the warmth of your heart. Feel this presence and know that you are never alone here in this world. Feel and know yourself as the essence of Spirit. This existence holds the truth of your connectedness to everything. Located in this space is guidance and courage along with pure, unconditional love. Encompass yourself in this energy. In your heart lies truth. God knows your heart and you don't have to prove yourself to anyone. As you gently rub your heart with your hand, repeat to yourself, "My only truth is God and God knows my truth." Repeat this several times until you become absorbed in the sensation of this reality.

Your soul is love and you, as Spirit, are love. Feel yourself stepping into this perfection and see yourself living in this physical world as a Godly being without any limitations. Sense your calm and compassionate disposition as you spread this energy and share it to everyone around you. Experience the breath of God behind your breath; feel the life force of God behind your every thought and action. Visualize yourself living every minute and every day of your life in this holy presence. Begin living in the truth that you are—a transcendental immortal and perfect image of God. Your physical and spiritual image is absolute truth. Breathe in truth . . . breathe out truth . . . breathe in truth . . . breathe out truth—you are love!

When you return from your journey, take a deep breath and reflect on the insights you received. Smile inwardly into your heart and thank your Godly self for the work you have done to accept life, yourself and others. Record any insights or awakenings in your copy of the *Reawakening the Soul Vision Quest Workbook.*

Introspection

What truths do I have about myself, about others and my earthly surroundings?

What would my experience be like if I truly felt and expressed myself as the presence of God?

How would I feel differently to be living in absolute truth?

EFT/Tapping

KC: Even though I don't know what the truth to life is anymore, I accept the way I feel.

KC: I seem to be inquiring as to what truth is to me, and I'm excited to explore this deeper.

KC: Even though truth is hard for me to comprehend, I accept the way I feel and I'm ready to grow.

Listen to
EFT Audio
to Feel
The Absolute
Truth of Your
Soul!

EB: What is truth?
SE: What is truth?
UE: Do I really know what truth is?
UN: My truth is different from another's perception of truth.
CP: So how can any of them really be correct?
CB: Isn't life just all a perception?
UA: And my perception is from what I believe to be true.
TH: And my belief was formed by my environment.

EB: So what really is true and what is not?
SE: And what does it all even matter?
UE: This is some deep stuff.
UN: There's a part of me that knows this deeper truth.
CP: And I feel that truth in my soul.
CB: That truth seems right.
UA: My soul is my higher self.
TH: Guiding me with wisdom.

EB: But most of the time, I feel guided by my lower self.
SE: My habits, moods and patterns.
UE: I want to change.
UN: And be guided by my soul.
CP: Then my perception would change.
CB: And my outer surroundings would change.
UA: Can I change my perception?
TH: To really see absolute truth?

EB: And feel absolute truth.
SE: What is absolute truth?
UE: The truth of perfection.
UN: My Creator is perfection.
CP: My Creator is truth.
CB: My soul knows this truth.
UA: Because this is my essence.
TH: My only truth is God.

EB: And God knows the truth.
SE: My heart knows the truth.
UE: And the "I" that I call myself knows the truth.
UN: In knowing this.
CP: I don't ever have to please the world.
CB: Because it doesn't matter.
UA: I feel the truth in my heart.
TH: And I know that's my truth.

"My only truth is God, and God knows the Truth."

~ Sundara A. Fawn

Unity

Unite in complete oneness with your Creator.

Unity

"Do not follow the ideas of others, but learn to listen to the voice within yourself. Your body and mind will become clear and you will realize the unity of all things."

~ Dogen

Affirmation

My great Creator flows through me.

Card Message

To remember your natural essence, which is being One with the Infinite is the goal of your existence. Uniting with your higher self begins by making a conscious choice in the way you perceive yourself. It requires paying attention to your conscious mind and the messages sent to you. If you feel uncomfortable when you listen to your consciousness, it's time to visit these beliefs and change them. Begin to peel off the layers of deception that hold you bound and replace them with the wisdom of truth. Your essence consists of goodness and love. When you open your eyes to see and feel God as the underlying reality, you live in the presence of peace.

The most important relationship to develop is a healthy and loving relationship within your self, with God. You must come to peace with yourself and forgive all past mistakes. (See Forgiveness) If you feel that you have hurt others, know that you acted to the best of your ability during that time and resolve to not do it again. Forgive yourself! Mentally change your consciousness to support your goodness. You know what improvements you wish to make, so set forth a conscious effort to change and improve yourself. Train your consciousness to support yourself with kind and loving words. This is self-love and when you learn how to love yourself and nurture your spirit you will be blessed with great rewards. You are never separate from God, nor will you ever be.

The excitement of realizing your oneness with God will be fully supported, as your own personal will aligns with the Divine will. You will come to know there is no separation between you and the world around you.

Unity means to feel the presence of Spirit that resides within your being and everything around you. Spirit is in every breath you take, every movement you make, every thought you think, every sound you hear and every word you speak. The holy presence of Spirit resides within you, is you, and consists of pure love. To come to the realization of the holy union between yourself and Spirit is your greatest treasure. You will reflect and express yourself as divinity itself and bring others back to themselves by your example. You will be aware that everyone in the world is your family.

When you experience yourself as Spirit, you will feel that the entire universe is connected to the same cosmic intelligence you are. Everything in existence is birthed from Spirit's consciousness. Your Creator is the world Soul out of which all souls have come. You are connected to all that exists in the universe. Learn to see the beautiful manifestation of Spirit in all persons, of whatever race or religion. Feel that you are part of a united world and give love and service to all. You will then feel Cosmic Love, which is what you are made up of.

Card Symbology

Upon looking into this image, you will see the use of the circle used in various ways. The circle symbol is universal, sacred and divine. It represents the infinite nature of energy and the inclusivity of the universe. It refers to the cycles of time, unity and oneness, infinity and perfection. The cycles of the moon and the rhythm of their energetic dance, links directly to the core of our being. The ring at the bottom of the painting depicts the genuine marriage between our soul and Spirit.

The circle is repeated again by the cycles of the moon and the cyclic progression the rose takes from bud into bloom. The fragrant and beauty that permeates from the rose as it blooms is reminiscent to our own growth toward our oneness with God. In the center is the sun with the sacred symbol of "aum" or "om" and reflects the perfection of our soul. The vibration of "aum" symbolizes the manifestation of God and is the reflection of the absolute reality without beginning or end and embracing all that exists.

The deer reflects ones own gentleness in thought, word and touch, to others and ourselves. The female deer symbolizes femininity and gracefulness. The male deer represents independence, purification and pride. He is known as the King of the Forest, the protector of its creatures. His antlers are connections to higher forms of attunement. As the deer enters deep into the forest of magic, they encourage us to explore our own magical and spiritual nature. When we explore our magic and spirituality, it must be with good intention, to harm no living being. We must enter the realm of the wild in the spirit of love and communion. We can learn the gift of caring and gentleness to help us overcome and put aside many testing situations. Only love, for ourselves and for others, helps us understand the true meaning of wholeness.

The dove represents peace, purity and love. Dove is birthed from the center of the sun/soul because when we realize our Unity by achieving our own peace, we create the world's vision of universal peace. The peace symbolized by dove is that of the deepest kind. It quiets our thoughts and allows us to find renewal in the silence of mind. In moments of stillness we are able to appreciate simple blessings.

Journey

Find a quiet place where you can relax undisturbed. Sit comfortably with your spine straight. Take a deep breath in, tensing your body from your feet to your head. Bring awareness to each body part, as you tense each muscle one by one, within the same inhale. As your entire body is tensed with energy, hold your breath until you are ready to exhale and release. As you exhale, make any audible sounds to expel all tension from your body. Repeat this exercise three times or until you feel relaxed. Gently begin allowing your natural breath to move in and out. With each inhale, silently chant: "I am in tune." With each exhale, chant: "With the Almighty." Repeat this chant several times as you naturally breathe in and out. Remain in this state for as long as necessary, feeling all distracting thoughts subside.

You are drawn deep into the cycles of consciousness. Everything in life flows from one stage into another as transformation is constantly taking place. This is the beauty in the harmony of life. You are a part of this movement and by reawakening your soul; you are constantly transforming your awareness to greater heights. You are like the rose bud, birthed out of the consciousness of Spirit, the Immutable Absolute. As you surrender to life's experiences, you grow in truth and beauty. Your wisdom is continually unfolding just like the petals on the precious rose. When you live your life from a heart of compassion and love, you open into a spectacular full bloom. Feel your self fully open, absorbed in the loving Oneness of God, acting and behaving as a Godly being. The more you love, the sweeter your aroma. Take a moment and breathe in your scent of essence. Now, feel how others gravitate to your heavenly bouquet of love. It is here where your fragrance permeates weaving throughout eternity.

Experience the Transcendental Video & Audio Journey on my Website to Feel Your Eternal Spirit!

You feel yourself flowing with the rhythm of oneness of the universe. The being of your essence is in harmony with the cycles of the moon. Reflecting the energy of the new moon, you withdraw into the depths of your own inner silence. In this darkness you recognize the stillness of your soul. In this silence, you feel your connection to your Creator. You respect this time as a period of self-reflection and planting new seeds of dreams. As your life cycle shifts into the rhythm of the full moon, you feel your energy bursting with light. You are highly active as you engage in the world around you. Your emotions peak and you may even feel a bit chaotic. But through conscious awareness, you know this is just a cycle that will pass and repeat itself. You feel the perfection of the cyclic rhythm and know there are gifts to be found in the duality of all the energies presenting themselves to you. The union of bringing your soul back to God creates a balanced state of mind through understanding the natural divine laws.

Two beautiful deer's appear before you. The spirit of the deer is a symbol of gentleness and heart energy. You sense the ways in which you are able to bring gentleness and grace in various aspects of your life, even in the most challenging moments. You feel the inspiration from the deer's qualities reflect unto you as you achieve ambitious goals and are able to tackle difficult situations smoothly with your special touch of gentleness and grace. The essence of serenity becomes your natural state of being.

Now, you relax into the union of your soul with spirit. You feel calm, whole, and yet extremely powerful! Your energy field is swirling and merging with all the universal energy. You feel spirit and nature dancing around you and within you as you feel your sacred connection to life. You are absorbed in the deep peace of your true nature. You are Spirit! In this peace you feel the spiritual dove being birthed from your consciousness into the oneness of all that exists. You relax into the sound vibration of aum, amen—the vibratory sound of creation.

When you return from your journey, take a deep breath and reflect on the insights you received. Smile inwardly into your heart and thank your Godly self for the work you have done to accept life, yourself and others. Record any insights or awakenings in your copy of the *Reawakening the Soul Vision Quest Workbook.*

Introspection

Do I allow myself the quiet time needed in order to feel the energy sustaining me?

Do I accept and embrace the ever-changing cycles that happen in my life?

How can I feel more unity with my Divine Creator?

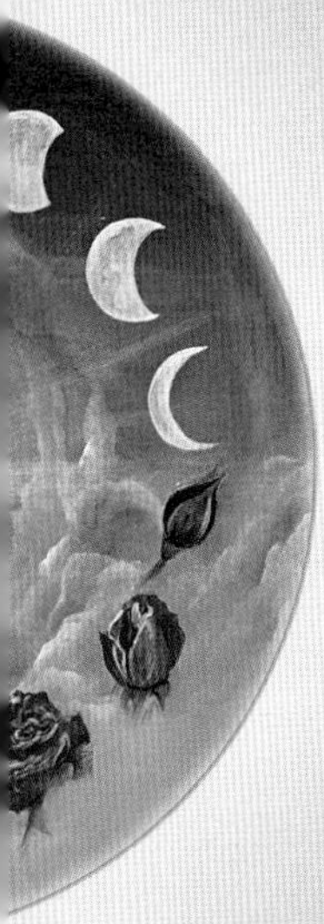

EFT/Tapping

KC: Even though at times I feel alone, I deeply and completely accept the way I feel.
KC: Even though at times I feel separate from Spirit, I am open to explore ways to feel more united.
KC: Even though I forget my true nature as Spirit, I am willing feel my spiritual nature.

EB: I feel separate.
SE: I feel alone.
UE: Who am I?
UN: I want to feel connected.
CP: I want to feel my true self.
CB: I want to feel my soul.
UA: I want to reawaken my consciousness.
TH: I tap and remember who I am.

EFT
Audio Available
to Feel
Your
Interconnection!

EB: I am divine.
SE: I am abundant.
UE: I am made in the image of God.
UN: I am almighty.
CP: I am love.
CB: I am goodness.
UA: I feel spirit pulsating in every cell of my body.
TH: I acknowledge the many cycles of life.

EB: I accept the emotional changes these cycles bring.
SE: I flow with grace in every aspect of my life.
UE: My thoughts are peaceful.
UN: My mind is quiet.
CP: In this stillness, I feel my unity with the world.
CB: This feels nice.
UA: This feels true to my being.
TH: I choose to live in this quiet peace.

EB: This is who I am.
SE: I am Spirit.
UE: And now, I shine my light as Spirit.
UN: As I live in this truth,
CP: I will reawaken others to this truth.
CB: This is true happiness.
UA: Helping others to help themselves.
TH: I am an example of love.

"Where there is unity there is always victory."

~ Publilius Syrus

Vision

Clearly see what you wish to create.

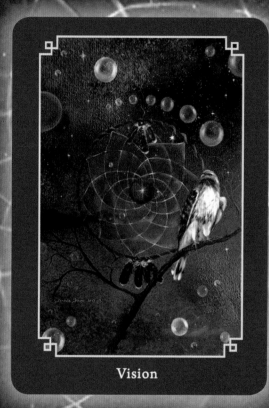

Vision

"Vision . . . It reaches beyond the thing that is, into the conception of what can be. Imagination gives you the picture. Vision gives you the impulse to make the picture your own."

~ Robert Collier

Affirmation

Vision expands my horizons. The more I dream, the more I can achieve.

Card Message

The red-tailed hawk is a visionary and messenger. Hawk is able to rise high above the ground, soaring on the breath of Spirit while extracting helpful information to bring back to earth. Hawk helps you to become aware of your dreams and encourages you to implement these dreams in the physical realm. Hawk inspires you to see with a broader perspective—a vantage point you cannot experience from the ground. Hawk invigorates you and inspires you to soar, to see and to reach your highest potential. The spirit of the hawk brings balance to your body, mind, and soul. The time has come to develop your spiritual awareness and connect with your higher self. When you learn to do this, you harness the power of your intuition.

Hawk has arrived in your life to help you clearly see the visions and messages that the Universe is sending your way. There is a special message from your soul that is being transmitted to you. The energy of the hawk will help you interpret this important message. This hawk may have shown up to tell you to be more observant and to pay closer attention as to how you are living your life. Are there ways in which you can be more authentic and spiritually centered? Do you have a dream that wishes to be birthed? The hawk may see something that you are not able to see clearly. Take time to be alone and pay attention to what you feel passionate about. The voice of your soul is trying to express itself through the feeling of passion. The hawk will provide wisdom to help you observe situations with clear vision. He has arrived to help you clarify your dreams. You have the ability to lead and influence others when you share your gifts. You may have to take more initiative and action in order for your ideas and dreams to come to fruition. Utilize the support that this beautiful red-tailed hawk has to offer.

Card Symbology

The red-tailed hawk sits upon a tree branch symbolizing his ability to bring Spirit from the heavens down to the earth. He is confident and sure of himself because he has transformed his heart and mind into pure intuition. The dream catcher that floats behind him signifies the web of life—the connection between spirit and matter. This web helps you to reach your goals and make good use of your ideas, dreams and visions. Through the power of the Great Spirit, the web filters your ideas and assists you in implementing your highest visions. The bubbles of light in the painting represent the essence of Spirit made manifest in the physical realm. This universal vibration, symbolized by free floating bubbles, exists in all physical matter.

Journey

Find a quiet place where you can relax undisturbed. Sit comfortably with your spine straight. Take a deep breath in, tensing your body from your feet to your head. Bring awareness to each body part, as you tense each muscle one by one, within the same inhale. As your entire body is tensed with energy, hold your breath until you are ready to exhale and release. As you exhale, make any audible sounds to expel all tension from your body. Repeat this exercise three times or until you feel relaxed. Gently begin allowing your natural breath to move in and out. With each inhale, silently chant: "My dreams." With each exhale, chant: "Are my visions." Repeat this chant several times as you naturally breathe in and out. Remain in this state for as long as needed, feeling all distracting thoughts subside.

You find yourself sitting within a galaxy of cosmic space. Mystical colors are moving all around you as they breathe their secret essence into your core. Your entire spiritual and physical being merges within the cosmic breath. As you breathe in and out, a rhythmic harmony synchronizes your life force to the cosmic life force. You feel so safe and complete in this space. You are absolutely fearless, free and alive. Relax into this oneness as you begin to feel yourself as pure vibrating Spirit.

You notice something taking form and emerging out of the cosmic breath. As it draws closer, you behold a mystical Native American dream catcher. You observe the intricate webs and dazzling sparkles of light that emanate from it. You feel magic happening at a deep soul level. In a sacred language, the web begins to share a story with you from the Lakota tradition. This story is about the web being formed by the cycles of life—how we begin our journey as infants and move through childhood on to adulthood. We complete this cycle in our old age when we must be taken care of again, just like when we were infants. As the web spins each cycle of life, there are many forces you must face—both perceived good and bad influences. These forces can assist or obstruct your har-

Experience the Transcendental Video & Audio Journey on my Website to Obtain Laser Focused VISION!!

monious nature. As you look into the web, clearly view your goals and life path. Are you making good use of your ideas, dreams and visions? Are you utilizing the good forces around you? Take time to ponder these questions as you revisit the dreams latent within your soul. Begin to see what dreams are asking to be called forth in your life. Hold these dreams close to your heart and nurture them.

A captivating red-tailed hawk has now arrived to guide you. As he speaks his mystical language, he saturates you with wisdom. He helps you to see situations from a different perspective; he gives you a vantage point aligned with absolute truth. You now possess the power of heightened observation as you clearly view your dreams. You know what you are passionate about and you see what tasks need to be accomplished to fulfill your dreams. The hawk infuses you with the power of direct focus, activating your passion and energizing you with the ability to take action. You now have crystal clear vision and take action with laser beam focus to create your dreams. Your spiritual awareness is heightened as you experience your oneness with cosmic consciousness, experiencing the Great Creator within yourself. You know that the time is right for you to lead and share your gifts to help others on their spiritual journey. You feel yourself soaring high into the sky as the heavens support your vision. You are now connected to the spiritual realms. You reach up to the heavens to extract valuable information and bring it back to earth. You feel the excitement to bring your wonderful ideas back to those who can benefit from them. You are no longer distracted by small details of your mundane daily existence, but rather consciously focused on your higher aspirations.

This gift of clear vision inspires you to take immediate action. You sense your clairvoyant abilities and know these skills will support your goals. You have a natural inclination to receive visions, either in dreams or awake, as your sensory abilities and intuition are now enhanced by the power of this hawk. Your visionary powers are now awakened and you are ready to begin the mission you were called here to do. With your reverence to the interconnectedness of all of life, you are now involved in making the world a better place. By applying your dreams and visions, you become a protector of the earth. When you share your gifts, you encourage and educate others to do the same. You now begin to move toward your soul purpose in a powerful way. Thank the hawk spirit for sharing his medicine and magic. Know that he is flying with you forever, guiding your way.

When you return from your journey, take a deep breath and reflect on the insights you received. Smile inwardly into your heart and thank your Godly self for the work you have done to accept life, yourself and others. Record any insights or awakenings in your copy of the *Reawakening the Soul Vision Quest Workbook.*

Introspection

What is my vision in life?

Am I focused on my goals and dreams?

What do I want to achieve?

How can I become more spiritually aware?

Am I working towards my creative life purpose?

EFT/Tapping

KC: Even though I'm not fully creating my dreams, I deeply and completely accept myself.

KC: Even though just thinking about achieving my dreams scares me, I choose to relax now.

KC: Even though I've placed my dreams on hold, I am willing and open to explore them again.

EB: What are my dreams?
SE: What are my goals?
UE: What do I feel passionate about?
UN: What is my life all about?
CP: Where is all my energy going each day?
CB: It doesn't feel safe to dream.
UA: I was taught to quit dreaming.
TH: Maybe I've shut down to my dreams.

EB: The thought of this makes me feel sad.
SE: I have a lot to share.
UE: But then again, who am I?
UN: I'm really a nobody.
CP: I can't change the world.

EFT Audio Available to Awaken Your Visionary Powers!

CB: But I do have special gifts.
UA: That only I can do.
TH: I need to recognize these gifts.

EB: And honor them.
SE: Because they are special,
UE: Just for me.
UN: From my Creator.
CP: Is there fear around my dreams?
CB: Can I start getting in touch with my dreams?
UA: Even if it's little by little.
TH: And step by step.

EB: I will make a small effort every day.
SE: And my effort may grow larger.
UE: To reach closer to my vision.
UN: To experience who I really am.
CP: By connecting with my Source.
CB: I want to spiritually awaken.
UA: And I am getting closer every day.
TH: I choose to make a conscious effort now.

EB: My Creator breathes through me,
SE: And lives through me,
UE: And creates through me.
UN: I allow my vision to be born.
CP: Because my vision,
CB: Is my Creator's vision.
UA: I have so much to give,
TH: I will now begin to share my gifts.

Wisdom

You possess knowledge within your soul that comes directly from God's encompassing truth.

Wisdom

"The teacher who is indeed wise does not bid you to enter the house of his wisdom but rather leads you to the threshold of your mind."
~ Kahlil Gibran

Affirmation

I am aligned with Spirit. I am wise.

Card Message

Wisdom comes from direct perception of truth, obtained through awareness and actual experience of your absolute existence as Spirit. Wisdom is guided by the soul's intuition, which comes from a calm, still mind. When you are connected to God and know yourself as a divine being, you are guided by wisdom.

Wisdom is to know that thought is spirit and its job is to create, grow, expand and flourish. You being a reflection of spirit are meant to do the same.

You grow in wisdom when you experience life as a gift and accept each of these gifts completely knowing that each one is for your spiritual advancement. Wisdom is the knowing that life is a dream, a gift, a story, and a movie—one that we are all playing in together.

Draw upon the well of Spirit that resides deep within the silence of your mind. Calm your thoughts and drink from the fountain of truth.

Wisdom is the ability to understand inner qualities, relationships and truth. Remembering your oneness with God is essential to know truth. This silent wisdom is in the palm of your hands. Be still and know that you are an image of God. To know this truth, you must have authority over your mind by dwelling upon the positive aspects of life. Keep your thoughts and actions in harmony with your real Self and you will bring forth peace and happiness.

He who is wisest conceives himself as Divine, and knows the purpose of life, and his own purpose in life. Living as this quality, he expresses himself fully and inspires others.

Wisdom is the ability to:

 Receive life's experiences as gifts manifested from your creative thought.

 Fully understand that everything - every experience, situation and circumstance was created by your thought.

 Be 100% accountable for every experience in your life.

Acknowledge and feel the higher Source operating through you.

 Be in the present moment using discernment when making decisions.

 Grow from perceived mistakes and see them as gifts of opportunity.

Card Symbology

The sun represents your own inner light, your soul. The hand symbolizes that wisdom is in the palm of your hands, in the seat of your soul and linked to your great Creator. Tapping into this wisdom is essential to the creation of life and how you contribute for the good of all.

The lotus flower portrays purity and beauty as it grows out of the murky darkness of the pond. The flower is a reflection of your own purity and wisdom that progresses from the lowest to highest states of consciousness. The lotus flower inspires you to continue to grow through the trials of your life so you can bloom and reach your highest potential. This spiritual unfolding can be achieved by fully surrendering to your Creator.

The lotus flower is a reminder of the beauty found in every aspect of life. When you unfold like the lotus, completely surrendered in the ocean of God, you enter a transcendental state of consciousness. You begin to understand the magic found in the silence of wisdom.

Journey

Find a quiet place where you can relax undisturbed. Sit comfortably with your spine straight. Take a deep breath in, tensing your body from your feet to your head. Bring awareness to each body part, as you tense each muscle one by one, within the same inhale. As your entire body is tensed with energy, hold your breath until you are ready to exhale and release. As you exhale, make any audible sounds to expel all tension from your body. Repeat this exercise three times or until you feel relaxed. Gently begin allowing your natural breath to move in and out. With each inhale, silently chant: "I listen to my soul." With each exhale, chant: "And live in wisdom." Repeat this chant several times as you naturally breathe in and out. Remain in this state for as long as needed, feeling all distracting thoughts subside.

Experience the Transcendental Video & Audio Journey on my Website to Hear the Wisdom of Your SOUL!

You are now floating within the clouds and space of the formless. You feel safe, supported, and completely free from all mental and physical worries. You merge with the universe and become space less. There is no time, only the eternal, present moment. In the chamber of silence, you have entered the realm of wisdom. The glorious sun magnifies her piercing rays of light, penetrating you with life force, activating you with God Source, permeating every space of your being with radiant rays of love. You are open and receptive, as you receive her words of wisdom:

> You are immortal. You consist of the living energy of Spirit. Every fiber of your being is the holy essence of Love. You are truth and you are love. You are now guided by the wisdom of your soul's intuition. You make conscious choices, with the absence of error. You listen in the depths of silence, as you are confident in making life-shifting decisions shaping your life of excellence. Breathe and feel the truth of your existence as a Godly being. You are whole and complete just as you are. Your mission is to express your creative, passionate self and share what you love. Share who you are. You are authentic and living your life, becoming great. You have the wisdom to speak your truth and how you feel. You ask for what you need with the faith in knowing that you will receive it.

You float upon the waters like the beautiful lotus unfolding and growing from the deep, dark murky depths of the water. You are continuously expanding your state of consciousness, just as the lotus petals of awareness unfold within your soul. You inwardly glance at the dark parts of your past and understand the blessings and the gifts they offered for your spiritual growth. You are awake and aware and know that each of life's experiences was created by your energy in order to bring yourself back to the remembrance of your true nature. Gratitude fills your body, because you understand truth at a soul level. You make decisions guided by wisdom rather than fear. You know you are One with all the cosmos. You are connected to cosmic intelligence. You know who you are, and you create and live in accordance to your soul's calling. You sing the song of truth; you live the life of wisdom; and you dance in the rhythm of oneness. You are happy, content with a deep sense of peace. You are reunited in wisdom with your beloved, your soul. Now go shine and share your wisdom.

When you return from your journey, take a deep breath and reflect on the insights you received. Smile inwardly into your heart and thank your Godly

Godly self for the work you have done to accept life, yourself and others. Record any insights or awakenings in your copy of the *Reawakening the Soul Vision Quest Workbook*.

Introspection

Am I willing to give myself the gift of silencing my mind in order to hear my soul?

Am I open to explore the wisdom of my soul?

Am I willing to seek wisdom without measure from God's all-possessing, all-bountiful hands?

EFT/Tapping

KC: Even though I don't feel confident in many of my decisions, I am open to explore ways to achieve wisdom.

KC: Even though it's hard for me to take full responsibility for everything happening in my life, I accept the way I feel.

KC: Even though I don't feel very wise cause I've made some bad Decisions, I deeply and completely accept myself.

Listen to EFT Audio to Reawaken Your Soul to Joy!

EB: Sometimes I don't feel very wise.
SE: I feel like I make many decisions from my emotions.
UE: And this seems to cause suffering.
UN: I'm ready to be guided by wisdom.
CP: I'm ready to make good choices.
CB: I know it's going to take some practice.
UA: But I'm willing to change.
TH: I'm tired of suffering from ignorance.

EB: I've made some bad choices in the past.
SE: That didn't feel very wise.
UE: Some left me feeling awful.
UN: But I accept them all.
CP: Because they have allowed me to build my character.
CB: Wisdom comes from understanding.
UA: And learning and growing from life's experiences.
TH: I now move into the place of wisdom.

EB: Where I feel joyously connected.
SE: Because wisdom is knowledge.
UE: And knowledge comes from the experience of truth.
UN: I need to be quiet to hear my guidance.
CP: Am I willing to allow myself this quite time?
CB: It would really change the course of my life.
UA: I now make decisions while I am calm.
TH: And my mind is still.

EB: I receive wisdom from my soul.
SE: And my soul is always aligned to truth.
UE: I am now am guided by wisdom.
UN: And I listen to my soul's intuition.
CP: By remembering who I am.
CB: I am spirit.
UA: I am wise.
TH: I hear the wisdom of my soul.

This painting is dedicated to Lord Jesus Christ and Lord Bhagavan Krishna—The Masters behind my Catholic roots and Science of Yoga journey.

He who perceives Me everywhere and beholds everything in Me, never loses sight of Me, nor do I ever lose sight of him.
The Bhagavad Gita VI:30

"But seek ye first the kingdom of God, and his righteousness; and all these things shall be added unto you."
Matthew 6:33

About the Author

Sundara Fawn is a mystic visionary artist, muralist and writer who shares her unique personal awareness, gained by many years of devotion to both the creative process and to her connection with the Divine. She demonstrates that the journey into an awareness of our divinity can be fun and creative as she shares beautiful artwork expressing God's infinite power.

Sundara's paintings are universal and honor the truth manifest in all religions as they express her commitment to experiencing absolute truth and sharing this truth with others. This focus on absolute truth is, in fact, one of the deep guiding passions of her life. In addition, her innate desire to express artistically led her to complete studies in painting at Northern Illinois University, where she earned both BFA and MFA degrees with honors.

As Sundara channels the Divine through her artwork, she brings forth inspirational writings. This special pairing of gifts leads to complementary works that are both beautiful and healing. Sharing these gifts in the form of art, guided meditations, videos and spiritual tools enables her to take others through a journey into Spirit to experience higher states of consciousness.

In recent years, she has developed her skills as a motivational speaker and leads workshops and online courses to empower others, along with offering individual opportunities for leadership in sharing her program.

The essence of nature is a primary influence. Through the communion found on daily hikes in the beautiful Blue Ridge Mountains of North Carolina, Sundara is continually inspired by the sermons given by the sacred voice of the woods. She is also a disciple of Paramahansa Yogananda, and shares deep insights gained through the study of Yogananda's teachings and techniques for meditation.

Sundara's art is recognized nationally and internationally and can be found on several book covers, CD jackets, cards and in numerous publications. She is also a professional graphic designer, layout artist and illustrator.

Through her passionate and creative gifts, she intuitively reaches out and touches the hearts of those who are ready for positive change.

Namaste'

Thank you for being on this wondrous journey with me! Only we determine how long it will take to obtain our inherent true happiness . . . it's all up to how much we are willing to apply ourselves! By working on multiple levels of consciousness, we can achieve liberation! But as with anything, it takes work. This work entails: commitment, perseverance, dedication, patience, wisdom, determination, practice and application. It also takes testing and experimenting for yourself to see what works. We learn and grow through our own personal and direct experience. I'm excited to celebrate with you—as you see the results for yourself!

When we bridge heaven and earth, heart and mind, body and soul, we become the rainbow prism of love! Let's keep having fun exercising our powerful minds and opening our loving hearts to align our will with divine will. Let's reawaken our souls back to their true nature and allow them to shine their brilliant diamond light!

Keep Shining!

Sundara Fawn

Please Stay Connected!

For further product information, workshop schedules, newsletter subscriptions, or to contact me:

Sundara.Fawn@gmail.com
www.SundaraFawn.com

www.facebook.com/SundaraDreams
www.twitter.com/SundaraFawn
www.pinterest.com/SundaraFawn
www.youtube.com/SundaraFawn

Notes And Permissions

Grateful acknowledgment to Self Realization Fellowship for the permission to use my beloved Gurudeva, Paramahansa Yogananda's quoted material. His wisdom and teachings are the inspiration of my work.

Page 10 - Paramahansa Yogananda, *Journey to Self-Realization*, Los Angeles, CA: Self-Realization Fellowship.

Page 69 - Paramahansa Yogananda, A "Para-gram" on Balance, Los Angeles, CA: Self-Realization Fellowship.

Page 145 - Paramahansa Yogananda, *The Divine Romance*, Los Angeles, CA: Self-Realization Fellowship.

Page 150 - Paramahansa Yogananda, *The Divine Romance,* Los Angeles, CA: Self-Realization Fellowship.

Page 186 - Paramahansa Yogananda, *Journey to Self-Realization*, Los Angeles, CA: Self- Realization Fellowship.

Page 215 - Paramahansa Yogananda, *Journey to Self-Realization*, Los Angeles, CA: Self- Realization Fellowship.

Page 228 - Paramahansa Yogananda, *Inner Peace*, Los Angeles, CA: Self-Realization Fellowship.

Page 231 - Paramahansa Yogananda, *Man's Eternal Quest*, Los Angeles, CA: Self-Realization Fellowship.

Page 244 - Paramahansa Yogananda, *Journey to Self-Realization*, Los Angeles, CA: Self- Realization Fellowship. "The ultimate Truth is God; and God is the ultimate Truth." pg 95 . . . . "What you are before God . . . pg 339.

10% of all proceeds from the sale of this book will be donated to Self-Realization Fellowship, founded by Paramahansa Yogananda.